Well Preserved

small batch preserving
for the new cook

Mary Anne Dragan

whitecap

Edited by Elaine Jones
Design, food photography and food styling
  by Michelle Mayne
Additional photography by Lionel Trudel
  (pages 43 and 267) and ©iStockphoto.com/
  Jill Chen (page i)

Sidebar images ©iStockphoto.com: Joe Biafore
(page 26); Valentyn Volkov (page 28); Juha
Huiskonen (page 33); Wolfgang Amri (page 49);
Doug Cannell (page 60); Stefano Tiraboschi
(page 69); Alina Solovyova-Vincent (pages 71, 125
and 169); Elena Schweitzer (page 81); MorePixels
(page 82); Tomasz Dlugosz (page 93); Monika
Adamczyk (page 98); Gustavo Andrade (page 101);
Ivan Mateev (page 103); Galayko Sergey (page 135);
Gabor Izso (page 173); Andi Berger (page 177); Tim
Scott (page 179); Tea Potocnik (page 186); Saskia
Massink (page 209); Robyn Mackenzie (page 216);
Marek Uliasz (page 261)

Printed in China

**Library and Archives Canada Cataloguing
in Publication**

Dragan, Mary Anne, 1959–
    Well preserved : small batch preserving for the
new cook / Mary Anne Dragan. -- Rev. 3rd ed.

Includes index.
ISBN 978-1-55285-988-9

    1. Canning and preserving. I. Title.

TX601.D72 2009   641.8'52   C2008-905610-8

The publisher acknowledges the financial support
of the Government of Canada through the Book
Publishing Industry Development Program (BPIDP)
and the Province of British Columbia through the
Book Publishing Tax Credit.

09 10 11 12 13   5 4 3 2 1

Preface v

Introduction 1

Jams 15

Jellies 37

Marmalades 61

Conserves 77

Preserves 85

Fruit Sauces 95

Fruit Butters 105

Pickles 117

Relishes 141

Chutneys 161

Ketchups 181

Infused Vinegars 193

Cooking with Preserves 211

Gifts from the Pantry 267

Index 275

Preface

hy try home preserving? Well, why not? The art of home preserving has never been more relevant than it is today.

Not so very long ago, preserving foods was essential for survival. But what was once a necessity has now become a pleasure. Today's cooks preserve food at home because they want to, not because they have to.

When *Well Preserved* was first published in 1998, the practice of home preserving was already experiencing a notable resurgence. Home gardeners, health-conscious individuals concerned about food additives and nutrition, and adventurous cooks were all turning to home preserving in an effort to combine the joy of creativity with a productive and satisfying activity . . . one that yielded delicious results.

Since that time, we have seen the advent of "Slow Food," an increasingly popular movement created to celebrate traditional foods and cooking methods and help keep rural, agricultural communities sustainable. The "100 Mile Diet," the practice of consuming only products grown or produced within 100 miles of one's home, encourages us to reap the benefits of good food locally sourced, and make this a regular part of daily life.

Today, more and more of us are eating organic produce or growing our own fruits and vegetables. Home preserving allows us to engage in a form of cooking that uses only the best ingredients—locally grown and seasonal. Food that is in season is at the peak of its freshness and flavor, and we can take advantage of seasonal surpluses of produce and create delectable specialties at home at a very reasonable cost. And we can be assured of natural, chemical-free food.

For those who have never considered home preserving, this book is intended to help them tackle the process with both pleasure and ease. Preserving food at home need not be a chore. Preserve your food in small batches—gathering just enough produce for one recipe will eliminate long preparation time, and you can complete the process while attending to other work in the kitchen. And get family and friends to join in the fun.

Welcome to the wonderful world of home preserving. You don't have to settle for store-bought anymore!

Introduction

hen I was a child growing up in Nova Scotia, everyone's mom did some kind of home canning. It always seemed to be a rather old-fashioned, outdated activity, at least as far as we kids were concerned. We couldn't understand why anyone would want to spend long, hot hours working in the kitchen, in the middle of the summer, when jams and pickles could be had at any grocery store.

Now I wonder why anyone would prefer a store-bought product, when it is so easy and so much fun to make delicious preserves at home. For the price of a basket of produce and an hour or two of your time, you can enjoy the exceptional taste and quality of a homemade jam, pickle, chutney or relish year-round, and savor the knowledge that you made it yourself.

Preserves are easier to make than you think. If you like cooking, you're going to love home preserving. There's a back-to-nature, homey goodness about it that makes it a very satisfying pastime. And provided that you follow some simple, basic techniques and observe the guidelines for selecting and preparing produce, proper hygiene and careful storage, preserving will be a successful and rewarding experience.

For a time, home preserving had become something of a lost art, but it is now enjoying a vigorous revival. The desire for excellent food without unnecessary preservatives has greatly contributed to its renewed popularity. Gardening and the preservation of home-grown produce have become a way of life for more and more people.

Food preservation is no longer the tedious, time-consuming activity of Grandmother's day. Thanks to modern equipment and innovations, preparation and cooking times have been dramatically reduced. Techniques are continually being refined so that foods can be safely preserved and still retain flavor, color, texture and nutrients. Although there are countless varieties of store-bought preserves to choose from, none can compare with the vibrant, glorious flavors of the ones you make yourself.

Homemade preserves generally contain less sugar and salt than their commercially produced counterparts, and because they contain no artificial additives designed to prolong shelf life, homemade preserves are usually more wholesome as well. You know exactly what is inside the jar because you put it there yourself. If you choose, you can make healthful, delicious preserves using organically grown fruits and vegetables.

Fat-free relishes and salsas allow you to enhance otherwise bland dishes and may take the place of rich sauces. Select only the freshest fruits and vegetables, and the best available ingredients for your preserves, as preserving cannot improve the quality of food, it simply maintains it. If only the best goes into the jar, you will have a truly superior final product.

Food preservation makes sense economically too. Homemade tastes twice as good as store-bought and costs about half as much. You can even create luxurious specialty items at a fraction of what they would cost at an upscale grocery store, while taking advantage of the abundance of fruits and vegetables in your summer garden or local farmer's market.

The art of preserving brings us closer to nature—we become more in tune with the passage of the seasons, it encourages us to use up and recycle and it places an emphasis on fresh, natural ingredients preserved for future use at their peak of perfection.

Not least, preserving is fun. There is plenty of room for imagination in home preserving, so after you have gained some confidence, experiment a little with your own inventive combinations of fruits, vegetables, herbs and spices. Who knows? You could be creating a favorite family recipe that will be cherished and handed down by future generations.

This book is designed to give you just a taste of preserving—to whet your appetite for it. All the preserves in this book can be safely canned at home with a minimum of equipment in a reasonable period of time. You will learn how to make several types of sweet preserves: jams and jellies and their relatives, marmalades, conserves, preserves, fruit sauces and butters. The next section covers savory condiments, such as pickles, relishes, chutneys and ketchups. There is a chapter on infusing vinegars with fresh fruit and herbs, and another with ideas on how to use your homemade preserves in a variety of mouth-watering recipes. The last chapter offers suggestions on how to give your preserves as gifts and ideas for creatively packaging and decorating them.

If you've never tried it, give home preserving a chance. By following the rules you can produce consistently excellent preserves with little time and effort. Your reward will be cupboards filled with mouth-watering condiments to complement every meal, and the satisfaction of rows of gleaming jars adorning your pantry shelves.

THE BASICS OF PRESERVING

What Is Preserving?

Preserving food means to store and protect it from spoilage so that it can be eaten safely at some time in the future. There are many methods of food preservation; some, like drying, date back to prehistoric times. Other methods of food preservation include fermenting, brining, salting and smoking. This book covers the preservation of foods in vacuum-sealed glass jars, a procedure known as preserving, or canning. The term canning sometimes causes confusion to those who are unfamiliar with it, since cans are not actually involved. In the past, some cooks did preserve food at home in cans, but today this is virtually unheard of.

Canning is generally understood to mean the process of preparing foods in airtight jars. It is one of the most reliable methods for preserving foods. In the 19th century, Nicolas Appert, a native of France, developed canning in response to Napoleon's request for a way to preserve foods for his troops. Appert's efforts laid the groundwork for modern canning. Not long afterwards, Louis Pasteur proved that food spoilage is caused by microorganisms present in air, water and soil. His discoveries led to further developments in preserving methods and equipment. Even today, methods for canning or preserving are constantly being reviewed and improved.

Why Does Food Spoil?

All food preservation methods are based on simple principles. To preserve foods safely and effectively, we must control enzymes and microorganisms naturally occurring in foods that can cause them to spoil. Containers of preserved food must also be thoroughly sealed to prevent the reintroduction of airborne microorganisms and to counteract oxidation.

Enzymes are organic substances in foods. They are absolutely essential for fruits and vegetables to ripen, but if left unchecked, the action of enzymes will ultimately cause food to spoil. For this reason, it is advisable to process fresh produce as soon as possible after picking.

Enzymatic action is destroyed by heat. Heat is also the easiest and most effective way to kill microorganisms. Most molds, yeasts and bacteria are killed at the temperature of boiling water. Most, but not all . . .

A dangerous bacterium, *Clostridium botulinum*, can form spores able to withstand extremely high temperatures. While heat will kill the bacteria, it encourages the formation of spores that, given the right conditions, can later germinate. Coincidentally, the conditions necessary for the spores to flourish and grow are exactly those that exist inside a jar of canned food: the absence of air and a moist environment. These bacteria produce a poisonous toxin that causes the deadly disease botulism.

C. botulinum cannot grow in the presence of acid, so high-acid foods such as fruits and other foods preserved with vinegar or lemon juice will prevent its growth, providing proper canning procedures are followed.

There are only two widely accepted methods for processing canned foods: the boiling water bath method and pressure canning. Both procedures use heat to destroy microorganisms and inactivate enzymes. Pressure canning is reserved for low-acid foods such as meat, poultry, fish or vegetables preserved without vinegar. The extended time and higher temperatures used in this procedure will destroy spores and bacteria not normally eliminated at the temperature of boiling water. Pressure canning requires specialized equipment—a pressure canner is a considerable investment.

All the preserves in this book may be safely processed using the boiling water bath method, as they contain sufficient acid to prevent the growth of bacteria.

How Does Preserving Actually Work?

Preserving arrests the spoilage of fresh food by heating it in a sealed container. The food is prepared and placed in hot, sterilized jars. It is then heated in the jars to a temperature sufficient to destroy spoilage agents. During the heating process, air remaining in the food and in the space at the top of the jar is driven out between the jar and the special canning jar lid.

As the jar and the contents cool, the vacuum that has been created inside the jar sucks the lid inward, holding it tightly in place until the jar is opened. This airtight seal prevents any further contamination unless the seal is broken. This allows preserves to maintain their flavor and quality for a long time without refrigeration.

It is certainly possible to make virtually any type of preserve without heat processing. Such unprocessed preserves must be kept refrigerated and used within a short period of time.

PRESERVING EQUIPMENT

Using the right equipment will make preserving easier, safer and more successful. Only a few basic utensils are required for small-scale preserving. Fortunately, most of you will already have everything that you need in your own kitchens. There are also some specially designed, inexpensive tools that will save time and frustration, making your experience a more pleasurable one. These are optional, but recommended. And if you really get into preserving, there are additional time-saving gadgets that you will long to have.

The Preserving Pot

Without a doubt the most important piece of equipment is the preserving pot. It should be a wide, heavy pot with a thick bottom that will distribute heat evenly. A lightweight stock pot, for example, will not do. The even distribution of heat will help prevent scorching in foods that contain a lot of sugar. Straight-sided pots are best—they are especially useful for measuring the depth of liquid when a recipe calls for boiling a mixture until its volume is reduced by half.

The pot must be large enough to allow foods to bubble up the sides without overflowing. Some fruit and sugar mixtures expand considerably during rapid boiling—the juice and foam can rise amazingly high (alarmingly high if your pot is too small). Believe me, it is no picnic cleaning boiled-over jam or jelly off the top of your stove. A wide-diameter pot also speeds evaporation and reduces cooking time. A pot that is about three times the volume of your food is ideal. Eight to ten quarts (8 to 10 L) is a good all-purpose size.

Stainless steel or enamel-lined cast iron pots are your best bets for preserving. Unlined cast iron, copper, aluminum or galvanized pots will react with acids that are naturally present in foods, resulting in unpleasant flavors and colors.

Other Essentials

- measuring cups (liquid and dry)
- measuring spoons
- a stiff vegetable brush
- selection of knives, including a sharp paring knife and a good, sturdy knife for chopping
- a cutting board
- a vegetable peeler
- a grater
- a citrus reamer or juicer
- a long-handled spoon for stirring, preferably with a metal bowl
- a slotted spoon
- a ladle
- a potato masher
- rubber spatulas
- tongs
- mixing bowls
- a colander, a sieve or both
- cheesecloth

- a timer
- hot pads or oven mitts
- rubber gloves
- jars, lids and screwbands (more on these below)
- a water-bath canner

Optional but Highly Recommended Tools

- a canning jar funnel (to fill jars without spilling)
- a jar lifter (to raise or lower jars into the boiling water bath)
- a jelly bag (to strain fruit pulp when making jelly)
- a candy thermometer (to determine when sweet preserves are sufficiently cooked)
- a food processor
- kitchen scales
- a citrus zester

Extras

- cake racks for cooling jars
- a cherry pitter
- a berry huller
- a food mill
- a magnetic lid lifter (for removing jar lids from hot water)
- a metal steamer or basket (for blanching tomatoes and peaches)

Canning Jars

Often called Mason jars after the inventive American John Mason, who pioneered their design, canning jars are now marketed under various brand names. Poor Mr. Mason apparently let his patent lapse, and other entrepreneurs were quick to jump on the bandwagon.

A complete box of canning jars will include the jars and a corresponding number of two-piece metal lids. These lids consist of a flat metal disc and a metal screwband (sometimes referred to as a ring). The underside of the disc is coated with an enamel that resists food acids. Take care not to scratch the discs to help prevent rusting. The edge of the disc is lined with a sealing compound which softens slightly when heated and covers the rim of the jar to form a seal. The metal screwband holds the disc in place and should be secured until fingertip tight. Do not overtighten. During heat processing, the two-piece lid allows steam to escape, changing pressure inside the jar.

Each time you make preserves, check your jars to ensure that they are not chipped or cracked. Check new jars, too, just to be sure. Wash all jars in hot, soapy water and carefully sterilize them before each use.

A box of canning jars contains one other thing: excellent instructions that explain how to safely and successfully use them. Follow these instructions.

Canning jars are made with two sizes of openings: standard mouth (2 3/8 inches/ 6 cm) and wide mouth (3 inches/7.5 cm).

You may come across a third size, the gem or jewel jar, which has an opening that falls somewhere in between. These jars are no longer being manufactured, but lids and screwbands are available for purchase to accommodate people who may still have these jars at home.

Keep in mind that processing times are determined by food type and jar size. The larger the jar, the longer it takes to process.

Jars are available in various sizes (capacities):

½ cup (4 fl. oz)	125 mL
½ pint (8 fl. oz)	250 mL (236 mL)
pint (16 fl. oz)	500 mL
quart (32 fl. oz)	1 liter
1½ quarts (48 fl. oz)	1.5 liters

The half-pint, pint and quart are most commonly used. The half-cup (125 mL) size is so tiny, I find it suitable only for gifts, when I want to give a variety of preserves in small, taster sizes.

The half-pint (250 mL) is an excellent size for jams and jellies. It may appear as 236 mL just to make things confusing, but you may use the 250 mL and 236 mL sizes interchangeably.

Jars larger than 1.5 L are not recommended. First, it is almost impossible to find a pot deep enough to handle jars this size. Second, it takes so long for heat to penetrate the food at the center of the jar

that the process would take far too long. Besides, who needs that much food in one jar? So do yourself a favor and stick to the more common sizes.

Select the size of jar and the diameter of the mouth according to the type of food that you are preserving. Another consideration is the size of your family. There is no point putting up jam in teensy-weensy jars if you have four teenage children.

Through experience, I have found that certain jars accommodate particular types of foods best. For each recipe, I have indicated the size of jar that I feel is most appropriate.

Liquid-type foods, such as jams, jellies, marmalades and ketchups, that pour easily when hot are best in standard-mouth jars. The narrow opening decreases the likelihood of splashing. For most people, the half-pint (250 mL) jars are most practical for sweet spreads.

Chunky or thick foods do best in wide-mouth jars as it is easier to ladle the preserves into a larger opening. Relishes, chutneys and butters are included in this group. Either a half-pint (250 mL) or a pint (500 mL) jar may be suitable. A half-pint, wide-mouth jar is generally sold as a jar for canning salmon, but these are perfect for small sizes of relish and chutney. Wide-mouth jars are also best for foods that need to be individually arranged inside the jars, such as some types of pickles. Quart (1 L) jars are recommended for large or long vegetables, such as whole cucumbers, beans or asparagus.

Canning jars are made of sturdy glass designed to withstand high temperatures and repeated handlings. Do not be tempted to recycle regular commercial jars. Using old mayonnaise or peanut butter jars may seem like a money-saving idea, but they are made from a lighter-weight glass that may shatter during filling or heat processing. Jars which are not specifically designed for canning also may not seal properly. Considering the time and effort you will spend on preserving, it is not worth risking accidents or food spoilage by using such jars.

A supply of canning jars may seem rather expensive initially, but remember, they are reusable. If you handle and store your jars carefully, you will be able to use them year after year. As long as they are in perfect condition, the jars and metal screwbands may be used time and time again, but the lids are designed for single use only. They will not seal properly if used a second time; throw them away once used. Replacement lids are available at a minimal cost. You must also discard screwbands that are bent or rusty. Nifty one-piece, screw-on plastic caps are available for refrigerator storage of your preserves. These are much more convenient than dealing with lids and screwbands every time you want to open up a jar. They are available in grocery stores and

most places that sell canning jars.

Buy your canning jars early in the spring or summer to ensure a good supply later on in the year. Many stores only carry jars during what they consider to be "the canning season" and they do not restock jars once they sell out, for fear of having to carry them over the winter. You may find it difficult to track down jars by mid-August.

Shop around for jars, as prices vary widely from place to place. Keep an eye open for sales. Garage sales, secondhand stores and rummage sales are good sources for reasonably priced jars, but you will usually need to buy new lids and screwbands. Once your friends discover that you are preserving, you will be showered with secondhand jars. (Could they have ulterior motives?) Some of these may be suitable. Always examine recycled jars very carefully to be sure they are not damaged.

THE PRESERVING PROCESS
How to Sterilize Jars

1. Wash the jars (including new jars) in hot, soapy water and dry thoroughly. Or simply run them through the regular cycle of your dishwasher.
2. Place the clean jars on a rack in a large pot. You can use the same pot you will be using for the water bath.
3. Cover the jars with water and bring to a boil.
4. Boil the jars for 15 minutes.

5. Turn off the heat, cover the pot and keep the jars hot until you are ready to fill them.

Preparing the Jar Lids

Only the jar lids, not the metal screw-bands, need advance preparation.

The sealing compound on the inside of the lid needs to be softened so it will adhere to the rim of the jar and seal the jar properly. Heating the lids in boiling water sterilizes the lids and also softens the sealing compound.

1. Place lids in a small pot of water.
2. Boil for 5 minutes—not longer.
3. Cover the pot and let the lids stand in hot water until you are ready to use them.
4. Use a nonmetallic utensil to remove the lids from the water. Metal tongs can scratch the lids' enamel surface, which can cause lids to rust. (A magnetic wand specially designed for this very purpose is available from canning-jar manufacturers.)

What Is Head Space?

When preserving food in jars, never fill the jars right to the rim. The space between the contents of the jar and the lid is known as the head space.

Head space allows room for expansion of the food during heat processing. It should be just enough to permit food to swell as it is heated without danger of it overflowing, but not so much that an excess of air would prevent a good vacuum seal from being formed.

Food that escapes the jar during heat processing does far more damage than just causing a big mess. Particles of food on the rims or threads of a jar can interfere with a perfect seal, and can contribute to the growth of mold. Mold on the outside of a jar will eventually force its way under the lid and ruin the seal, causing the food inside to spoil.

If you leave too large a head space, the air inside the jar may prevent a proper seal from forming. Excess air may also cause foods to discolor due to oxidation.

Most preserves require about a $1/4$-inch (6 mm) head space, while pickles require a $1/2$ inch (1.2 cm), but density, shape and particular characteristics of foods can all affect head-space specifications.

Food density, jar size and processing methods determine the required head space for different foods in different jars.

Releasing Air Bubbles

Sometimes air is trapped between the food and the jar as the food is placed inside during packing. Air bubbles (pockets of air) can prevent liquid from completely covering or surrounding the food, and may contribute to food spoiling. Air bubbles are more likely to happen with some types of foods than with others. Relishes and pickled vegetables and fruits are particular culprits.

After the jars are packed, run a thin nonmetal object, such as a plastic knife or spatula, around the inside of each jar, between the food and the glass. This will dislodge the bubbles. Do not use a metal knife or any sharp utensil which could make tiny scratches or nicks in the glass. The high temperatures during heat processing stress the glass and may cause it to break along these weakened spots.

If additional space is created at the top of the jar after the air bubbles have been released, add more liquid to the jar to return it to the proper level before closing it. The correct head space helps to create a good vacuum seal.

If you don't dislodge air bubbles, you may find that once the food cools and the liquid settles, there will be extra space at the top of the jar between the food and the lid. Certain foods, like pickles, may end up protruding above the level of the liquid. This is unattractive and foods at the top of the jar will soon discolor. It is best to refrigerate such jars and use the preserves as soon as possible.

The Boiling Water Bath

Unless they are to be kept refrigerated, all preserves must be processed in a boiling water bath. Many people believe that it is not necessary to heat process certain types of preserves, such as jams or jellies, but experts agree that this additional step must be taken to ensure that homemade preserves are safe to eat.

Despite your most scrupulous efforts at cleanliness, bacteria, molds and spores may be present in the foods you are preserving. Airborne microorganisms may also contaminate foods as they are being placed into jars.

Heat processing in a boiling water bath will destroy any microorganisms that may be lurking in your homemade preserves. For safety's sake, do not omit this vital procedure.

Any large pot will do for a water bath canner provided that it meets certain requirements.

The pot must be deep enough to allow at least 2 inches (5 cm) of water to cover the jars when they are placed inside, as well as permitting sufficient space for boiling. A pot about 10 inches (25 cm) deep is good for pints (500 mL); allow about 12 inches (30 cm) for quart (1 L) jars.

The pot must be large enough to hold several jars at a time so that they are not touching one another, allowing the water to circulate freely around them. (Jars that are packed in too tightly could crack as they expand with the heat.)

There must be room at the bottom of the pot for a metal rack, such as a cake rack, to elevate the jars slightly. (You can improvise a rack for elevating jars by tying several old canning rings (screwbands) together and placing them right side up inside the bottom of the pot.) The pot should be no more than 4 inches (10 cm) greater in diameter than the burner that you will be using. And finally, your canner must have a snug-fitting lid.

Of course, there are pots specifically designed for water bath canning. These large deep pots, usually made from enamel-coated metal or stainless steel, come equipped with a specially fitted, basket-shaped rack to hold your jars of preserves in place and have high or folding handles that enable you to lift the entire rack full of jars from the boiling water. A genuine water bath canner is an excellent investment if you plan to do a lot of preserving.

Precisely when you prepare the boiling water bath depends on how long it will take to make your preserves. There is no point having the water boiling while foods are being chopped up, for example, or if they have to be soaked.

The boiling water bath should be ready to go as soon as your jars are filled, so that the hot jars can immediately be placed in the pot. (Never place cold or room temperature jars into boiling water.)

If you are using the same pot that you used to sterilize the jars, then it is very easy. After all the jars have been filled and any extras removed from the pot, simply turn the heat to high, cover the pot and bring the water to a boil. Since the water is already hot, this won't take long.

ADJUSTMENTS FOR ALTITUDE

Altitude affects certain aspects of preserving. Water boils at a lower temperature at higher altitudes, due to decreased atmospheric pressure. This affects two preserving operations: testing for the gel stage using a thermometer and processing preserves in a boiling water bath.

Testing for the gel stage: At elevations up to 1,000 feet (300 m), the gel stage for preserves is reached at 220°F (104°C). Temperatures that refer to the gel stage in this book are for such elevations. To determine the gel stage at elevations above 1,000 feet (300 m), add 8°F (4°C) to the boiling point of water at your elevation.

The boiling water bath: At altitudes higher than 1,000 feet (300 m), increase processing and jar sterilization time. At 1,001 to 3,000 feet (300 to 900 m), add 5 minutes to processing and jar sterilization time indicated in recipe. At 3,001 to 6,000 feet (900 to 1,800 m), add 10 minutes.

The jars will displace the water as they are put in the pot, causing the water level to rise considerably. There is usually enough water in the canner to cover the jars sufficiently. However, it is convenient to have an extra pot of hot water simmering just in case you need to add some. You don't want to have to start boiling cold water at this stage.

If your canner has a basket, fill it with the jars and lower it carefully into the water. If you are using a regular pot, place the jars inside, one by one, onto the rack in the bottom of the pot, standing them upright so that none of them are touching any others. It is very helpful to have a proper jar lifter for this, so that you don't scald your hands with the boiling water. If you don't have a jar lifter, wear rubber gloves to protect your hands. For small jam-sized jars, you can use a nonmetallic utensil to grasp the tops of the jars and then place them in the canner. Larger jars will have to be placed in by hand. If you are performing this tricky operation, don't fill the canner as full at the outset, but do have the extra pot of hot water standing by. The lower level of water in the canner will allow you to safely put the jars into the pot without burning yourself. Top up the water to cover the jars using the water in the smaller pot. Whew! This is sounding a lot more complicated than it really is.

Once the jars are in the canner, cover it and let the water return to a boil. Start timing from the moment the water starts to boil again. Lower the heat a bit if necessary to keep the water from overflowing, but make sure that the water remains at a steady boil.

When the time is up, remove the jars and place them on a wire rack or a heatproof surface to cool. Allow enough space for air to circulate freely around the jars. Never place the jars on a cold surface—they could crack.

How to Know When Jars Are Sealed

- You can hear it. As they cool, most jar lids will make a popping sound—music to the ears of home preservers! If you tap the lid with a spoon, a clear ringing sound indicates the seal is complete.
- You can see it. If you hold the jar at eye level, you can see a slight indentation in the center of the lid (the surface is concave). A flat or bulging lid isn't sealed.
- You can feel it. Push down on the center of the lid with your finger. A properly sealed jar will not respond to pressure on its lid. If the lid gives then pops back up when your finger is removed, the jar is not sealed.

A final way to check for properly sealed jars is to remove the screwband. If the lids are sealed, you can lift the jar by the lid.

Be patient. Give the jars a chance to seal. Some take up to 24 hours.

You do not need to perform all of these tests to be certain that your jars are sealed. They are included more for reassurance than anything else. The fingertip pressure test is adequate.

Occasionally, a jar will appear to have sealed, then later on the lid will pop back up again. For this reason, it's a good idea to check jars once they have cooled and once again before you use the preserves.

Reprocessing unsealed jars is not recommended. Refrigerate unsealed jars and use them as soon as possible.

STORING YOUR PRESERVES

Storing preserved foods, even in a small city apartment, is not a big problem. Foods that are preserved in jars have an advantage over frozen foods in that preserves require no special equipment to keep them. While not all of us are fortunate enough to have a separate, temperature-controlled pantry or root cellar, most homes have several places that are suitable for keeping preserves.

Cool, dark and dry—these are the words to remember when storing your preserves.

- Ideally, the temperature should be 40 to 50°F (5 to 10°C), but this is not always possible. Even properly processed foods will lose vitamins and nutrients above 50°F (10°C) and if the temperature is high enough, certain types of bacteria can reactivate and begin to grow inside the jars. Keep preserves away from extra warm areas near furnaces, fireplaces, heating pipes and vents.

  Guard preserves from freezing. Freezing will not cause spoilage, but since foods expand as they freeze, the seals could be damaged or the jars could break. If the cool place that you have in mind is subject to freezing, wrap the jars in newspapers or blankets to insulate them.

- Light also destroys vitamins and can cause certain types of preserves to fade

ABOUT MICROWAVE PRESERVING

If you enjoy microwave cooking in general, you may want to try processing foods using the microwave.

The microwave can be used to make small amounts of preserves, but they will require very frequent stirring to prevent sticking or scorching, especially towards the end of the cooking time.

The most success is likely with very small batches using a maximum of 1 to 2 cups (240 to 475 mL) of fruit. Larger quantities tend to boil over.

I have found that it is more trouble to constantly open and close the door of the microwave than it is to stir a pot on top of the stove. And unless you are going to store your microwave preserves in the refrigerator, you must still sterilize your jars and process your preserves in boiling water—so you're using the stove anyway.

Consult a microwave cookbook for more information on microwave preserving.

or darken unappetizingly. As attractive as they are, your preserves must be stored out of sight, away from the light.

- A dry storage area is crucial. Dampness or humidity can cause metal jar lids to rust.

- Arrange preserves in such a way that you can have good "stock rotation," using up the older foods before the newer ones. Well-made preserves should remain in good condition even after the next season comes along, provided they have been stored properly. After prolonged storage, however, flavor and quality will definitely suffer. It is not recommended to keep homemade preserves longer than one year—six months is best. If you find that you still have jars of one thing or another once the new season has arrived, make a mental note to prepare less of that particular item the next time.

- Don't forget to label your preserves. You may be able to tell the difference now, but six months later blueberry jam and blackberry jam will look exactly alike. And it's not always easy to tell which pickles are the mild ones and which are extra hot.
- Always check your jars for any signs of spoilage before using the preserves. Discard any jars that are even remotely questionable.

BASIC STEPS FOR SUCCESSFUL PRESERVING

1. Read the recipe carefully.
2. Check that you have all the ingredients and equipment you need before you start.
3. Select the correct size and type of jars, ensuring that they are not chipped or cracked.
4. Wash the jars thoroughly, then sterilize the jars and lids and keep them hot until you are ready to use them.
5. Prepare the water bath canner.
6. Place the prepared preserves into the hot jars as directed in the recipe. Work quickly so that everything remains hot. Leave the recommended head space.
7. Release air bubbles if necessary.
8. Carefully wipe the rims of the jars free of any spilled food.
9. Place the lids on the jars, sealing compound side down, and screw on the rings (screwbands) until fingertip tight.
10. Transfer the jars to the boiling water bath.
11. Boil the jars for the amount of time indicated in the recipe. Start timing once the water has returned to a boil.
12. Remove the jars and place them upright on a heatproof surface in a draft-free place to cool. Do not retighten screwbands.
13. Cool the preserves undisturbed for 24 hours.
14. Once the jars have cooled, test for a seal. Refrigerate any jars that have not sealed properly.
15. Remove the screwbands and wipe jars carefully with a damp cloth.
16. Label the jars clearly, indicating the type of preserve and the date.
17. Store preserves in a cool, dark, dry place.

Jams

Soft Strawberry Jam 21

Ruby Red Raspberry Jam 22

Jumbleberry Jam 24

Spiced Blackberry and Apple Jam 25

True Blueberry Jam 26

Apricot Jam 28

Butterscotch Peach Jam 29

Peach Melba Jam 30

Gingered Pear Jam 31

Rhubarb and Carrot Jam 32

Strawberry Rhubarb Jam 33

Kiwi Lime Jam 34

Plum Jam 36

Jams

Jam is so simple to make that perhaps the expression "as easy as pie" should be revised to "as easy as jam." (I don't know about you, but I find pie-making to be a rather daunting task!)

Easy, economical and satisfying to make, a batch of homemade jam can be whipped up in as little as one hour from start to finish, although some recipes take a little longer. Making jam requires no special equipment—everything you need is already in your kitchen.

The taste of fresh fruit shines through homemade jam, unmasked by the excessive amounts of sugar and preservatives found in commercial products. You will find that the jams you make yourself have a slightly different texture than store-bought jams. Home-made jams tend to be of a softer consistency, set but not solid.

The beauty of jam is that there is a certain amount of room for error, if it doesn't thicken as much as you would like—it still tastes terrific.

Unlike some other types of preserves that take time to mature, jam is ready to eat as soon as you make it. But don't limit your enjoyment of jam to breakfast—jam can en-hance many types of desserts. It makes an excellent filling for bars and cookies, or it can be sandwiched between the layers of a rich, homemade cake. (Try raspberry jam with chocolate cake.) Fill small tart shells with custard and a dollop of jam, then top with fresh fruit; or thin jams with juice or alcohol to make marvelous, instant fruit sauces.

Many old recipes call for sealing jars of preserves using melted paraffin wax. Doubtless a great number of seasoned home preservers still seal jams and jellies using this method, but wax seals are no longer recommended as they do not always provide an airtight seal. As the wax cools, it can pull away from the sides of the jar, exposing the surface of the preserves to air. Tiny bubbles in the wax may open, creating holes through which air and microorganisms can enter, allowing mold to develop.

A bit of jam added to plain, nonfat yogurt gives a boost of flavor and sweetness without too many extra calories. A spoonful of jam has about half as many calories as the same amount of butter; use jam instead of butter if you are watching your weight.

So delight your family and friends—simmer up a pot of old-fashioned, home-made jam. Your kitchen will be filled with mouth-watering aromas and visions of sweet surprises to come. What a treat it will be to enjoy a luscious, fresh-testing jam, made from the finest of juicy summer fruits, on a cold wintry morning in January. That is, if it lasts that long!

THE ESSENTIALS OF MAKING JAM

Jam is essentially just a mixture of mashed-up fruit and sugar, cooked together until thickened. The basic principle of making jam is to have a proper balance of fruit, sugar, pectin and acid. This will ensure a good set, meaning the jam will be soft enough to spread, but firm enough not to run off your toast.

Fruit

As in all preserving, it is crucial to use only the freshest, top-quality produce. The ideal is a mixture of ripe and slightly underripe fruit, as underripe fruit contains more natural pectin, critical in helping the jam to set. A good ratio is three-quarters ripe fruit to one-quarter slightly underripe, but not green, fruit. Never use overripe or mushy fruit. Wash the fruit carefully, even if it is to be peeled.

Sugar

The correct amount of sugar is necessary for a jam to thicken properly. Sugar acts as a preservative and adds flavor and texture to the jam. Do not reduce the amount of sugar called for in jam recipes unless you are prepared to store your jam in the refrigerator. Unless otherwise specified, sugar means white granulated sugar.

For those with special concerns about sugar, it is possible to make sweet preserves using reduced amounts of sugar or sugar substitutes, using modified pectin or gelatin. Special recipes are required.

Pectin

Pectin is a naturally occurring substance found in all fruits. Pectin causes jam to thicken. If all fruits contained the same amounts of pectin, making jam would be a cinch. But the amount of pectin varies not only from one fruit to another, but even within groups of fruits, that is, by variety. The pectin content is also determined by the degree of ripeness of the fruit; even growing conditions can have an effect. A wet year will produce plump, juicy fruit with less pectin; a dry year results in drier, smaller fruit with a higher pectin content. Fruits rich in pectin make good jam quickly and easily. High- and low-pectin fruits can be combined to achieve a desirable pectin level.

Another solution is to use a commercial pectin product. Commercial pectins are made from citrus fruits or apples. They can be used with any fruit to assure the formation of a gel. This book does not contain many recipes using commercial pectin, as excellent, reliable recipes are found inside every package. I have only included commercial pectin in those recipes where a gel could not be obtained in a reasonable amount of time without it (see next chapter, on Jellies).

The jams in this chapter are made by the traditional "long cook" method—without the use of commercial pectin. Long-cooked jams use less sugar than those made with commercial pectin and, I believe, have a more intense fruit flavor.

Acid

Jams will not thicken properly without the presence of acid. Many fruits naturally contain sufficient acid, but others require the addition of an acid, usually lemon juice, to help the jam to gel. Underripe fruit has a higher acid content than fully ripe fruit.

THE BASICS OF MAKING JAM

1. For long-boil jams, select a mixture of ripe and slightly underripe fruit (three-quarters ripe to one-quarter slightly underripe fruit is a good ratio).

MAKING JAM OR JELLY FROM FROZEN FRUIT

So many berries ripen at the same time of year! Sometimes it's hard to keep up with jam or jelly making during the summertime, when there is so much to do. If you haven't the time (or the inclination) to make berry jam or jelly in season, you can freeze fresh berries for use at any time of the year.

Berries should be frozen as soon as possible after picking. Rinse the berries and stem or hull them if necessary. Gently pat the berries dry using paper towels. Place the berries in a single layer on trays or cookie sheets lined with waxed paper. Freeze until solid, about 2 hours.

As you are aware, accurate measurements are very important in jam and jelly making. Because frozen berries tend to collapse somewhat as they thaw, it is advisable to measure your berries as you pack them into their containers once they are frozen. Measure the berries in the quantities required for a single recipe. Transfer them to freezer bags or plastic containers, label clearly with the type of berry and the amount, and freeze.

Do not add sugar to fruit that is being frozen for jam and jelly making—berries freeze perfectly well without it. For the best flavor use frozen berries within one year.

To make jam or jelly using frozen berries, simply remove the measured berries from the freezer and thaw the fruit in the refrigerator until only a few ice crystals remain. Then just follow your favorite recipe.

2. Rinse or wash the fruit briefly under running water. Don't allow the fruit to soak in water for long periods of time.

3. Prepare the fruit as directed in the recipe (peel and/or chop or crush). Some recipes call for precooking hard fruits (such as pears) or stone fruits

(such as peaches) briefly, in water or their own juices. Others require you to leave the fruit and sugar to stand for a short time to allow juices to form.

4. Bring the jam to a boil. Count the cooking time from the moment the jam starts to boil vigorously.

5. Once the jam starts to boil, it should be stirred often to prevent pieces of fruit from sticking to the bottom of the pot.

6. Cooking times for jam may vary in minutes depending on the type of fruit and the amount of pectin present. Most jams are ready when the jam holds its shape somewhat on a spoon. It will thicken more as it cools.

7. A candy thermometer is useful to indicate when the jam is cooked. The stage is between 218°F and 222°F (103°C and 105°C)—it varies slightly depending on the pectin content of the fruit. A good median figure is 220°F (104°C). Adjustments may also need to be made for altitude (see page 11). You do not have to be as precise with jam as you do with jelly. You can also use the plate test, described on page 42, if you like.

8. When the jam is cooked, remove it from the heat. Stir and skim off any foam that has collected on the surface of the jam (a metal spoon with a shallow bowl does the best job of this). To reduce the amount of foam somewhat, add ½ tsp (2.5 mL) of butter to the fruit and sugar mixture before it starts to boil.

9. Some recipes call for stirring the jam briefly (2 to 5 minutes) to help prevent pieces of fruit from rising to the surface and floating at the top of the jam. This is usually the case with jams that are made from hard or stone fruits.

10. Carefully pour or ladle the hot jam into the hot, sterilized jars. You can use a small pitcher or measuring cup for pouring; a ladle and canning jar funnel are more useful for thicker jams.

11. Leave a ¼-inch (6 mm) head space at the top of the jars. Carefully wipe the rims of the jars to ensure that there is no spilled jam that might interfere with a good seal. Use a clean cloth or paper towel dipped in hot water (you can use the water from the pot that held your jars).

12. Seal the jars according to the manufacturer's directions.

13. Process the jars in a boiling water bath for 10 minutes.

Soft Strawberry Jam

MAKES ABOUT SIX 8 OZ (250 ML) JARS

This jam is slightly soft and runny, but oh so delicious.
The natural, fruity taste of the strawberries really shines
through. Rinse the berries briefly before hulling to keep
them from absorbing too much water.

8 cups • 2 L sliced strawberries

6 cups • 1.5 L sugar

⅓ cup • 80 mL lemon juice

PREPARE the preserving jars.

In your preserving pot, crush the strawberries lightly with a potato masher. Simmer over medium-low heat for 10 minutes. Add the sugar and lemon juice, stirring until the sugar is dissolved. Increase the heat to medium-high and boil rapidly, stirring often, for 15 to 20 minutes or until it is slightly thickened. Test for set, if desired.

Remove from the heat. Stir for 2 to 3 minutes and skim off the foam if necessary. Pour the jam into hot, sterilized jars, leaving a ¼-inch (6 mm) head space. Wipe the rims clean. Seal according to manufacturer's directions. Process the jars in a boiling water bath for 10 minutes.

STRAWBERRY LIME JAM Add the finely grated zest of 1 lime to the strawberries during the initial cooking. Substitute lime juice for lemon juice.

STRAWBERRY MINT JAM After the jam has been removed from the heat and the foam has been skimmed off, stir in 2 Tbsp (30 mL) chopped fresh mint.

STRAWBERRY ORANGE JAM Slice an orange thinly, discarding the ends and seeds. Chop very finely by hand or in a food processor. Add to the strawberries during the initial cooking.

Ruby Red Raspberry Jam

MAKES ABOUT FOUR 8 OZ (250 ML) JARS

The fragile raspberry must be handled carefully. Vulnerable to mold once picked, they should be refrigerated and used as soon as possible.

4 cups • 950 mL raspberries
3 cups • 720 mL sugar
¼ cup • 60 mL lemon juice

PREPARE the preserving jars.

In your preserving pot, gently crush the raspberries with a potato masher. Add the sugar and let stand for 1 hour.

Bring to a boil over medium-high heat; stir in the lemon juice. Boil rapidly, stirring often, for 15 to 20 minutes, or until it starts to thicken. Test for set if desired.

Remove from the heat. Stir and skim off the foam if necessary. Pour the jam into hot, sterilized jars, leaving a ¼-inch (6 mm) head space. Wipe the rims clean. Seal according to manufacturer's directions. Process the jars in a boiling water bath for 10 minutes.

BLACKBERRY JAM Simply replace the raspberries with blackberries for a mouth-watering jam.

PICTURED» Ruby Red Raspberry Jam and Soft Strawberry Jam (page 21).

Jumbleberry Jam

MAKES ABOUT FOUR TO FIVE 8 OZ (250 ML) JARS

If you freeze extra berries while they are in season, you can make homemade jam at any time of the year. This also will allow you to combine fruits that are generally not in season at the same time. If you use frozen berries, thaw them first.

2 cups • 475 mL strawberries

2 cups • 475 mL blackberries

1 cup • 240 mL blueberries

1 cup • 240 mL cranberries

3½ cups • 840 mL sugar

¼ cup • 60 mL lemon juice

PREPARE the preserving jars.

Combine the berries and sugar in your preserving pot. Mash them thoroughly with a potato masher. Add the lemon juice. Bring to a boil over medium heat and simmer, stirring often, 20 to 25 minutes, or until thickened. Test for set if desired.

Remove from the heat. Stir and skim off the foam if necessary. Pour the jam into hot, sterilized jars, leaving a ¼-inch (6 mm) head space. Wipe the rims clean. Seal according to manufacturer's directions. Process the jars in a boiling water bath for 10 minutes.

Spiced Blackberry and Apple Jam

MAKES ABOUT FIVE TO SIX 8 OZ (250 ML) JARS

A delightful, piquant, subtly spiced jam.

  2 cups • 475 mL peeled, cored and
      chopped apples
  ½ cup • 120 mL red wine vinegar
  1 lemon, zest only, coarsely grated
  3 cups • 720 mL blackberries
  3 cups • 720 mL sugar
  ¼ tsp • 1.2 mL each ground nutmeg, cinnamon
      and cloves

PREPARE the preserving jars.

Combine the apples, vinegar and lemon zest in your preserving pot. Bring to a boil over medium heat. Cover and simmer for 10 minutes, until the apples begin to soften, stirring occasionally. Stir in the remaining ingredients. Simmer for 20 to 25 minutes, stirring often, until the jam thickens. Test for set if desired.

Remove from the heat. Stir and skim off the foam if necessary. Pour the jam into hot, sterilized jars, leaving a ¼-inch (6 mm) head space. Wipe the rims clean. Seal according to manufacturer's directions. Process the jars in a boiling water bath for 10 minutes.

HINT: ADD APPLES TO JAM

Adding apples to a jam recipe is an excellent way to stretch fresh fruit and you will boost the pectin level at the same time. The unobtrusive flavor of apples will not mask the taste of the other fruit. Be sure to use a variety of apple that breaks down easily when cooked, such as McIntosh, unless you prefer a chunky jam.

Wild lowbush blueberries are common in the east, but on the west coast we are more apt to find the highbush cultivated varieties. Wild berries are generally considered to be more flavorful for eating fresh, but either kind are good for preserving.

Although the blueberry closely resembles another wild fruit, the huckleberry, they are not related. Blueberries contain many tiny edible seeds; huckleberries have ten seeds that are relatively large and stony. Huckleberries are tarter than blueberries and are not cultivated.

Blueberries are botanically related to the English bilberry, also known as the whortleberry. The French *myrtille* is the same fruit.

In North America, blueberries are harvested from May to September, but the peak season is in July and August.

Select firm plump berries that are fresh and dry in appearance. Overripe fruit has a dull lifeless look to it. Blueberries range in color from light blue to blue-black, depending on variety. The silver bloom seen on blueberries is a pearly coating that is a natural protective wax.

Blueberries are a pleasure to prepare. There is no peeling, pitting or hulling; just sort them and pick out the odd stem or two.

Blueberries have a long shelf life compared to other berries; they will keep in the refrigerator up to 2 weeks. Wash them just before using.

True Blueberry Jam

MAKES ABOUT FOUR TO FIVE 8 OZ (250 ML) JARS

Select plump, blue-black berries, avoiding any that are shriveled. Wild blueberries are wonderful if you can get them.

6 cups • 1.5 L blueberries
4 cups • 950 mL sugar
¼ cup • 60 mL lemon juice

PREPARE the preserving jars.

In your preserving pot, crush the blueberries thoroughly with a potato masher. Add the sugar and lemon juice. Bring to a boil over medium-high heat and boil rapidly, stirring often, for 15 to 20 minutes. Test for set if desired.

Remove from the heat. Stir and skim off the foam if necessary. Pour the jam into hot, sterilized jars, leaving a ¼-inch (6 mm) head space. Wipe the rims clean. Seal according to manufacturer's directions. Process the jars in a boiling water bath for 10 minutes.

BLACK AND BLUE JAM Replace half the blueberries with blackberries. After crushing berries and adding sugar, let stand for 1 hour. Follow directions for blueberry jam, adding an extra 2 Tbsp (30 mL) lemon juice and 2 tsp (10 mL) finely grated lemon zest.

APRICOT PITS AND KERNELS

If you crack open an apricot pit, you will find a kernel inside that has a strong smell and taste of almonds. Plums, cherries and peaches have such kernels as well.

Many old-time recipes instruct you to place these kernels in a cheesecloth bag and cook them with the other ingredients to impart an almond flavor to some preserves. This practice is no longer recommended, as these kernels contain a cyanide compound—hydrocyanic acid—which can be toxic.

Although some may say that there is no danger in using just a few kernels, as the amount of hydrocyanic acid would be minimal, I say, why take the chance?

Apricot Jam

MAKES ABOUT FIVE TO SIX 8 OZ (250 ML) JARS

Because apricots have little natural pectin, apple juice is added to increase the likelihood of a good set. Nevertheless, this will still be a rather soft jam.

4½ cups • 1.1 L pitted, chopped apricots
⅓ cup • 80 mL apple juice
4 cups • 950 mL sugar
2 Tbsp • 30 mL lemon juice

PREPARE the preserving jars.

Combine the apricots and apple juice in your preserving pot. Bring to a boil over medium heat, cover and simmer about 10 minutes, until the apricots are tender, stirring occasionally.

Add the sugar and lemon juice, stirring until the sugar dissolves. Bring to a full boil over medium-high heat, then reduce the heat to medium. Simmer 15 to 20 minutes, stirring almost constantly, until the jam has thickened. Test for set if desired.

Remove from the heat and stir for 3 to 5 minutes. Pour the jam into hot, sterilized jars, leaving a ¼-inch (6 mm) head space. Wipe the rims clean. Seal according to manufacturer's directions. Process the jars in a boiling water bath for 10 minutes.

Butterscotch Peach Jam

Try to select freestone rather than clingstone peaches—
they are so much quicker to prepare, as the flesh of the
peach easily separates from the pit.

> 6 cups • 1.5 L peeled, cored and chopped
>   peaches
> ⅓ cup • 80 mL lemon juice
> 5 cups • 1.2 L brown sugar

PREPARE the preserving jars.

Combine the peaches and lemon juice in your preserving pot. Crush the fruit
with a potato masher. Bring to a boil over medium heat, cover and simmer for
10 minutes, stirring occasionally. Stir in the brown sugar. Increase the heat to
medium-high and cook, stirring often, for about 20 to 25 minutes, until slightly
thickened. Test for set if desired.

Remove from the heat and stir the jam for 3 to 5 minutes. Skim off the foam
if necessary. Ladle the jam into hot, sterilized jars, leaving a ¼-inch (6 mm)
head space. Wipe the rims clean. Seal according to manufacturer's directions.
Process the jars in a boiling water bath for 10 minutes.

Peach Melba Jam

MAKES ABOUT FOUR TO FIVE 8 OZ (250 ML) JARS

Peach Melba is a classic dessert created by the great French chef Escoffier in honor of a famous opera singer named Nellie Melba. Despite the fact that the quantity of peaches is four times that of the raspberries, the raspberry-red color will prevail.

4 cups • 950 mL peeled, pitted and
   chopped peaches
¼ cup • 60 mL lemon juice
1 cup • 240 mL raspberries
4 cups • 950 mL sugar

PREPARE the preserving jars.

Combine the peaches and lemon juice in your preserving pot. Mash thoroughly with a potato masher. Bring to a boil over medium heat. Cover and simmer for 10 minutes, stirring occasionally. Stir in the raspberries and sugar. Increase the heat to medium-high and boil rapidly, stirring often, for 20 to 25 minutes, or until the jam begins to thicken. Test for set if desired.

Remove from the heat. Stir and skim off the foam if necessary. Pour the jam into hot, sterilized jars, leaving a ¼-inch (6 mm) head space. Wipe the rims clean. Seal according to manufacturer's directions. Process the jars in a boiling water bath for 10 minutes.

Gingered Pear Jam

I can eat this straight from the jar! To save time, use a food processor fitted with a shredding disc to chop the pears.

one 3-inch (7.5 cm) cinnamon stick

1 tsp • 5 mL whole cloves

6 cups • 1.5 L peeled, cored and
   chopped pears

¼ cup • 60 mL lemon juice

4½ cups • 1.1 L sugar

¼ cup • 60 mL chopped candied ginger

PREPARE the preserving jars. Put the cinnamon stick and cloves into a cheesecloth bag and tie the top with string.

Combine the pears and lemon juice in your preserving pot. Bring to a boil over medium heat. Cover and simmer for 10 minutes, stirring often.

Add the cheesecloth bag of spices and the sugar and ginger; stir until the sugar is dissolved. Cook over medium heat, stirring often, for 20 to 25 minutes, or until the mixture thickens. Be careful, as the jam may tend to stick to the bottom of the pot towards the end of the cooking time. Test for set if desired.

Remove from the heat and discard the spice bag. Stir the jam and skim off the foam if necessary. Ladle the jam into hot, sterilized jars, leaving a ¼-inch (6 mm) head space. Wipe the rims clean. Seal according to manufacturer's directions. Process the jars in a boiling water bath for 10 minutes.

HOW TO MAKE A CHEESECLOTH SPICE BAG

A cheesecloth bag allows for the easy removal of whole spices from your preserving pot once the preserves are cooked. It is also very useful for straining liquids.

Cheesecloth is a loosely woven, lightweight cloth. You can usually find it at the grocery store.

Cut a double thickness of cheesecloth about 4 inches (10 cm) square. Place the spices in the center and gather up the corners to form a pouch. Tie it tightly at the top with string.

To extract all of the spicy goodness, place the spice bag in a small bowl when you remove it from the preserves. Tilt the bowl over the preserving pot and use the back of a spoon to press the bag and allow all the flavored juices to drip back into the pot. Discard the spice bag.

Rhubarb and Carrot Jam

MAKES ABOUT FOUR 8 OZ (250 ML) JARS

An unusual combination that tastes terrific, this jam can
easily be made at any time of year using frozen rhubarb.

> 4 cups • 950 mL rhubarb, chopped into ½-inch
> (1.2 cm) dice
> 4 cups • 950 mL grated carrots
> 2 oranges, juice and finely grated zest
> 2 lemons, juice and finely grated zest
> 6 cups • 1.5 L sugar

MIX all the ingredients together in your preserving pot. Cover and let stand
overnight.

The next day, bring the mixture to a boil over medium heat, stirring
occasionally.

Prepare the preserving jars.

Simmer the mixture for 25 to 40 minutes, stirring often, until the jam begins
to thicken. It is a good idea to use a thermometer to test for set with this jam
as the cooking time can vary widely. When the thermometer registers 220°F
(104°C), remove from the heat and test again using the plate test (see "How to
Test for Gel," page 42). If the jam is not thick enough, cook it a little longer, but
stir it constantly, as it may begin to stick to the bottom of the pot.

When the jam is ready, remove it from the heat and stir for 2 to 3 minutes.
Ladle the jam into hot, sterilized jars, leaving a ¼-inch (6 mm) head space.
Wipe the rims clean. Seal according to manufacturer's directions. Process the
jars in a boiling water bath for 10 minutes.

Strawberry Rhubarb Jam

MAKES ABOUT FOUR TO FIVE 8 OZ (250 ML) JARS

One of spring's first crops, rhubarb turns a rather unappetizing brown color when cooked. But team it with strawberries and you have this sweet-tart, rose-colored jam. Use less rhubarb and more strawberries or vice versa, if you prefer.

3 cups • 720 mL rhubarb, chopped into ½-inch (1.2 cm) dice
4 cups • 950 mL sugar
3 cups • 720 mL sliced strawberries
¼ cup • 60 mL lemon juice

COMBINE the rhubarb and sugar in your preserving pot. Let stand for 2 hours.

Prepare the preserving jars.

Add the strawberries and lemon juice and bring to a boil over medium heat, stirring until the sugar is dissolved. Increase the heat to medium-high and boil rapidly, stirring often, for 20 to 25 minutes, or until the jam is slightly thickened. Test for set if desired.

Remove from the heat and stir for 3 to 5 minutes. Skim off the foam if necessary. Pour into hot, sterilized jars, leaving a ¼-inch (6 mm) head space. Wipe the rims clean. Seal according to manufacturer's directions. Process the jars in a boiling water bath for 10 minutes.

ABOUT RHUBARB

There are red and green varieties of rhubarb, but both become brown when cooked. Select firm, crisp, thick stalks showing good color. Avoid rhubarb that is limp, stringy or hollow-looking. Rhubarb wilts quickly at room temperature. It will keep refrigerated, in a plastic bag, for 3 to 5 days.

To prepare rhubarb, cut off the root end and pull away any stringy bits. Always be sure to remove all the green leaves from rhubarb stalks—they are toxic. Wash the stalks well and cut them into pieces—most recipes call for 1-inch (2.5 cm) or ½-inch (1.2 cm) dice.

Rhubarb freezes easily. Simply place the washed, chopped rhubarb into freezer bags or plastic containers and freeze. Measure rhubarb before freezing and note the amount on the label to simplify using it in recipes later on.

Kiwi Lime Jam

MAKES ABOUT THREE 8 OZ (250 ML) JARS

You may do as you choose, but I like to add a couple of drops of green food coloring to this jam. The resulting color, a gorgeous emerald green, is far more attractive than the army green that you'll get without it.

8 large, firm but ripe kiwis

2 Tbsp • 30 mL finely grated lime zest

6 Tbsp • 90 mL fresh lime juice

3 cups • 720 mL sugar

a few drops of green food coloring (optional)

PEEL the kiwis and shred them in a food processor, or slice them and then chop finely. Combine all the ingredients except the food coloring in your preserving pot. Let stand for 30 minutes, until the sugar is dissolved and the juices begin to flow.

Prepare the preserving jars.

Bring the fruit to a boil over medium-high heat. Boil rapidly, stirring constantly, for 15 to 20 minutes. Test for set using a thermometer or the plate test (see "How to Test for Gel," page 42).

Remove from the heat, stir and skim off the foam if necessary. Carefully add 1 or 2 drops of food coloring if desired. (Be judicious in your use of food coloring. Your jam should be a nice, natural kiwi green. Start by adding 1 drop, then stir well and look at the color. Remember, you can always add more, but you can't take it out!)

Pour the jam into hot, sterilized jars, leaving a $1/4$-inch (6 mm) head space. Wipe the rims clean. Seal according to manufacturer's directions. Process the jars in a boiling water bath for 10 minutes.

NOTE One lime will yield approximately 2 Tbsp (30 mL) of lime juice and 2 tsp (10 mL) of lime zest.

Plum Jam

Plums are available in a bewildering variety of colors and sizes. Each has its own distinct flavor. Any type of plum can be used to make this tasty jam, and the nicest thing is, you don't have to peel or chop the fruit.

2 lb • 900 g plums, stems removed

1 cup • 240 mL water

3 cups • 720 mL sugar

2 Tbsp • 30 mL lemon juice

PREPARE the preserving jars.

Combine the plums and water in your preserving pot and bring to a boil over medium heat. Reduce the heat to medium-low. Cover and simmer for about 20 minutes, stirring occasionally, until the plums are soft. The plum pits will rise to the surface; fish them out with a slotted spoon. Add the sugar and lemon juice. Increase the heat to medium and cook, stirring often, for 20 to 25 minutes, or until thickened. Test for set if desired.

Remove from the heat. Stir and skim off the foam if necessary. Pour into hot, sterilized jars, leaving a ¼-inch (6 mm) head space. Wipe the rims clean. Seal according to manufacturer's directions. Process the jars in a boiling water bath for 10 minutes.

PLUM APPLE JAM Replace water with 1 cup (240 mL) apple juice and add 1 lb (454 g) apples, peeled, cored and coarsely chopped, to your preserving pot. Increase sugar to 4 cups (950 mL) and use the juice and finely grated zest of 1 whole lemon.

Jellies

Basic Apple Jelly 44

Cranberry and Apple Jelly 45

Apple Mint Jelly 46

Quince Jelly Scented with Vanilla 48

Honey Lemon Jelly 50

Summer Berry Jelly 51

Blackberry Jelly 53

Grape Jelly 54

Red Currant Jelly 55

Rosemary and Red Wine Jelly
with Orange 56

Red Pepper and Orange Jelly 59

Jalapeño Pepper Jelly 60

Jellies

There's no escaping it—making jelly is a little trickier than making jam. The aim of jelly making is to get the stuff to gel—and that requires a little extra care and precision. A runny jam is still jam, but there's no disguising an unset jelly—it's a syrup!

Like jam, jelly requires a careful balance of fruit, pectin, sugar and acid. Fruits that are high in pectin will form a gel naturally; others need the assistance of additional pectin, either homemade or commercially prepared.

It is possible to make your own homemade pectin extract from apples or citrus fruit, but it is a rather time-consuming process. With a few exceptions, the recipes here call for fruits that are rich enough in pectin to form a gel naturally. I have also included a few special recipes that use commercial pectin, as some delicious, popular varieties of jelly simply cannot be made without it.

The traditional method of making jelly involves a two-step process. First, the fruit is simmered in water or its own juice, then the juice is carefully strained away from the fruit pulp. For the richest flavor in the finished jelly, a minimal amount of water is added; this varies according to the juiciness of the fruit.

In the second step, the fruit juice and an appropriate amount of sugar are boiled until the mixture reaches the gel stage. The volume of sugar and the cooking time are dependent on the amount of pectin in the fruit juice.

This method is only suitable for pectin-rich fruits such as apples, quinces and currants. To make jellies from low-pectin fruits, such as strawberries, raspberries or cherries, you must either combine the juice with the juice of a high-pectin fruit, or use a commercial pectin product to assist the gelling process.

Commercial pectin manufacturers include detailed, reliable recipes with their products, which enable you to make jelly from virtually any type of fruit, whether the fruit contains sufficient natural pectin or not. These recipes must be followed to the letter to ensure success. Don't attempt to use commercial pectin recipes without adding the pectin product. They won't work.

The recipes in this book that contain commercial pectin follow the methods recommended by the manufacturers. Don't alter the amounts of fruit or sugar specified in the recipes.

There are two basic varieties of commercial pectin: dry (powdered) pectin, sometimes referred to as pectin crystals, and liquid pectin. Liquid pectin comes in foil-wrapped envelopes, two to a package. When using liquid pectin, be sure to read the recipe carefully to be certain that you are using the correct amount. There is also a relatively new type of dry pectin, specially developed for recipes using reduced amounts of sugar.

Each type of pectin requires that you follow a slightly different procedure—they are not interchangeable in recipes. Dry pectin crystals are mixed with the unheated fruit or fruit juice before cooking. The sugar is added later on. Liquid pectin is added to the boiling fruit or juice and sugar during the cooking.

When using commercial pectin, cook for the recommended time, but no longer. You do not increase the likelihood of a gel by prolonging the cooking time, in fact, quite the opposite. For while pectin is activated by heat, it is deactivated by extended cooking.

You will find mention of the term "a full rolling boil" in some recipes, especially those using commercial pectin. A full rolling boil is reached when the jelly mixture is boiling so hard that no matter how much you stir it, the boiling will not subside.

Jellies may take some time to set. Some jellies made using commercial pectin will set within hours, others may take as long as a week or two. It is best to leave jellies undisturbed until they have set firmly.

EASY STEPS TO MAKING JELLY
Step One: Extract the Juice

1. Use three-quarters ripe fruit and one-quarter slightly underripe fruit. Jelly can also be made successfully with frozen fruit (see page 19 for more information).

2. Wash the fruit briefly in cold water; do not allow the fruit to soak in water.

3. Cut stone or hard fruits, such as peaches or pears, into small pieces. Do not peel or core fruits, as the peels and cores contain most of the pectin necessary to cause the juice to gel. Berries and small fruits such as grapes are crushed rather than cut up.

4. Place the prepared fruit in your preserving pot and add the amount of water indicated in the recipe. The harder the fruit, the more water is generally required. Many soft fruits and berries contain sufficient juice so that no additional water is needed.

5. Cover the pot, bring to a boil and simmer until the fruit is very soft and the juices are flowing. Berries only need about 10 to 15 minutes; hard fruits may take as long as 30 minutes to cook sufficiently.

6. Remove the pot from the heat and transfer the mixture to a dampened jelly bag (or a colander lined with a double thickness of cheesecloth) suspended over a large bowl. The clear juice will drip through the bag and into the bowl below, leaving the solids behind. This can be a rather slow process—it is best to allow the juice to drip overnight, or at least several hours. Do not squeeze the bag.

NOTE You can prepare the juice one day and make jelly a day or two later. And if you decide that you don't want to make jelly after all, the extracted fruit juice diluted with a little water or soda is an excellent drink. Extracted juice can also be frozen for future jelly-making ventures.

Step Two: Make the Jelly

Measure the juice into your preserving pot and add the amount of sugar called for in the recipe.

7. You can extract as much juice as you have fruit—in great batches if you like—but do not make jelly using more than 6 cups (1.5 L) of fruit juice at a time. Four cups (950 mL) is usually a good amount. Large volumes of juice have to be boiled for a longer time, decreasing the likelihood of a good set. Also, since the juice and sugar mixture usually triples in volume as it boils, most pots are not large enough to accommodate larger batches. It really doesn't take much longer to cook several batches of jelly, and the results will be superior.

8. Bring the juice and sugar to a boil over high heat, then reduce the heat slightly if necessary to keep the pot from boiling over. Boil rapidly, stirring often to prevent scorching. You can greatly reduce the amount of foam by adding $1/2$ tsp (2.5 mL) of butter to the mixture before it starts to boil.

9. Insert a thermometer in the boiling liquid once it starts to get syrupy. The jelly is done when it reaches 220°F

USING A JELLY BAG

If you are going to make serious amounts of jelly, you may want to invest in a jelly bag. It is easy to manage and can save a considerable amount of messing around.

A jelly bag is a cloth pouch made from a closely woven fabric that, by means of a metal frame, can be suspended over a bowl. It is used for straining cooked fruit in order to achieve a clear juice. Jelly bags can be purchased from cookware shops. However convenient, though, a jelly bag is not essential.

jellies

41

JELLY THAT FAILS TO SET

It sometimes happens that jelly just won't gel—no matter how long you cook it. If your jelly will not sheet from a spoon or pass the plate test, even though it has reached the gel point according to your thermometer, it probably isn't going to gel. More cooking will only make it gluey and gummy, so give up gracefully.

Runny fruit jelly makes a lovely thick syrup for pancakes or desserts. Savory "jelly" can be used as a glaze for roast meats or to enhance sauces.

(104°C), or 8°F (4°C) above the boiling point of water at your elevation. You may also determine doneness by using gel tests, described below. (Remove the jelly from the heat while performing a gel test.)

10. Remove the pot from the heat and skim any foam off the surface of the jelly.

11. Stir the jelly briefly and pour it into hot, sterilized jars. Process the jars in a boiling water bath for 5 minutes. The processing time for jelly is the briefest of any type of preserve as the heat from the boiling water bath can penetrate the liquid jelly very quickly.

12. Once processed, allow jellies to stand undisturbed until they are set. Some may take as long as 48 hours. Sometimes jellies made with commercial pectin can take up to 2 weeks to set—believe it or not!

HOW TO TEST FOR GEL

The following tests will help you to determine if your preserves have cooked sufficiently to form a gel. You can use a combination of tests to be extra sure.

When you are performing either the plate or sheet test, remove the pot from the heat so that the mixture doesn't continue to cook. If your gel test fails, cook the mixture a little longer, then try again. Keep cooking and testing until the mixture passes the test.

The temperature test

Using a candy or jelly thermometer is the easiest and most accurate method. Stir the hot mixture, then immerse the thermometer in it, making sure that the bulb does not touch the bottom of the pot. Continue cooking until the temperature reaches 220°F (104°C), or 8°F (4°C) above the temperature of boiling water at your elevation.

The cold plate test

Place a small plate in the freezer. Towards the end of the cooking time, place a spoonful of the hot mixture on the plate. Return the plate to the freezer for 2 minutes, then check to see if the mixture has gelled.

The sheet test

This is the traditional method for jellies, but it's not recommended for jams. The sheet test can be tricky for beginners, because it may not be obvious what you are looking for. Dip a cold metal spoon into the boiling mixture, then raise it above the pot, away from the steam. Wait about 20 seconds, then slowly tilt the spoon and allow the mixture to drip off the spoon and back into the pot. If the mixture forms 2 drops that flow together to form a "sheet" (a wide drop that sort of hangs from the spoon), then the gel stage has been reached.

JELLY TROUBLES

Sometimes things can go wrong, no matter how careful you are. Here are some possible explanations as to why your jelly may be less than perfect.

Failure to set

- Fruit lacked pectin or acid.
- Jelly was overcooked, causing pectin to break down.
- Jelly was undercooked; too little evaporation caused a weak set.
- Too much water was added during juice extraction.
- Insufficient sugar was used.

Crystallization

- Too much sugar was used.
- There was too little acid.
- Jelly was overcooked.
- There was a delay in sealing the jars.
- Tartrate crystals were present (in grape jelly).

Cloudy jelly

- The jelly bag was squeezed, forcing particles of fruit pulp into the juice.
- Too much underripe fruit was used (it contains more starch than sugar).

"Weeping" jelly (liquid separates from the solids)

- Too much acid.

Mold

- Improper sterilization.
- Jars were poorly sealed.

Always discard moldy jelly!

Basic Apple Jelly

MAKES ABOUT FOUR TO FIVE 8 OZ (250 ML) JARS

A classic jelly, apple jelly can be used as a base for many
varieties of herbal jelly as well.

3 lb • 1.4 kg firm tart apples

sugar

CHOP the apples coarsely, removing the stems and blossom ends. Do not peel
or core. Place the apples in your preserving pot, adding enough water to completely cover the fruit, about 5 cups (1.2 L).

Cover the pot and bring to a boil over medium heat. Simmer for 20 to
25 minutes, stirring occasionally, until the apples are very soft. Crush the
apples using a potato masher and cook for another 2 to 3 minutes. Remove
from the heat.

Transfer the mixture to a dampened jelly bag or a colander lined with a
double thickness of cheesecloth. Let the juice drip through overnight.

The next day, measure the juice; there should be about 4 cups (950 mL).
Discard the pulp. Prepare the preserving jars.

In your processing pot, combine the apple juice and ¾ cup (180 mL) of sugar
for each cup (240 mL) of juice. Bring to a boil over high heat and boil rapidly,
stirring constantly, for 15 to 20 minutes, or until the mixture starts to get syrupy.
Test for gel and when the gel stage has been reached, remove from the heat. Stir
and skim off the foam if necessary.

Pour the jelly into hot, sterilized jars, leaving a ¼-inch (6 mm) head space.
Wipe the rims clean. Seal according to manufacturer's directions. Process the
jars in a boiling water bath for 5 minutes.

SPICED APPLE JELLY Add one 2- to 3-inch (5 to 7.5 cm) cinnamon stick (broken),
2 tsp (10 mL) whole cloves, 1 tsp (5 mL) whole allspice and ½ cup (120 mL) cider
vinegar to the apples during the initial cooking.

CRABAPPLE JELLY Substitute an equal amount of red-skinned crabapples for
the apples.

Cranberry and Apple Jelly

MAKES ABOUT FOUR TO FIVE 8 OZ (250 ML) JARS

You can use either fresh or frozen cranberries for this delectable jelly. It is tart enough to accompany roast meats.

3 cups • 720 mL cranberries

6 large apples, coarsely chopped

sugar

COMBINE the cranberries and apples in your preserving pot. Add enough water to cover the fruit. Cover the pot and bring to a boil over medium heat. Simmer for 20 to 25 minutes, stirring occasionally, until the fruit is very soft. Crush the fruit using a potato masher and cook for another 2 to 3 minutes. Remove from the heat. Transfer the mixture to a dampened jelly bag or a sieve lined with a double thickness of cheesecloth. Let the juice drip through overnight.

The next day, measure the juice; there should be about 4 cups (950 mL). Discard the pulp. Prepare the preserving jars.

In your preserving pot, combine the juice with an equal amount of sugar. Bring to a boil over high heat and boil rapidly, stirring constantly, for about 15 minutes, or until the jelly tests done.

Remove from the heat, stir and skim off the foam if necessary. Pour the jelly into hot, sterilized jars, leaving a ¼-inch (6 mm) head space. Wipe the rims clean. Seal according to manufacturer's directions. Process the jars in a boiling water bath for 5 minutes.

Apple Mint Jelly

MAKES ABOUT FOUR TO FIVE 8 OZ (250 ML) JARS

A natural accompaniment to roast lamb or chops, this versatile jelly also makes a lovely glaze for fresh fruit tarts. I consider its golden color to be most appealing, but if you must have it green, stir in a couple of drops of green food coloring just before it goes into the jars.

3 lb • 1.4 kg firm tart apples

1 lemon

1 small bunch of fresh mint, roughly chopped,
   about 1–1½ cups (240–360 mL)

1 cup • 240 mL cider vinegar

sugar

CHOP the apples coarsely, removing the stems and blossom ends. Do not peel or core. Cut the lemon in half lengthwise and slice it thinly. Place the apples and lemon in your preserving pot and add just enough water to barely cover the fruit.

Cover the pot and bring to a boil over medium heat. Simmer for 20 to 25 minutes, stirring occasionally, until the apples are very soft. Add the chopped mint and vinegar and simmer for another 10 minutes. Remove from the heat.

Crush the mixture with a potato masher, then cover the pot and let stand for 10 minutes. Transfer the mixture to a jelly bag or a colander lined with a double thickness of cheesecloth. Let the juice drip through overnight.

The next day, prepare the preserving jars. Measure the juice; there should be about 5 cups (1.2 L). Combine the juice and an equal amount of sugar in your preserving pot. Bring to a boil over high heat and boil rapidly, stirring constantly, for 15 to 20 minutes, or until the jelly tests done.

Remove from the heat. Stir and skim off the foam if necessary. Pour the jelly into hot, sterilized jars, leaving a ¼-inch (6 mm) head space. Wipe the rims clean. Seal according to manufacturer's directions. Process the jars in a boiling water bath for 5 minutes.

APPLE LEMON BALM JELLY Substitute 1 to 1¹⁄₂ cups (240 to 360 mL) chopped fresh lemon balm for the mint.

APPLE BASIL JELLY Substitute 1 to 1¹⁄₂ cups (240 to 360 mL) chopped fresh basil for the mint.

APPLE ROSE GERANIUM JELLY Substitute 1 to 1¹⁄₂ cups (240 to 360 mL) chopped rose geranium leaves for the mint.

Quince Jelly Scented with Vanilla

MAKES ABOUT FOUR TO FIVE 8 OZ (250 ML) JARS

Rather a forgotten, old-fashioned fruit, quinces are rarely available in markets or fruit stands. I'd never seen a quince until I discovered them growing in my own yard! A splendid ornamental shrub with lovely red flowers, quinces mature in the autumn, and when they are ripe have an incredible fragrance.

Quinces are so hard and astringent they are not usually eaten raw. They remain hard even when ripe, which makes them rather difficult to prepare. Rub off any fuzz on the skin of the fruit using a dry towel. Wash and remove the stems and blossom ends, but do not peel or core. Cut them into small pieces.

4 lb • 1.8 kg quinces, cut into pieces

1 vanilla bean

sugar

2 Tbsp • 30 mL lemon juice

PLACE the quince pieces and the vanilla bean in your preserving pot and add enough water to completely cover them. Cover and bring to a boil over medium heat. Simmer, stirring occasionally, for about 45 minutes, until the quinces are very soft. Mash the quince pulp with a potato masher and cook for another 5 minutes. Remove from the heat. Remove the vanilla bean.

Transfer the mixture to a dampened jelly bag or a colander lined with a double thickness of cheesecloth. Let the juice drip through overnight.

The next day, measure the juice; there should be about 4 cups (950 mL). Discard the pulp. Prepare the preserving jars.

In your preserving pot, combine the quince juice and ¾ cup (180 mL) sugar for each 1 cup (240 mL) of juice. Add the lemon juice. Bring to a boil over high heat and boil rapidly, stirring often, for about 20 to 25 minutes, or until the jelly tests done. Stir more often towards the end of the cooking time to prevent scorching.

Remove from the heat, stir and skim off foam if necessary. Pour the jelly into hot, sterilized jars, leaving a ¼-inch (6 mm) head space. Wipe the rims clean. Seal according to manufacturer's directions. Process the jars in a boiling water bath for 5 minutes.

NOTE If you cannot use a vanilla bean, substitute ½ tsp (2.5 mL) pure vanilla extract, adding it just before the jelly is poured into the jars.

ABOUT VANILLA

Vanilla comes from the pod fruit of a vine native to Central America, a member of the orchid family. Vanilla must be pollinated by hand and has a long, complex curing process, which explains why it is so expensive.

Vanilla pods, or beans, have a superior flavor to vanilla extract, but pure vanilla extract is infinitely preferable to a synthetic substitute.

Although expensive, vanilla beans are well worth the price. They will keep for months in an airtight container; stored in a canister of sugar, a vanilla bean will impart a rich mellow flavor to the sugar. Vanilla beans may be used many times over, as long as they are carefully washed and dried after each use.

Honey Lemon Jelly

MAKES ABOUT THREE TO FOUR 8 OZ (250 ML) JARS

Use a light, delicately flavored honey for this magically sweet treat. There are two important things to note about this jelly. Honey jelly really boils up when it is cooking so take care that the pot does not boil over. It also sets up very quickly when it is removed from the heat, so do not delay in filling the jars.

2 cups • 475 mL honey

1 cup • 240 mL sugar

⅔ cup • 160 mL freshly squeezed lemon
   juice, strained

2 tsp • 10 mL finely grated lemon zest

½ cup • 120 mL water

one 3 oz (85 mL) pouch liquid pectin

PREPARE the preserving jars.

Combine the honey, sugar, lemon juice, lemon zest and water in your preserving pot. Bring to a boil over medium heat and stir in the pectin. Continue to cook and stir until the mixture reaches a full, rolling boil that cannot be stirred down. Boil hard for exactly 1 minute. Remove from the heat, stir and skim off the foam if necessary.

Quickly pour the jelly into hot, sterilized jars, leaving a ¼-inch (6 mm) head space. Wipe the rims clean. Seal according to manufacturer's directions. Process the jars in a boiling water bath for 5 minutes.

Summer Berry Jelly

MAKES ABOUT FOUR TO FIVE 8 OZ (250 ML) JARS

A happy marriage of four of summer's finest fruits. The gooseberries provide the pectin necessary to achieve a good set.

    2 cups • 475 mL cherries, stemmed and pitted
    2 cups • 475 mL raspberries
    2 cups • 475 mL strawberries, hulled
    2 cups • 475 mL gooseberries
    sugar
    2 Tbsp • 30 mL lemon juice

PLACE the fruit in your preserving pot and crush it with a potato masher. Add just enough water to barely cover the fruit. Bring to a boil over medium heat. Cover and simmer for about 15 minutes, stirring occasionally, until the fruit is very soft. Remove from the heat.

Transfer the mixture to a dampened jelly bag or a colander lined with a double thickness of cheesecloth. Let the juice drip through overnight.

The next day, measure the juice; there should be about 4 cups (950 mL). Discard the pulp. Prepare the preserving jars.

In your preserving pot, combine the juice and an equal amount of sugar. Add the lemon juice. Bring to a boil over high heat and boil rapidly, stirring constantly, for about 10 to 15 minutes, or until the jelly tests done.

Remove from the heat, stir and skim off the foam if necessary. Pour the jelly into hot, sterilized jars, leaving a $\frac{1}{4}$-inch (6 mm) head space. Wipe the rims clean. Seal according to manufacturer's directions. Process the jars in a boiling water bath for 5 minutes.

Blackberry Jelly

Also known as bramble jelly, blackberry jelly is an excellent choice for those who love the taste of fresh blackberries, but cannot tolerate the seediness of blackberry jam.

10 cups • 2.4 L blackberries

½ cup • 120 mL water

3 Tbsp • 45 mL lemon juice

sugar

IN your preserving pot, crush the blackberries with a potato masher. Add the water and lemon juice. Cover and simmer over medium heat for 15 minutes, stirring occasionally, until the blackberries are really mushy. Remove from the heat.

Transfer the mixture to a dampened jelly bag or a colander lined with a double thickness of cheesecloth. Let the juice drip through overnight.

The next day, measure the juice; there should be about 4 cups (950 mL). Discard the pulp. Prepare the preserving jars.

In your preserving pot, combine the juice and an equal amount of sugar. Bring to a boil over high heat and boil rapidly, stirring often, for about 15 to 20 minutes, or until the jelly tests done.

Remove from the heat, stir and skim off the foam if necessary. Pour the jelly into hot, sterilized jars, leaving a ¼-inch (6 mm) head space. Wipe the rims clean. Seal according to manufacturer's directions. Process the jars in a boiling water bath for 5 minutes.

GLAZE A FRESH FRUIT TART WITH JELLY

For a 9- or 10-inch (23 or 25 cm) fresh fruit tart, melt ½ cup (120 mL) of jelly with about 1 Tbsp (15 mL) water or juice over low heat, stirring until smooth.

Brush the warm mixture over the cooled tart. Sprinkle with chopped nuts, if desired. When the glaze has set, the tart is ready to serve.

jellies

Grape Jelly

MAKES ABOUT FOUR TO FIVE 8 OZ (250 ML) JARS

Grapes naturally contain tartaric acid, which will form crystals in the finished jelly if you do not allow the juice to settle after it is extracted. Do not omit this extra step.

4 lb • 1.8 kg dark red or blue grapes

1 tart apple

¾ cup • 180 mL water

sugar

STEM the grapes and coarsely chop the apple, removing the stem and blossom ends. Combine the grapes, apple and water in your preserving pot. Cover and bring to a boil over medium heat. Simmer for about 20 minutes, stirring occasionally, until the fruit is very soft. Remove from the heat.

Transfer the mixture to a dampened jelly bag or a colander lined with a double thickness of cheesecloth. Let the juice drip through overnight. Cover the juice and refrigerate for 8 to 10 hours to allow the tartrate crystals to settle to the bottom of the pot. Strain the juice a second time, taking great care not to disturb the sediment. Discard the sediment.

Prepare the preserving jars.

Measure the juice into your preserving pot; there should be about 4 cups (950 mL). Add ¾ cup (180 mL) of sugar for each 1 cup (240 mL) of juice. Bring to a boil over high heat and boil rapidly, stirring constantly, for about 15 to 20 minutes, or until the jelly tests done.

Remove from the heat, stir and skim off the foam if necessary. Pour the jelly into hot, sterilized jars, leaving a ¼-inch (6 mm) head space. Wipe the rims clean. Seal according to manufacturer's directions. Process the jars in a boiling water bath for 5 minutes.

Red Currant Jelly

A brilliant red jewel-like jelly with a tart flavor, Red Currant Jelly is traditionally served with meats. There is no need to stem the currants when preparing the juice.

4 lb • 1.8 kg red currants

1 cup • 240 mL water

sugar

PLACE the currants in your preserving pot, and crush them, using a potato masher. Add the water and simmer over medium heat until the currants are soft, about 10 minutes. Remove from the heat.

Transfer the pulp to a dampened jelly bag or a colander lined with a double thickness of cheesecloth, and allow to drip through overnight.

The next day, prepare the preserving jars.

Measure the juice into your preserving pot, adding $^{3}/_{4}$ cup (180 mL) of sugar for each 1 cup (240 mL) of juice. Bring to a boil over high heat and boil rapidly, stirring constantly, for about 10 to 15 minutes, or until the jelly tests done.

Remove from the heat. Stir and skim off the foam if necessary. Pour the jelly into hot, sterilized jars, leaving a $^{1}/_{4}$-inch (6 mm) head space. Wipe the rims clean. Seal according to manufacturer's directions. Process the jars in a boiling water bath for 5 minutes.

Rosemary and Red Wine Jelly with Orange

MAKES ABOUT FOUR TO FIVE 8 OZ (250 ML) JARS

This is a distinguished jelly with an assertive rosemary flavor. Use a robust, full-bodied red wine—the intensity of flavor and color of the jelly depend on using a wine with character.

¾ cup • 180 mL fresh rosemary leaves, chopped

1 orange, zest only, removed in thin strips

2 cups • 475 mL red wine

½ cup • 120 mL red wine vinegar

4 cups • 950 mL sugar

one 3 oz (85 mL) pouch liquid pectin

RINSE the rosemary under running water, shake well, then pat dry with paper towels. Strip the rosemary leaves from the stems, measure and chop coarsely.

Place the rosemary leaves in your preserving pot. Twist the strips of orange zest (as if you were twisting lemon zest to drop into a martini) over the pot to extract the fragrant drops of oil in the skin. Drop the zest into the pot. Add the wine and vinegar and bring to a boil over high heat. As soon as it boils, remove from the heat. Cover the pot and let the mixture steep for 30 minutes.

Strain the mixture through a sieve lined with a double thickness of dampened cheesecloth, pressing on the herbs to extract as much liquid as possible. Discard the herbs. Prepare the preserving jars.

Combine the extracted liquid and the sugar in your preserving pot. Bring to a boil over high heat, stirring often. When the mixture reaches a full boil, stir in the pectin. Cook and stir until the mixture reaches a full rolling boil that cannot be stirred down. Boil hard for exactly 1 minute, stirring constantly. Remove from the heat. Stir and skim off any foam that has formed.

Pour the jelly into the hot, sterilized jars, leaving a ¼-inch (6 mm) head space. Wipe the rims clean. Seal according to manufacturer's directions. Process the jars in a boiling water bath for 5 minutes.

ROSEMARY AND RED WINE JELLY WITH GARLIC Omit the orange and add 3 to 4 sliced garlic cloves with the rosemary.

ROSEMARY AND ORANGE JELLY Substitute orange juice for the wine and 3 Tbsp (45 mL) lemon juice for the vinegar. Add 1 Tbsp (15 mL) finely grated orange zest when the jelly is removed from the heat. Stir 3 to 5 minutes to distribute the zest evenly in the jelly.

ADDING CHOPPED HERBS TO JELLY

You can add fresh chopped herbs to your jelly after the jelly has been removed from the heat.

Once you have skimmed off the foam, add ¾ to 1 cup (180 to 240 mL) fresh chopped herbs, such as basil, mint or tarragon. Stirring for 3 to 5 minutes will help keep the herbs suspended in the jelly, but they do tend to float to the top. You can tilt the jars from time to time as the jelly cools to distribute the herbs more evenly.

jellies

Red Pepper and Orange Jelly

MAKES ABOUT SIX TO SEVEN 8 OZ (250 ML) JARS

What is commonly known as pepper jelly is actually more of a jellied relish. For those who may be unfamiliar with the substance by any name, it is a truly addictive snack when served with cream cheese and crackers. This version contains orange juice and zest for a little extra zip.

    3–4 medium-large red bell peppers

    1¼ cups • 300 mL cider vinegar

    ¼ cup • 60 mL orange juice

    ¼ cup • 60 mL finely grated orange zest

    6 cups • 1.5 L sugar

    two 3 oz (85 mL) pouches liquid pectin

    ½–1 tsp • 2.5–5 mL hot pepper sauce, to taste

IT'S tricky to say how many peppers this will take because they vary so much in size. Cut them into small chunks, discarding the stems, ribs and seeds. Purée in a food processor until finely and uniformly chopped. Use a spatula to scrape down the sides of the bowl once or twice during processing. Measure out 2 cups (475 mL).

Prepare the preserving jars.

Combine the peppers, vinegar, orange juice, zest and sugar in your preserving pot. Bring to a boil over high heat. Reduce the heat to low, cover and simmer for 10 minutes. Increase the heat to high and bring the mixture to a full boil, stirring constantly. Stir in the pectin. Continue to stir over high heat until the mixture returns to a full boil, then boil hard for 1 minute.

Remove from the heat and stir in the hot pepper sauce. Skim off the foam if necessary. Stir for 3 to 5 minutes (this helps to keep the peppers and zest from floating to the tops of the jars).

Pour the jelly into hot, sterilized jars, leaving a ¼-inch (6 mm) head space. Wipe the rims clean. Seal according to manufacturer's directions. Process the jars in a boiling water bath for 5 minutes.

PURÉEING

You must use a food processor for this recipe because the peppers must be ground finely enough to extract some juice, and this cannot be achieved by simple chopping.

jellies

Hot peppers must be handled with caution. They release fumes and oils that can cause excruciating pain to the sensitive tissues of your eyes, nose, lips, even your fingertips, especially if you have any cuts or abrasions. The alkaloid capsaicin that is present in hot peppers is used as the active ingredient in pepper spray. The white membrane inside the pepper, holding the seeds, is the hottest part.

Always wear rubber gloves when handling hot peppers. Medical-type latex gloves are great because you can throw them out when you're finished, but regular rubber gloves are fine too. Just be sure to wash them carefully after each use to remove any remaining oils. And don't forget to wash utensils you have used as well.

Jalapeño Pepper Jelly

MAKES ABOUT SIX TO SEVEN 8 OZ (250 ML) JARS

No joke—this stuff is really hot! To make a milder version, simply reduce the amount of jalapeño pepper and substitute an equal volume of green pepper. As long as the total volume of peppers is equal to 2 cups (475 mL), it doesn't matter what kind they are.

25–30 medium jalapeño peppers

1½ cups • 360 mL cider vinegar

6½ cups • 1.6 L sugar

½ tsp • 2.5 mL salt

two 3 oz (85 mL) pouches liquid pectin

a few drops of green food coloring
    (optional)

TO prepare the peppers, cut them into chunks, discarding the ribs, stems and seeds. Chop the pepper chunks in the food processor until they are finely and uniformly ground. Measure out 2 cups (475 mL).

Prepare the preserving jars.

Combine the 2 cups (475 mL) of peppers, vinegar, sugar and salt in your preserving pot. Bring to a boil over high heat, stirring occasionally. Once the mixture has reached a full boil, stir constantly. Boil for 5 minutes. Stir in the pectin, and when the mixture has returned to a full rolling boil, boil for exactly 1 minute.

Remove from the heat. Stir and skim off any foam from the surface of the jelly. Stir the jelly for 3 to 5 minutes (this will help keep the peppers from floating to the tops of the jars). At this time, add the food coloring, if desired. (If you don't mind the drab olive green color of cooked green peppers, or have objections to the use of food coloring, by all means leave it out. But I must confess, I find the jelly to be much prettier if it is included.)

Pour the jelly into hot, sterilized jars, leaving a ¼-inch (6 mm) head space. Wipe the rims clean. Seal according to manufacturer's directions. Process the jars in a boiling water bath for 5 minutes.

Marmalades

Traditional English Marmalade 65

Orange Marmalade 66

Lemon-Lime Marmalade 68

Amber Marmalade 70

Chunky Apple Marmalade with
Ginger 71

Peach Orange Marmalade 72

Carrot Marmalade 73

Pumpkin Marmalade 74

Zany Zucchini Marmalade 75

Winter Marmalade 76

Marmalades

The word *marmalade* is said to derive from the Portuguese word for quince, *marmelo*. A marmalade is a soft jam- or jelly-like preserve based on citrus fruit, usually oranges. Marmalades may be thick and chunky or soft and tender. The texture depends on the method used to soften the citrus skin before the marmalade is cooked.

The bitter Seville orange is the principal ingredient in traditional English marmalade, but marmalades may be made from any citrus fruit: oranges, lemons, limes, grapefruits or tangerines, either singly or in combination. Delightful marmalade may also be prepared by partnering citrus fruits with compatible fruits or vegetables . . . everything from apples to zucchini. Some marmalades are flavored with ginger or other spices, or enhanced by the addition of liqueurs or a good Scotch whisky!

To my mind, one of the nicest things about marmalade is its season—January to February. Citrus fruit is at its finest at this time of year and also at its most inexpensive. And this is the only time you can find the elusive Seville orange, prized by marmalade enthusiasts for its thin skin, acidic flavor and high pectin content.

After the excitement of Christmas is over, there is no better way to brighten up a dull January day than to bring home a basket of citrus fruit from the market and set to work making marmalade. By happy coincidence, the beginning of the year is always a quiet time on the preserving calendar, so you won't be distracted by other fruits and

FRUIT "BUTTERS"

Jam or marmalade combined with softened butter makes a delightful spread for muffins, croissants, quick breads or waffles.

Cream ½ cup (120 mL) jam or marmalade and ⅓ cup (80 mL) butter together until smooth. Transfer the fruit butter to a small crock or decorative serving dish and chill until ready to serve. Serve at room temperature.

For a sweeter spread, add ½ tsp (2.5 mL) sifted icing sugar. For a tarter spread, add ½ tsp (2.5 mL) lemon juice or 2 tsp (10 mL) finely grated orange zest. For a spicy spread, add ½ tsp (2.5 mL) cinnamon or 2 tsp (10 mL) finely chopped candied ginger.

vegetables clamoring for your attention.

Marmalade does require a little extra time to make, as there are some preliminary preparations that must be done to ensure that your marmalading venture is a successful one.

Some marmalades may take a couple of days to prepare. This is because the tough skin of the citrus fruit needs to be softened before it can be made into marmalade. This may be achieved by soaking the fruit for several hours or overnight and by precooking the fruit in water prior to adding the sugar. Some recipes call for boiling the fruit whole, then chopping it up; in other recipes, the fruit is very thinly sliced, then precooked. A third method involves boiling the zest in several changes of water, then cooking the zest, pulp and juice with water.

In some ways, making marmalade is less complicated than making jam or jelly. Citrus fruits contain plenty of pectin, so there is little danger the marmalade will fail to set. In fact, many marmalades will thicken considerably after cooling, so care must be taken not to overcook them.

Once the peel is softened, it is cooked until tender and the sugar is added. The process moves quickly after this. It is best to use a candy thermometer to gauge the progress of your marmalade as it can reach the gel stage quite quickly. Upon reaching the gel stage, the marmalade must immediately be removed from the heat, skimmed free of foam if necessary, and stirred briefly for a few minutes. The stirring helps to distribute the fruit or zest evenly throughout the mixture.

Not all marmalades are bittersweet. The addition of noncitrus fruit can temper the traditional bitterness of marmalade, making it more palatable to the uninitiated. Once you develop a taste for it, however, you will appreciate the complex flavors and distinctive tang that define a true marmalade.

Traditional English Marmalade

MAKES ABOUT FIVE TO SIX 8 OZ (250 ML) JARS

Early in January keep your eyes peeled for Seville oranges.
They have a very short season and can be difficult to find.
Be sure to make enough to last the whole year through!

2 lb • 900 g Seville oranges

3 medium lemons

8 cups • 2 L sugar

PREPARE the preserving jars.

Scrub the oranges and lemons well and discard the little stem ends. In your preserving pot, place the whole oranges and lemons, and add enough water to cover them. Cover the pot and bring to a boil over medium heat. Simmer for 1 to 1½ hours, or until the fruit can be easily pierced with a metal skewer. Drain the fruit in a colander, reserving the liquid. When the fruit is cool enough to handle, slice it in half lengthwise. Then place the cut side down and slice very thinly, reserving the seeds. Place the seeds in a cheesecloth bag.

Pour the reserved liquid back into the pot and add the sugar. Cook and stir over low heat until the sugar is dissolved. Increase the heat to medium and simmer the liquid for 10 minutes, stirring often. Stir in the sliced fruit and the bag of seeds. Boil and stir until the marmalade reaches the gel point, about 25 to 30 minutes. Test for gel using the thermometer or plate test.

Remove from the heat and discard the bag of seeds, squeezing it out well first. Skim any foam that may have formed and stir for 2 to 3 minutes to distribute the fruit evenly. Pour the marmalade into hot, sterilized jars, leaving a ¼-inch (6 mm) head space. Wipe the rims clean. Seal according to manufacturer's directions. Process the jars in a boiling water bath for 10 minutes.

SPIRITED SEVILLE MARMALADE. Stir in 3 Tbsp (45 mL) orange-flavored liqueur, such as Cointreau or Triple Sec, or the same amount of Scotch whisky just before the marmalade is poured into the jars.

DARK SEVILLE MARMALADE. Substitute dark brown sugar for the regular sugar and add 1 Tbsp (15 mL) molasses when the sugar is added.

Orange Marmalade

MAKES ABOUT SIX TO SEVEN 8 OZ (250 ML) JARS

A lively fresh flavor is the hallmark of this popular marmalade.

2 cups • 475 mL orange slices
 (2–3 medium oranges)
2 cups • 475 mL lemon slices
 (about 3 medium lemons)
6 cups • 1.5 L water
sugar

PREPARE the preserving jars.

To prepare the fruit, cut the oranges and lemons in half lengthwise, then into quarters. Slice them as thinly as possible, discarding the ends but reserving the seeds. Place the seeds in a cheesecloth bag.

Combine the orange, lemon, the bag of seeds and the water in your preserving pot. Bring to a boil over high heat. Reduce the heat to medium and simmer until the fruit is tender, about 30 to 40 minutes. Remove from the heat. Discard the bag of seeds, squeezing it out well first.

Measure the fruit and liquid and add an equal volume of sugar to the pot. Bring to a boil over medium-high heat and boil, stirring often, for 20 to 30 minutes. Test for the gel stage using a thermometer or the plate test.

Remove from the heat. Skim off the foam if necessary. Stir for 3 to 5 minutes to prevent floating fruit. Pour the marmalade into hot, sterilized jars, leaving a $1/4$-inch (6 mm) head space. Wipe the rims clean. Seal according to manufacturer's directions. Process the jars in a boiling water bath for 10 minutes.

Lemon-Lime Marmalade

MAKES ABOUT SIX TO SEVEN 8 OZ (250 ML) JARS

A true tart and tangy marmalade. Not for the faint of heart! The skin of the lime is extremely tough; be sure to slice the fruit very thinly.

> 2 cups • 475 mL lemon slices
>   (about 3 medium lemons)
> 2 cups • 475 mL lime slices (about
>   4 medium limes)
> 7 cups • 1.75 L water
> sugar

PREPARE the preserving jars.

To prepare the fruit, cut the lemons and limes in half lengthwise, then again into quarters. Slice the fruit as thinly as possible, discarding the ends and reserving the seeds. Place the seeds in a cheesecloth bag.

Combine the fruit, the bag of seeds and the water in your preserving pot. Cover and let stand at room temperature overnight.

The next day, bring to a boil over high heat, then reduce the heat to medium and simmer until the fruit is very tender, about 45 to 50 minutes. Remove from the heat. Discard the bag of seeds, squeezing it out as much as possible.

Measure the fruit and liquid. Add an equal volume of sugar. Bring to a boil over medium-high heat and boil, stirring often, for 25 to 35 minutes. Test for the gel stage using a thermometer or the plate test.

Remove from the heat. Skim off the foam if necessary. Stir for 3 to 5 minutes to prevent floating fruit. Pour the marmalade into hot, sterilized jars, leaving a $1/4$-inch (6 mm) head space. Wipe the rims clean. Seal according to manufacturer's directions. Process the jars in a boiling water bath for 10 minutes.

ABOUT LEMONS

Lemons are an invaluable asset to the home preserver. Although in North America we generally don't preserve lemons on their own, they are probably used in more preserving recipes than any other fruit.

In many recipes, lemons provide the necessary acidity that, in conjunction with pectin and sugar, causes sweet preserves to form a gel. Lemon juice is often added to raise the acidity of low-acid foods to a level that allows those foods to be safely processed in a boiling water bath.

Lemons are also used as a flavor enhancer. A touch of lemon juice will heighten the taste of most foods, sweet or savory. Grated lemon zest enlivens many preserves, conserves and chutneys.

Lemon juice, when sprinkled over cut fruits such as apples, bananas and pears, helps to inhibit browning. Such foods may also be placed in an acidic "bath" of water and lemon juice for the same effect. Lemon juice can also be useful as a mild bleaching agent that helps to keep white vegetables from discoloring during cooking.

Choose plump, firm lemons that feel slightly oily to the touch. They should be bright yellow with no traces of green.

The best lemons will feel heavy for their size and have a fine-textured skin. Thicker-skinned lemons that are lighter generally contain less juice, but are easier to grate for their zest.

In recipes that call for both juice and zest, always grate the zest first, before halving the fruit and extracting the juice. The zest contains the desirable aromatic oils. Avoid the white pith as much as possible; it is very bitter. A vegetable peeler may be helpful in removing large pieces of zest, and a zester is a useful cook's tool that will remove the zest in long thin shreds.

If you wish to extract the juice of a whole lemon, it helps to soften the fruit first by rolling it around on a table or countertop beneath the palm of your hand. The juice will flow more freely, and you will get more of it. Room-temperature lemons will yield more juice than those straight from the refrigerator.

One medium-sized lemon will yield about 2½ to 3 Tbsp (38 to 45 mL) juice and about 1 Tbsp (15 mL) grated zest.

Amber Marmalade

MAKES ABOUT SEVEN TO EIGHT 8 OZ (250 ML) JARS

Savor the contrasting flavors and textures of this distinctive marmalade.

6 medium oranges

1 medium lemon

2 medium limes

4 cups • 950 mL water

4 cups • 950 mL pineapple, cut in ½-inch
   (1.2 cm) dice

sugar

½ tsp • 2.5 mL ground ginger

CUT the oranges, lemon and limes in half lengthwise. Placing the cut side down, slice the fruit very thinly, discarding the ends but reserving the seeds. Place the seeds in a cheesecloth bag. Combine the sliced fruit, water and the bag of seeds in your preserving pot. Cover and cook over low heat for 1 hour, stirring occasionally. Remove from the heat, uncover and cool. When cool, replace the cover and let stand at room temperature overnight.

The next day, squeeze out the cheesecloth bag and discard. Bring the mixture to a boil over medium heat. Add the pineapple. Simmer, partially covered, for about 35 to 40 minutes, or until the pineapple is tender. Stir occasionally.

Remove the mixture from the heat. Prepare the preserving jars. Measure the fruit mixture and add an equal volume of sugar to the pot. Stir in the ginger. Return to the heat, stirring constantly until the sugar dissolves. Increase the heat to medium-high and cook rapidly, stirring often, for 15 to 20 minutes. Test for the gel stage, using the thermometer or plate test.

Remove from the heat. Skim off the foam, if necessary. Stir for 3 to 5 minutes to prevent floating fruit. Ladle into hot, sterilized jars, leaving a ¼-inch (6 mm) head space. Wipe the rims clean. Seal according to manufacturer's directions. Process the jars in a boiling water bath for 10 minutes.

Chunky Apple Marmalade with Ginger

MAKES ABOUT SIX 8 OZ (250 ML) JARS

Brighten up an early-morning breakfast or a lazy Sunday brunch by serving this sprightly marmalade on hot toast, muffins or biscuits.

2 oranges

1 lemon

6 cups • 1.5 L peeled, chopped apples

1½ cups • 360 mL water

4½ cups • 1.1 L sugar

¼ cup • 60 mL chopped candied ginger

ABOUT GINGER

In its many forms, ginger is one of the most commonly used spices. Fresh ginger root (see page 177) has a strong, distinctive taste. Powdered ginger is the dried, ground root. Candied or crystallized ginger may be chopped and used in any number of sweet and savory preserves, from jams to chutneys; it is much less sharp-tasting than the fresh. Yet another form of ginger is stem ginger preserved in syrup—a very sweet, mild-flavored confection. Pickled ginger (preserved in vinegar) is a very popular condiment in Japan.

CUT the orange and lemon in half lengthwise, discarding the ends and seeds. Place the cut side down and slice the fruit very thinly. Cut the slices into small pieces (do not chop finely). Put the chopped fruit in a small pot and add just enough water to cover it. Simmer over medium heat for about 30 minutes, until the peel is tender. Drain, reserving the fruit. Prepare the preserving jars.

Combine the cooked orange and lemon, apples and water in your preserving pot. Bring to a boil over medium heat. Reduce the heat and simmer for about 10 minutes, until the apples are tender. Stir in the sugar and ginger. Increase the heat to medium and boil rapidly, stirring almost constantly, for 15 to 20 minutes, until thickened. Test for the gel stage, using the thermometer or plate test.

Remove from the heat. Skim off the foam if necessary. Stir for 3 to 5 minutes to prevent floating fruit. Ladle into hot, sterilized jars, leaving a ¼-inch (6 mm) head space. Wipe the rims clean. Seal according to manufacturer's directions. Process the jars in a boiling water bath for 10 minutes.

Peach Orange Marmalade

MAKES ABOUT SIX TO SEVEN 8 OZ (250 ML) JARS

The addition of almond extract gives this marmalade an intriguing flavor, but it is optional. Just be sure that you add it after the marmalade is removed from the heat.

> 2 oranges
>
> 1 lemon
>
> 5 cups • 1.2 L finely chopped, unpeeled peaches
>
> 3½ cups • 840 mL sugar
>
> ½ tsp • 2.5 mL almond extract (optional)

PREPARE the preserving jars.

Grate the zest from the oranges and lemon. Place the zest in a small bowl and add enough boiling water to cover. Set aside.

Slice away as much of the white pith from the fruit as possible, preferably in large pieces. Chop the fruit very finely, reserving the seeds. Tie the seeds in a cheesecloth bag.

Drain the water from the zest. Combine the peaches, chopped oranges and lemon, zest, sugar and the cheesecloth bag in your preserving pot. Mix thoroughly.

Bring to a boil over medium heat. Boil rapidly, stirring often, for 25 to 30 minutes, until thickened. Test for the gel stage, using the thermometer or plate test.

Remove from the heat. Discard the cheesecloth bag, squeezing it out as much as possible. Skim off the foam if necessary. Stir for 3 to 5 minutes to prevent floating fruit. Stir in the almond extract, if desired. Pour into hot, sterilized jars, leaving a ¼-inch (6 mm) head space. Wipe the rims clean. Seal according to manufacturer's directions. Process the jars in a boiling water bath for 10 minutes.

Carrot Marmalade

MAKES ABOUT FOUR TO FIVE 8 OZ (250 ML) JARS

This bright orange marmalade is a natural served with poultry or game and equally good as a breakfast treat.

1 orange

1 lemon

4 cups • 950 mL grated raw carrots

3 cups • 720 mL sugar

½ tsp • 2.5 mL salt

USING the coarse side of a box grater, grate the zest from the orange and lemon. Set the zest aside. Using a sharp knife, remove as much of the white pith as possible and discard. Cut the fruits in half, extract the juice and set aside. Chop the orange and lemon pulp into small pieces.

Combine the orange and lemon zest, juice and pulp in your preserving pot. Mix in the remaining ingredients. Let stand for 1 hour. Prepare the preserving jars.

Bring the mixture to a boil over medium heat, stirring occasionally. Simmer gently, stirring often, for 30 minutes, or until thickened. Test for the gel stage using the thermometer or plate test.

Remove from the heat. Skim off the foam if necessary. Stir for 3 to 5 minutes to prevent floating fruit. Pour the marmalade into hot, sterilized jars, leaving a ¼-inch (6 mm) head space. Wipe the rims clean. Seal according to manufacturer's directions. Process the jars in a boiling water bath for 10 minutes.

Pumpkin Marmalade

MAKES ABOUT FOUR TO FIVE 8 OZ (250 ML) JARS

A rather unusual marmalade with a thick, chunky texture and an excellent citrusy flavor.

1 orange

2 lemons

3 cups • 720 mL water

1 small pumpkin, about 3 lb (1.4 kg)

4 cups • 950 mL sugar

CUT the orange and lemons in half lengthwise. Place the cut side down and slice the fruit very thinly, discarding the ends but reserving the seeds. Cut the slices into small pieces (do not chop finely). Place the seeds in a cheesecloth bag.

In your preserving pot, combine the fruit, water and the bag of seeds. Bring to a boil over medium heat. Reduce the heat, cover and simmer until the fruit is tender, about 30 minutes. Remove the bag of seeds, squeeze it out well and discard.

While the fruit is cooking, prepare the pumpkin. Carefully cut the pumpkin in half and remove the seeds. Cut the pumpkin into chunks, then peel and cut away the stem ends. Dice the pumpkin into small pieces, about $\frac{1}{2}$ inch (1.2 cm) square and $\frac{1}{8}$ inch (3 mm) thick. (Don't worry about being exact; these measurements are only to give you the approximate size.) You should end up with about 8 cups (2 L) of pumpkin. If you have extra, cook it up for dinner.

Add the sugar to the fruit mixture and cook over low heat, stirring until the sugar is dissolved, about 10 minutes. Prepare the preserving jars.

Add the 8 cups (2 L) of prepared pumpkin and increase the heat to medium-high. Cook rapidly, stirring often, for about 45 to 60 minutes, or until thickened. Test for the gel stage, using the thermometer or plate test.

Remove from the heat. Skim off the foam if necessary. Stir for 3 to 5 minutes to prevent floating fruit. Pour the marmalade into hot, sterilized jars, leaving a $\frac{1}{4}$-inch (6 mm) head space. Wipe the rims clean. Seal according to manufacturer's directions. Process the jars in a boiling water bath for 10 minutes.

Zany Zucchini Marmalade

MAKES ABOUT SIX 8 OZ (250 ML) JARS

Another in the never-ending search for new ways to use up extra zucchini . . . if only all vegetables grew as prolifically!

2 oranges

2 lemons

5 cups • 1.2 L grated zucchini
  (about 4 medium zucchini)

5 cups • 1.2 L sugar

2 Tbsp • 30 mL lemon juice

PREPARE the preserving jars.

Slice the oranges and lemons thinly, discarding the ends and seeds. Chop very finely or process in a food processor until finely chopped, but not puréed.

Combine all the ingredients in your preserving pot. Bring to a boil over medium-high heat. Cook rapidly, stirring constantly, until the mixture thickens, about 20 to 25 minutes. Test for the gel stage, using the thermometer or plate test.

Remove from the heat. Skim off the foam if necessary. Stir for 3 to 5 minutes to prevent floating fruit. Pour the marmalade into hot, sterilized jars, leaving a ¼-inch (6 mm) head space. Wipe the rims clean. Seal according to manufacturer's directions. Process the jars in a boiling water bath for 10 minutes.

Winter Marmalade

MAKES ABOUT EIGHT TO NINE 8 OZ (250 ML) JARS

Easily and quickly made with dried fruit and canned pineapple, Winter Marmalade is perfect for holiday gift giving. The larger yield of this recipe will give you plenty of marmalade to treat your friends and enough left over to treat yourself!

1 lb • 454 g dried apricots

¼ lb • 113 g dried cranberries

1 orange

one 14 oz (398 mL) can of crushed pineapple

1 lemon, juice and finely grated zest

1½ cups • 360 mL sugar

CUT the apricots into small pieces with scissors. Place the apricots and cranberries in a bowl and pour boiling water over them, just enough to cover. Set aside to soak for at least 1 hour.

Drain the fruit, reserving ¾ cup (180 mL) of the liquid.

Slice the orange thinly, discarding the ends and seeds. Chop finely.

Prepare the preserving jars.

Combine all the ingredients, including the reserved soaking liquid, in your preserving pot. Bring to a boil over medium-high heat, stirring occasionally. Reduce the heat to medium and simmer, stirring often, for 45 to 60 minutes, or until thickened. Test for the gel stage, using the thermometer or plate test.

Remove from the heat. Skim off the foam if necessary. Stir for 3 to 5 minutes to prevent floating fruit. Ladle the marmalade into hot, sterilized jars, leaving a ¼-inch (6 mm) head space. Wipe the rims clean. Seal according to manufacturer's directions. Process the jars in a boiling water bath for 10 minutes.

Conserves

Grape Pecan Conserve 80

Spiced Pear, Peach and Citrus
Conserve 81

Plum Orange Conserve with Figs 82

Papaya Nectarine Conserve 83

Cranberry, Rum and Raisin Conserve 84

Conserves

onserves are essentially jams that have been dressed up by the addition of dried fruits and nuts. They are usually made from two or more fruits, often including a citrus fruit, and frequently contain spices or alcohol.

Conserves are very versatile. You can serve them as you would a jam, on morning toast or muffins, or offer them as imaginative toppings for desserts. A spicy, tart conserve can provide a distinctive contrast to salty dishes like ham, or a delicious foil to rich meats like roast pork, duck or goose.

The method for making conserves is exactly the same as the procedure for making jam. The fruit and sugar are boiled together until thickened but, unlike jams, nuts or alcohol or both are stirred into conserves during the final minutes of cooking. These ingredients do not require cooking and are added at the last minute so that the nuts will maintain their texture, and the alcohol its intense flavor. The alcohol in any conserve is always optional—leave it out if you like. Feel free to experiment with different combinations of dried fruits and nuts, substituting almonds for walnuts or prunes for raisins, according to your personal preference. Just keep the amounts the same.

Grape Pecan Conserve

MAKES ABOUT FIVE 8 OZ (250 ML) JARS

Crunchy and sweet, this first-rate conserve makes a wonderful topping for toast or a luscious condiment with roast pork or chicken.

2 lb • 900 g seedless green or red grapes

1 lemon

1 orange

3 cups • 720 mL brown sugar

¼ cup • 60 mL lemon juice

1 cup • 240 mL pecans, lightly toasted

⅓ cup • 80 mL brandy or rum (optional)

STEM the grapes and slice them in half. Cut the lemon and orange in quarters lengthwise, then slice thinly, discarding the ends and seeds.

In your preserving pot, combine the grapes, lemon and orange slices, sugar and lemon juice. Mix well, cover and let stand for 2 to 3 hours, to allow the juices to develop.

Prepare the preserving jars.

Bring the fruit and sugar mixture to a boil over medium heat and simmer, stirring often, for 45 to 60 minutes, until thickened. Test for gel if desired. Stir in the pecans. Cook 1 minute longer. Remove from the heat. Stir in the brandy or rum. Skim off the foam if necessary.

Ladle the conserve into hot, sterilized jars, leaving a ¼-inch (6 mm) head space. Wipe the rims clean. Seal according to manufacturer's directions. Process the jars in a boiling water bath for 10 minutes.

Spiced Pear, Peach and Citrus Conserve

MAKES FIVE TO SIX 8 OZ (250 ML) JARS

Autumn is the ideal time to make this luscious conserve. Choose fruit that is ripe, but not too soft or juicy.

one 3-inch (7.5 cm) cinnamon stick,
    broken in half

½ tsp • 2.5 mL whole cloves

2 lemons

1 orange

5 pears, peeled, cored and chopped

5 peaches, peeled, pitted and chopped

½ cup • 120 mL orange juice

4 cups • 950 mL sugar

1 cup • 240 mL toasted slivered almonds

ABOUT CLOVES

Cloves are the dried, unopened floral buds of a tropical evergreen tree that is a member of the myrtle family. The highly aromatic, spicy-sweet flavor of cloves is indispensable in many varieties of preserves. Whole cloves resemble small tacks. They have a biting sharp flavor; use them sparingly to avoid overwhelming other tastes. Whole cloves are always removed after cooking. Ground cloves are less pungent than whole cloves.

PREPARE the preserving jars. Put the cinnamon stick and cloves into a cheesecloth bag and tie the top with string.

Thinly slice the lemons and orange, discarding the ends and seeds. Chop very finely. Place in a small pot and add enough water to barely cover the fruit. Cover and simmer over low heat until the peel is very tender, about 20 to 30 minutes, adding additional water if necessary to keep the fruit moist. Drain and set aside.

Combine the pears, peaches and orange juice in your preserving pot. Cover and simmer over medium heat, stirring often, until the fruit is soft, about 10 minutes. Add the chopped lemon and orange, sugar and spice bag. Increase the heat to medium-high. Simmer, stirring often, for another 20 to 30 minutes, until the conserve has thickened. Test for the gel stage if desired. Stir in the almonds. Cook 1 minute longer. Remove from the heat. Discard the spice bag.

Ladle the conserve into hot, sterilized jars, leaving a ¼-inch (6 mm) head space. Wipe the rims clean. Seal according to manufacturer's directions. Process the jars in a boiling water bath for 10 minutes.

ABOUT TOASTING NUTS

Toasting nuts intensifies their flavor and will add a delicious new dimension to your conserves (and to other recipes too).

As toasted nuts become stale more quickly than raw nuts, you should only prepare the amount that you need for a single recipe.

To toast nuts in the oven, spread shelled nuts in a single layer on a baking sheet or cake pan and toast in a preheated 350°F (175°C) oven for 7 to 10 minutes, or until they are golden brown. Watch them carefully, stirring the nuts every couple of minutes, as the nuts around the perimeter will brown more quickly.

Always let toasted nuts cool completely before using.

To remove the skin from hazelnuts, transfer the nuts while still warm to a clean dish towel. Rub vigorously to remove most of the loose, papery skins.

To toast nuts in the microwave, spread the nuts in a microwave-safe dish, and microwave uncovered on high heat for 5 to 10 minutes, or until the nuts are golden brown. Cashews and Brazil nuts seem to brown more quickly than other types of nuts.

Plum Orange Conserve with Figs

MAKES FIVE TO SIX 8 OZ (250 ML) JARS

Select firm, dark red or purple plums for this rich, elegant conserve. Make extra for Christmas gifts.

1 orange
6 cups • 1.5 L pitted, chopped plums
½ cup • 120 mL orange juice
3½ cups • 840 mL brown sugar
1 cup • 240 mL chopped dried figs
1 cup • 240 mL chopped toasted walnuts

PREPARE the preserving jars.

Thinly slice the orange, discarding the ends and seeds. Chop very finely. Combine the orange, plums and orange juice in your preserving pot. Bring to a boil over medium heat. Simmer, stirring occasionally, until the plums are tender, about 15 minutes. Add the sugar and figs and cook another 15 to 20 minutes, until the conserve has thickened. Stir in the walnuts. Cook 1 minute longer. Remove from the heat.

Ladle the conserve into hot, sterilized jars, leaving a ¼-inch (6 mm) head space. Wipe the rims clean. Seal according to manufacturer's directions. Process the jars in a boiling water bath for 10 minutes.

Papaya Nectarine Conserve

MAKES FIVE TO SIX 8 OZ (250 ML) JARS

Chock-full of ripe, succulent fruit, this conserve is delectable served with scones for an old-fashioned afternoon tea.

4 cups • 950 mL peeled, seeded, chopped
    papaya

4 cups • 950 mL pitted, chopped nectarines

¼ cup • 60 mL lemon juice

2 tsp • 10 mL finely grated lemon zest

6 cups • 1.5 L sugar

1 cup • 240 mL chopped dried apricots

½ tsp • 2.5 mL nutmeg

PREPARE the preserving jars.

In your preserving pot, combine the papaya, nectarines and lemon juice and zest. Cover and simmer over medium heat for about 15 minutes, stirring occasionally, until the fruit is tender. Add the sugar, apricots and nutmeg, and cook another 15 to 20 minutes, until the mixture thickens, stirring often. Test for the gel stage if desired. Remove from the heat.

Ladle the conserve into hot, sterilized jars, leaving a ¼-inch (6 mm) head space. Wipe the rims clean. Seal according to manufacturer's directions. Process the jars in a boiling water bath for 10 minutes.

Cranberry, Rum and Raisin Conserve

MAKES SIX TO SEVEN 8 OZ (250 ML) JARS

Quick and simple to make, this conserve can also be made using frozen cranberries. No need to thaw them— just rinse and sort.

2 oranges

3 cups • 720 mL cranberries

1 cup • 240 mL cranberry or orange juice

2 cups • 475 mL brown sugar

1 cup • 240 mL dark raisins

1 cup • 240 mL coarsely chopped, toasted Brazil nuts

½ cup • 120 mL dark rum

PREPARE the preserving jars.

Slice the oranges thinly, discarding the ends and seeds. Chop very finely. Combine the orange, cranberries, cranberry or orange juice, brown sugar and raisins in your preserving pot. Bring to a boil over medium heat. Simmer, stirring often, for about 15 minutes, or until thickened. Stir in the Brazil nuts and rum and cook 1 minute longer. Remove from the heat.

Ladle the conserve into hot, sterilized jars, leaving a ¼-inch (6 mm) head space. Wipe the rims clean. Seal according to manufacturer's directions. Process the jars in a boiling water bath for 10 minutes.

Preserves

Classic Strawberry Preserves 89

Sweet Cherry Preserves in
Almond Syrup 91

Plum Preserves with Orange Zest 92

Gingered Apple Preserves 93

Brandied Peach Preserves 94

Preserves

The word *preserves* describes preserved foods as a group, but it also refers to a particular subgroup of preserved foods—a unique type of sweet spread, similar to jam, but requiring much more painstaking preparation. Preserves are a showcase for only the choicest fruit, making maximum use of its natural, juicy sweetness. Reserve your preserves for those occasions when you really want to make an impression, a show-off brunch, or a tea with your mother's friends. They are treasures to spoon up and savor with your most elegant "company's coming" desserts.

Preserves are made from whole, small fruits, like berries or cherries, or uniform pieces of larger fruits, like peaches or pears. The fruit for preserves is never crushed or chopped as it is for jam—the goal is to have identifiable pieces of fruit that retain their color, texture and shape. The chunks of fruit are tender and plump, suspended in a clear jelly-like syrup. The consistency of preserves is dependent on the amount of pectin present in the fruit; slightly underripe fruit is best.

Techniques for making preserves vary considerably, depending on the type of fruit that is being used. Soft fruits are usually layered with sugar for several hours, allowing their juices to develop. Layering is simply alternating layers of sugar and fruit in the pot; in effect, combining the two without stirring them. This helps to keep the fruit intact. Hard fruits—pears or apples, for example—are simmered in water or a sugar syrup to tenderize them and draw out their natural juices.

Preserves often take two to three days to prepare. One reason for this is the standing time, during which the juices are extracted. The other reason is that many types of preserves are partially cooked, then poured into shallow dishes to encourage evaporation. During this process, the fruits steep in their syrup, absorbing sugar and becoming plump and juicy. This usually takes 12 to 24 hours.

As a result of these advance procedures, the final cooking time for preserves is reduced. The mixture is boiled rapidly for a brief period until the syrup thickens and the fruit appears translucent. The rapid cooking yields a fresh fruit flavor that is much more intense and concentrated than that of regular jams.

Classic Strawberry Preserves

MAKES FIVE TO SIX 8 OZ (250 ML) JARS

Don't be dismayed if your preserves end up syrupy instead of set—the pectin content of strawberries can vary tremendously. Strawberry preserves make a glorious dessert sauce. Select firm, slightly underripe (but not green!) strawberries, of uniform size, if possible.

6 cups • 1.5 L strawberries, about 3–3½ lb
   (1.4–1.6 kg)
5 cups • 1.2 L sugar
⅓ cup • 80 mL lemon juice

HULL the strawberries, but do not crush them. Layer the strawberries and sugar in your preserving pot. Cover and let stand at room temperature for 3 to 4 hours. Bring to a boil over low heat, stirring very gently until the sugar is dissolved. Increase the heat and boil rapidly for 15 minutes, stirring gently or shaking the pot often to prevent scorching. Stir in the lemon juice. Pour the mixture into 1 or 2 shallow, heatproof pans. Let stand, uncovered, until cool. Cover with cheesecloth or a dish towel and leave in a cool place for 24 hours.

The next day, prepare the preserving jars. Return the mixture to your preserving pot and bring it quickly to a boil over medium-high heat. Boil rapidly for 10 to 15 minutes, shaking the pot or stirring gently to prevent scorching, until the syrup has thickened slightly.

Remove from the heat. Stir gently for about 5 minutes to prevent floating fruit. Skim off the foam if necessary. Ladle the preserves into hot, sterilized jars, leaving a ¼-inch (6 mm) head space. Wipe the rims clean. Seal according to manufacturer's directions. Process the jars in a boiling water bath for 10 minutes.

Sweet Cherry Preserves in Almond Syrup

MAKES SIX TO SEVEN 8 OZ (250 ML) JARS

This preserve is delectable spooned over ice cream or cheesecake. Heavenly with chocolate.

8 cups • 2 L sweet, firm cherries
6 cups • 1.5 L sugar
3 Tbsp • 45 mL lemon juice
1 tsp • 5 mL almond extract

WORKING over a bowl to catch the juice, pit the cherries and cut any extra-large ones in half. (See "About Pitting Cherries," page 103.)

Layer the cherries and sugar together in your preserving pot. Cover and let stand for 1 to 2 hours at room temperature, to draw out the juices.

Bring the mixture to a boil over low heat, stirring gently until the sugar is dissolved. Increase the heat to medium and boil for 10 minutes, shaking the pot occasionally or stirring very gently to prevent scorching. Remove from the heat. Stir in the lemon juice.

Pour the mixture into 1 or 2 shallow, heatproof pans and let stand until cool. Cover loosely with cheesecloth or a dish towel and leave in a cool place for 12 to 18 hours or overnight.

The next day, prepare the preserving jars. Transfer the mixture to your preserving pot and bring to a boil over medium-high heat. Boil rapidly for 10 minutes, until slightly thickened. Stir gently or shake the pot often to prevent scorching.

Remove from the heat and skim off the foam if necessary. Add the almond extract, and stir for 5 minutes to prevent floating fruit. Ladle the preserves into hot, sterilized jars, leaving a ¼-inch (6 mm) head space. Wipe the rims clean. Seal according to manufacturer's directions. Process the jars in a boiling water bath for 10 minutes.

Plum Preserves with Orange Zest

MAKES FIVE TO SIX 8 OZ (250 ML) JARS

Plum delicious! Damson or prune plums make the best
preserves.

> 6 cups • 1.5 L halved, pitted firm plums,
>   about 3 lb (1.4 kg)
> ½ cup • 120 mL orange juice
> ½ cup • 120 mL water
> 4½ cups • 1.1 L sugar
> 1 Tbsp • 15 mL grated orange zest

COMBINE the plums, orange juice and water in your preserving pot. Simmer
gently over medium heat for 10 minutes. Using a slotted spoon, carefully remove
the plums from the liquid and place them in a shallow, heatproof pan. Add the
sugar and orange zest to the liquid in the pot, bring to a boil over medium heat
and simmer for 15 minutes, stirring occasionally. Remove from the heat and
skim off the foam if necessary. Pour the syrup over the plums. Let stand uncovered until cool, then cover loosely with cheesecloth or a dish towel and let stand
in a cool place for 12 to 18 hours or overnight.

The next day, prepare the preserving jars. Transfer the plums and syrup to
your preserving pot and bring it to a boil over medium heat. Boil rapidly for
10 to 15 minutes until the mixture is slightly thickened. Stir gently or shake the
pot often to prevent scorching.

Remove from the heat. Ladle the preserves into hot, sterilized jars, leaving a
¼-inch (6 mm) head space. Wipe the rims clean. Seal according to manufacturer's directions. Process the jars in a boiling water bath for 10 minutes.

Gingered Apple Preserves

MAKES ABOUT SIX 8 OZ (250 ML) JARS

This is for people with a real sweet tooth. Use firm, tart apples such as Granny Smiths. Sliced preserved ginger may be purchased either in jars or in bulk. A 4 to 6 oz (125 to 170 mL) jar will be about the right amount for this recipe. You don't have to be exact.

5 cups • 1.2 L sugar

2 cups • 475 mL water

one 3-inch (7.5 cm) cinnamon stick

8 cups • 2 L peeled, sliced apples, about
    3 lb (1.4 kg), cut ¼ inch (6 mm) thick

3 Tbsp • 45 mL lemon juice

1 Tbsp • 15 mL finely grated lemon zest

½–¾ cup • 120–180 mL sliced preserved
    ginger in syrup

ABOUT CINNAMON

Cinnamon is the dried bark of a tropical evergreen laurel tree. It is closely related to another spice, cassia, and the two are used interchangeably; in fact, cassia is often sold as cinnamon. Sweet and fragrant, cinnamon may be used to enhance a variety of preserves, from spiced jams to pickles. Cinnamon sticks may be added whole to flavor liquids, or broken and combined with other spices in a cheesecloth bag for easy removal. Ground cinnamon may be used in place of cinnamon sticks, but it may cause cloudiness in clear liquids. A universally popular spice, cinnamon is a component of spice mixtures from all over the world.

COMBINE the sugar, water and cinnamon stick in your preserving pot. Bring to a boil over high heat, stirring often. Reduce the heat to medium, and simmer the mixture for 10 to 15 minutes. Prepare the preserving jars.

Toss the apple slices with the lemon juice and zest in a bowl. Drain the ginger, reserving the syrup, and slice thinly. Add the lemony apples, ginger and reserved syrup to the preserving pot. Simmer gently over medium heat for 35 to 40 minutes, until the syrup is slightly thickened and the apples appear translucent. Stir very gently or shake the pot often to prevent scorching.

Remove from the heat. Discard the cinnamon stick. Divide the apple slices equally among the hot, sterilized jars. Pour the syrup over to cover, leaving a ¼-inch (6 mm) head space. Wipe the rims clean. Seal according to manufacturer's directions. Process the jars in a boiling water bath for 10 minutes.

Brandied Peach Preserves

MAKES FIVE TO SIX 8 OZ (250 ML) JARS

A rich, intensely flavored preserve, accented with brandy.
If you like, substitute apricots and Amaretto for the
peaches and brandy. Apricots do not need to be peeled.

8 cups • 2 L peeled peaches (use mature but
    underripe peaches), sliced about ½ inch
    (1.2 cm) thick
6 cups • 1.5 L sugar
½ cup • 120 mL lemon juice
½ cup • 120 mL brandy

IN your preserving pot, layer the peaches and sugar together. Cover and let stand in a cool place overnight to draw out the juices.

The next day, bring the mixture to a boil over low heat, stirring gently until the sugar is dissolved. Increase the heat to medium and simmer for 10 minutes, shaking the pot occasionally or stirring gently to prevent scorching. Remove from the heat and stir in the lemon juice. Pour into 1 or 2 shallow, heatproof pans and let stand until cool. Cover loosely with cheesecloth or a dish towel and leave in a cool place overnight.

The next day, prepare the preserving jars. Transfer the mixture to your preserving pot and bring it to a boil over medium-high heat. Boil rapidly for about 15 minutes, until the syrup has thickened slightly and the peaches look translucent. Stir gently or shake the pot often to prevent scorching.

Remove from the heat. Skim off the foam if necessary. Add the brandy and stir for 5 minutes to prevent floating fruit. Ladle the preserves into hot, sterilized jars, leaving a ¼-inch (6 mm) head space. Wipe the rims clean. Seal according to manufacturer's directions. Process the jars in a boiling water bath for 10 minutes.

Fruit Sauces

Honeyed Applesauce 98

Pineapple, Strawberry and Rhubarb
Dessert Sauce 100

Honeyed Peach and Blueberry
Compote 101

Spiced Pear Sauce 102

Spirited Cherry and Raspberry
Compote 103

Blackberry Orange Sauce with Port 104

Fruit Sauces

 reserved fruit sauces, sometimes referred to as compotes, are a wonderful staple to have on hand in the pantry—just waiting to enhance a variety of appetizers, main courses and desserts.

A fresh-tasting, tart fruit sauce is a lively companion to a veal pâté or chicken terrine. For the main course, pair a savory fruit sauce, such as Spiced Pear Sauce, with a crown roast of pork. Sauces with berries or cherries are a natural with chicken or duck.

Fruit sauces really shine at dessert time. Sweet fruit sauces can dress up any number of desserts, from simple ice cream or pound or angel food cake to an elegant trifle, cheesecake or dessert soufflé. Serve them spooned over poached fruit, rice pudding or gingerbread. You will no doubt find endless uses for these versatile toppings.

Simple concoctions of fruit, sugar and often juice or alcohol, fruit sauces are like a thinner version of jam, containing more fruit and less sugar.

Fruit sauces are simple to make. The fruit and sugar are simply simmered together until the fruit is cooked. Timing is not crucial and there is no need to test for a set. Then just pour the sauce into jars, process it and stash it away for a luscious taste of summer that you will enjoy year-round.

The queen of fruit sauces, applesauce is terrific with everything from pancakes to pork chops. Mix it half and half with plain yogurt for a healthy treat, or bake it into muffins, cakes or quick breads. Applesauce is sensational spooned over baked squash, yams or sweet potatoes.

You can vary applesauce by mixing apples with other fruits. Pears, peaches and plums can lend an intriguing flavor to applesauce, and citrus juices and zests really punch up the taste. Berry applesauce can be made simply by adding cooked berry purée to your favorite homemade applesauce.

Honeyed Applesauce

MAKES ABOUT FIVE TO SIX 1-PINT (500 ML) JARS

Applesauces can be made with any variety of apple, but the texture of the sauce may vary depending on the apple that is used. Some varieties of apples break down completely when cooked, while others tend to remain chunky. Experiment with different varieties of honey to lend a unique flavor to your applesauce.

6 lb • 2.75 kg apples

2 cups • 475 mL apple juice or cider

1 cup • 240 mL water

¼ cup • 60 mL lemon juice

½ cup • 120 mL honey, or to taste

1½ tsp • 7.5 mL cinnamon, or to taste

pinch of nutmeg

PREPARE the preserving jars. Peel and core the apples and cut into 1-inch (2.5 cm) chunks.

Combine the apples, apple juice or cider, water and lemon juice in your preserving pot and bring to a boil over medium heat. Reduce the heat to medium-low and simmer until the apples are very soft, 30 to 45 minutes, stirring often. Mash the apples thoroughly, using a potato masher. Stir in the honey and spices. Simmer for another 15 minutes, stirring constantly.

Remove from the heat. Ladle the applesauce into hot, sterilized jars, leaving a ¼-inch (6 mm) head space. Release the air bubbles if necessary. Wipe the rims clean. Seal according to manufacturer's directions. Process the jars in a boiling water bath for 20 minutes for either pints (500 mL) or quarts (1 L).

Pineapple, Strawberry and Rhubarb Dessert Sauce

MAKES SEVEN TO EIGHT 8 OZ (250 ML) JARS

A magical combination of three fruits that seem to have a natural affinity for each other.

7 cups • 1.75 L rhubarb, cut into ½-inch
    (1.2 cm) dice
2 cups • 475 mL fresh pineapple, cut into
    ½-inch (1.2 cm) dice OR one 19 oz (540 mL)
    can drained pineapple tidbits
2 cups • 475 mL sliced strawberries
¼ cup • 60 mL lemon juice
4 cups • 950 mL sugar

PREPARE the preserving jars.

Combine the rhubarb, pineapple, strawberries and lemon juice in your preserving pot. Simmer over medium-low heat until the juices begin to form, then cover and simmer for 15 minutes, stirring often. Add the sugar, stirring to dissolve. Return the mixture to a boil and simmer, stirring often, for 20 minutes.

Remove from the heat. Stir 2 to 3 minutes and skim off the foam if necessary. Pour into hot, sterilized jars, leaving a ¼-inch (6 mm) head space. Wipe the rims clean. Seal according to manufacturer's directions. Process the jars in a boiling water bath for 10 minutes.

Honeyed Peach and Blueberry Compote

MAKES ABOUT SIX TO SEVEN 8 OZ (250 ML) JARS

This is a sensational sauce for a cheesecake or spooned over rich vanilla ice cream. Use fully ripe peaches.

- 5 cups • 1.2 L sliced, peeled peaches
- 5 cups • 1.2 L blueberries
- 1 cup • 240 mL orange juice
- 2 cups • 475 mL sugar
- 1 cup • 240 mL honey
- ⅓ cup • 80 mL lemon juice
- one 3-inch (7.5 cm) cinnamon stick, broken in half

PREPARE the preserving jars.

Combine the peaches, blueberries and orange juice in your preserving pot. Bring to a boil over medium heat. Cover and simmer for 10 minutes, stirring occasionally. Add the remaining ingredients, stirring until the sugar is dissolved. Return the mixture to a boil and simmer, stirring often, for 15 to 20 minutes, or until the sauce is slightly thickened.

Remove from the heat. Discard the cinnamon sticks. Ladle the sauce into hot, sterilized jars, leaving a ¼-inch (6 mm) head space. Wipe the rims clean. Seal according to manufacturer's directions. Process the jars in a boiling water bath for 10 minutes.

SPIRITED PEACH AND BLUEBERRY COMPOTE Add ¼ cup (60 mL) of peach schnapps or brandy before bottling.

ABOUT HONEY

Honey varies in color, aroma and flavor, depending on the type of flowers from which the bees have gathered the nectar. As a rule, the lighter the honey is in color, the milder the flavor will be. Clover honey, for example, is a delicate, light honey, while buckwheat honey is dark and strongly flavored.

Honey is sweeter than sugar, so when substituting honey for sugar, less honey is normally used.

Honey has a distinctive taste, which may mask more delicate flavors, so it is not suitable for use in all recipes.

Honey is so thick it is sometimes tricky to measure. Lightly grease your measuring cup or spoon so that the honey will come out more readily and use a rubber spatula to remove every last bit.

Spiced Pear Sauce

MAKES ABOUT FIVE TO SIX 8 OZ (250 ML) JARS

Absolutely divine served warm over homemade ginger-bread, with a scoop of vanilla ice cream alongside.

8 large, juicy, ripe pears

¾ cup • 180 mL brown sugar, or more to taste

2 Tbsp • 30 mL lemon juice

1½ tsp • 7.5 mL ground ginger

1 tsp • 5 mL cinnamon

½ tsp • 2.5 mL ground cloves

PREPARE the preserving jars. Peel, core and dice the pears.

Combine all the ingredients in your preserving pot. Bring to a boil over medium heat. Reduce the heat to low. Simmer, partially covered, for 20 to 25 minutes, or until the pears are soft. Stir occasionally.

Remove from the heat and mash vigorously with a potato masher until the mixture is fairly smooth. Return to a boil over medium-low heat, and cook for another 10 minutes, stirring constantly. Taste the pear sauce and add additional sugar, if necessary. Once the pear sauce is uniformly hot and bubbling, remove from the heat.

Spoon the sauce into hot, sterilized jars, leaving a ¼-inch (6 mm) head space. Wipe the rims clean. Seal according to manufacturer's directions. Process the jars in a boiling water bath for 10 minutes.

Spirited Cherry and Raspberry Compote

MAKES ABOUT FIVE TO SIX 8 OZ (250 ML) JARS

This gorgeous dessert sauce partners exceptionally well with anything chocolate: chocolate mousse, chocolate terrine, even good old chocolate cake.

Chambord is a raspberry liqueur made in France. Kirsch is made from cherries.

- 6 cups • 1.5 L tart cherries, pitted
- 3 cups • 720 mL raspberries
- 4 cups • 950 mL sugar
- ¼ cup • 60 mL lemon juice
- ⅓ cup • 80 mL Chambord liqueur, or kirsch

PREPARE the preserving jars.

Combine the cherries, raspberries and sugar in your preserving pot. Let stand for 15 minutes to allow the juices to develop. Stir in the lemon juice. Bring to a boil over medium heat. Simmer, stirring often, for 15 to 20 minutes, until slightly thickened.

Remove from the heat. Stir and skim off the foam if necessary. Stir in the Chambord liqueur. Pour the sauce into hot, sterilized jars, leaving a ¼-inch (6 mm) head space. Wipe the rims clean. Seal according to manufacturer's directions. Process the jars in a boiling water bath for 10 minutes.

ABOUT PITTING CHERRIES

When pitting cherries, always work over a bowl to catch the inevitable drops of cherry juice. Less juice will drip out if the cherries are chilled prior to pitting. Slit the cherries using a small, sharp knife, then use the tip of the knife to pop out the pit.

You may also use a cherry pitter—a handy, plunger-type gadget that pushes the pit right through the cherry, leaving only a small, neat hole. Cherry pitters are available in most cookware stores.

fruit sauces

Blackberry Orange Sauce with Port

MAKES ABOUT FIVE TO SIX 8 OZ (250 ML) JARS

Don't go out and buy the most expensive port that you can find. (Save that for drinking!) Any moderately priced ruby port will do fine.

6 cups • 1.5 L blackberries

4 cups • 950 mL sugar

1 cup • 240 mL orange juice

¼ cup • 60 mL lemon juice

¼ cup • 60 mL grated orange zest

½ cup • 120 mL port

PREPARE the preserving jars.

Combine the blackberries and sugar in your preserving pot and crush them with a potato masher. Add the orange and lemon juices and orange zest.

Bring to a boil over medium heat, then simmer for 20 minutes, stirring often. Remove from the heat and skim off the foam if necessary. Stir in the port.

Pour the sauce into hot, sterilized jars, leaving a ¼-inch (6 mm) head space. Wipe the rims clean. Seal according to manufacturer's directions. Process the jars in a boiling water bath for 10 minutes.

Fruit Butters

Apple Butter 110

Wild Blackberry Butter 111

Pear Orange Butter 112

Quick Cranberry Butter 113

Plum Butter 114

Peach, Mango, Nectarine or
Papaya Butter 116

Fruit Butters

Fruit butters have a venerable tradition in the history of preserving. But until quite recently, they seemed to have fallen out of favor with home preservers, perhaps because they take a little extra time to prepare.

These old-fashioned favorites are now reappearing on pantry shelves, as we discover that fruit butters are among the most flavorful, versatile and arguably the most wholesome of homemade preserves.

Fruit butters are a tremendous way to utilize ripe or slightly overripe fruits that are not suitable for other types of preserves. Natural sugars are at their peak in such fruits, therefore very little extra sugar is needed, and the intense fruit flavors are concentrated.

And fear not—virtuous fruit butters contain no butter at all. The name simply refers to their smooth, velvety texture. They can be used *instead* of butter on your morning toast or muffins, for fewer than half the calories, and offer a change of pace from jams or jellies. For this reason, fruit butters are a more healthful choice for those who are monitoring fat, sugar or caloric intakes.

Fruit butters taste as good with meats and entrées as they do for breakfast, and can be incorporated into sauces and baked goods as well.

Fruit butters require no special skills to make, but they are a little time-consuming. Plan to make fruit butter on a day when you have lots of time to spend in the kitchen, as it does demand a fair amount of attention. Perhaps you can have another project on

COOKING FRUIT BUTTERS IN THE OVEN

Fruit butters may also be cooked in the oven and many cooks prefer this method. It requires less stirring and tends to be less messy.

You still have to prepare the fruit purée in a pot on top of the stove (Step One). The difference is in Step Two.

A preserving pot is not suitable for cooking fruit butters in the oven. Use a large, shallow roasting pan made of stainless steel, glass or enamel-coated metal. It is important to have the maximum surface area of the butter exposed to the heat to encourage evaporation. Cook the butter, uncovered, at 325°F (165°C) until thick, stirring occasionally.

the go and you can switch from one to the other to make the best use of your time.

Fruit butters are not as delicate as some preserves that require precise timing and careful balancing of pectin, acid and sugar. Butters don't actually gel, but thicken naturally during a long, slow cooking process—that gradually reduces the fruit pulp to a thick spreadable consistency.

Patience is a prerequisite, however, as it is essential to stir the butter almost constantly to prevent scorching, especially during the end of the cooking period.

But don't let this discourage you. If you persevere, you will be rewarded with a silky-smooth, naturally sweet, heavenly tasting ambrosia that will make all your efforts worthwhile.

HOW TO MAKE FRUIT BUTTERS

Most traditional recipes for fruit butter were developed as a way to use up surplus fruit and therefore generally do not specify amounts.

Fruit butters, like jellies, are prepared in two steps—the first step readies the fruit for cooking in the second step. But this is where the similarities end.

Step One: Prepare the Fruit Purée

1. Place cut-up hard fruits or berries in your preserving pot. Hard fruits, such as apples or pears, should be cut into chunks, but do not need to be peeled.
2. Add water or juice if using hard fruits.

Crush the fruit if using soft berry-like fruits. No water is necessary as they will simmer in their own juice.

3. Cover and simmer until the fruit is very soft, stirring often.
4. For fruit with peels or pits, pass the fruit through a sieve or food mill. Soft fruits may be puréed in a blender or food processor.

NOTE You can prepare fruit butter up to this point, then refrigerate the purée and continue with Step 2 later on.

Step Two: Cook the Fruit Butter

5. Measure the purée back into the preserving pot.
6. Add the appropriate amount of sugar. Usually this will be one-third to half as much sugar as you have purée. If you are using honey instead of sugar, it is added later on in the cooking process, as the mixture reduces and starts to thicken.
7. Stir over low heat to dissolve the sugar; continue to simmer the butter over low heat until it is very thick.
8. Stir the butter almost constantly to prevent scorching; this is especially important once it begins to thicken. Use a long-handled spoon, as fruit butters tend to spatter.
9. Towards the end of the cooking time, once the butter has thickened somewhat, add the spices. This is

also the time to add honey if you are using it.

10. To determine if the butter is ready, draw your spoon through the center of the butter, making a trough. If the trough doesn't immediately fill with liquid, the butter is done. You can also test by dropping a teaspoonful of butter onto a chilled plate. If no juice oozes away from the more solid mass of the butter, it is ready to be put into jars.

11. Can the butter as you would any other type of sweet preserve, although due to its thickness it is usually best to spoon the butter into the jars. Butters tend to trap air bubbles because of their density, so be sure to release any pockets of air by running a nonmetal utensil around the inside of the glass.

12. Process the jars of butter in a boiling water bath, as directed in the recipe.

Apple Butter

MAKES SIX TO SEVEN 8 OZ (250 ML) JARS

In the past, people cooked apple butter outside in massive kettles slung over an open fire. Lucky you!

5 lb • 2.25 kg tart apples

2 cups • 475 mL apple juice or cider

1½–2 cups • 360–475 mL brown sugar

2 Tbsp • 30 mL lemon juice

1 Tbsp • 15 mL cinnamon

½ tsp • 2.5 mL each ground cloves, allspice
   and nutmeg

CORE the apples and chop them coarsely. Combine the apples and apple juice or cider in your preserving pot. Bring to a boil over medium heat. Reduce the heat to low, cover and simmer for about 20 minutes, or until the apples are tender. Stir occasionally. Remove from the heat. Pass the mixture through a sieve or food mill.

Measure the purée back into your preserving pot. Add ½ to ⅔ cup (120 to 160 mL) of sugar for each cup of purée, depending on the tartness of the apples. Add the lemon juice and mix well. Cook over low heat, stirring almost constantly, for 35 to 45 minutes, or until thickened. Stir in the spices during the last 10 to 15 minutes of the cooking time. Test for doneness if desired.

Remove from the heat. Spoon the butter into hot, sterilized jars, leaving a ¼-inch (6 mm) head space. Release the air bubbles. Wipe the rims clean. Seal according to manufacturer's directions. Process the jars in a boiling water bath for 10 minutes.

Wild Blackberry Butter

Blackberries are free for the picking along many road-
sides or in deserted lots. Use fully ripe, juicy berries for
this butter.

8 cups • 2 L blackberries

6 large apples, about 2 lb (900 g)

sugar

½ tsp • 2.5 mL ground cloves

½ tsp • 2.5 mL cinnamon

PLACE the blackberries in your preserving pot and crush them with a potato
masher. Core the apples and chop them coarsely. Add the apples to the
blackberries.

Bring to a boil over medium-low heat. Cover and simmer for about 30 minutes, or until the apples are soft, stirring often. Remove from the heat and pass
the mixture through a sieve or food mill.

Prepare the preserving jars.

Measure the purée back into the preserving pot and add ½ to ¾ cup (120 to
180 mL) of sugar for each cup of purée. Taste as you add the sugar: the amount
will depend on your own personal preference as well as the sweetness or tartness
of the berries.

Stir well to dissolve the sugar and simmer over low heat, stirring often, for
45 to 60 minutes. Once the butter starts to get quite thick, towards the end of
the cooking time, add the spices. Stir constantly from this point on to prevent
scorching. Test for doneness if desired.

Remove from the heat. Spoon the butter into hot, sterilized jars, leaving a
¼-inch (6 mm) head space. Release the air bubbles. Wipe the rims clean. Seal
according to manufacturer's directions. Process the jars in a boiling water bath
for 10 minutes.

fruit butters |

Pear Orange Butter

MAKES FIVE TO SIX 8 OZ (250 ML) JARS

A sweet, silky butter subtly spiked with orange and ginger.

4 lb • 1.8 kg ripe, juicy pears
1 cup • 240 mL orange juice
3 Tbsp • 45 mL lemon juice
2 cups • 475 mL sugar, or to taste
½ tsp • 2.5 mL ground ginger

CORE the pears and chop them coarsely. Combine the pears, orange juice
and lemon juice in your preserving pot and bring to a boil over medium heat.
Reduce the heat to low. Cover and simmer for about 30 minutes, until the pears
are very soft, stirring occasionally. Remove from the heat and pass the mixture
through a sieve or food mill.

Prepare the preserving jars.

Return the purée to the pot and add the sugar, stirring until it is dissolved.
Simmer over medium-low heat, stirring almost constantly, for 40 to 50 minutes,
or until the butter is very thick. Stir in the ginger during the last 10 to 15 minutes of the cooking time. Test for doneness if desired.

Remove from the heat. Spoon the butter into hot, sterilized jars, leaving a
¼-inch (6 mm) head space. Release the air bubbles. Wipe the rims clean. Seal
according to manufacturer's directions. Process the jars in a boiling water bath
for 10 minutes.

Quick Cranberry Butter

MAKES SIX TO SEVEN 8 OZ (250 ML) JARS

This butter is much less time-consuming than most. Cranberries are full of pectin, causing the butter to thicken up quickly.

10 cups • 2.4 L cranberries

1½ cups • 360 mL cranberry juice

1½ cups • 360 mL honey or maple syrup, or to taste

½ tsp • 2.5 mL ground allspice

COMBINE the cranberries and juice in your preserving pot. Cover and cook over medium-low heat until the cranberries are soft, about 20 to 30 minutes, stirring occasionally. Cool the mixture slightly, then purée it in a blender or food processor until smooth.

Prepare the preserving jars.

Return the cranberry purée to the preserving pot and add the honey or maple syrup and allspice. Simmer over low heat, stirring constantly, about 15 to 20 minutes, until the butter is thick. Test for doneness.

Remove from the heat. Spoon the butter into hot, sterilized jars, leaving a ¼-inch (6 mm) head space. Release the air bubbles. Wipe the rims clean. Seal according to manufacturer's directions. Process the jars in a boiling water bath for 10 minutes.

USING HONEY IN FRUIT BUTTERS

You may prefer to use honey instead of sugar to sweeten fruit butters. Remember that all honeys have a definite flavor, and will impart that to your butter. For this reason, a mild, light-colored honey is the best choice.

You will need much less honey than sugar, usually about half the amount. The honey is added near the end of the cooking time, at the same time that you add the spices. Simply taste the fruit mixture and add enough honey to sweeten it to your liking.

Plum Butter

Serve this mellow, richly flavored butter with roast pork or turkey, or as a spread on fruit or nut quick breads.

12 cups • 3 L coarsely chopped, pitted plums

1 cup • 240 mL water

4 cups • 950 mL sugar, or to taste

½ tsp • 2.5 mL cinnamon

½ tsp • 2.5 mL ground cloves

COMBINE the plums and water in your preserving pot. Cover and simmer over medium heat for about 20 minutes, or until the plums are tender. Stir occasionally. Remove from the heat. Pass the mixture through a sieve or food mill (or if you don't mind the barely discernible bits of skin, purée in a food processor).

Prepare the preserving jars.

Return the purée to the preserving pot. Stir in the sugar until it is dissolved. Simmer over medium-low heat, stirring almost constantly, for 30 to 40 minutes, or until the mixture is somewhat thickened. Stir in the spices during the last 10 to 15 minutes of the cooking time. Test for doneness if desired.

Remove from the heat. Spoon the butter into hot, sterilized jars, leaving a ¼-inch (6 mm) head space. Release the air bubbles. Wipe the rims clean. Seal according to manufacturer's directions. Process the jars in a boiling water bath for 10 minutes.

Peach, Mango, Nectarine or Papaya Butter

MAKES SEVEN TO EIGHT 8 OZ (250 ML) JARS

Only ripe, juicy, succulent fruits will do for this recipe. I like to use lemon juice with peaches or nectarines and lime juice with mangos and papayas. Pure ambrosia!

10 cups • 2.4 L chopped, peeled fruit

⅔ cup • 160 mL orange juice

⅓ cup • 80 mL lemon or lime juice

2 cups • 475 mL sugar, or to taste

½ tsp • 2.5 mL ground ginger

½ tsp • 2.5 mL nutmeg

COMBINE the fruit, orange juice and lemon or lime juice in your preserving pot. Bring to a boil over medium heat. Reduce the heat to low, cover and simmer for about 20 minutes, or until the fruit is very soft. Stir often. Remove from the heat. Cool the mixture slightly, then purée it in a blender or food processor until smooth.

Prepare the preserving jars.

Return the purée to the preserving pot and stir in the sugar. Simmer over medium-low heat, stirring almost constantly, for 35 to 40 minutes, until thickened. Add the spices during the last 10 to 15 minutes of the cooking time. Test for doneness, if desired.

Remove from the heat. Spoon the butter into hot, sterilized jars, leaving a ¼-inch (6 mm) head space. Release the air bubbles. Wipe the rims clean. Seal according to manufacturer's directions. Process the jars in a boiling water bath for 10 minutes.

Pickles

Simply Good Dill Pickles 125

Authentic Bread and Butter Pickles 126

Pickled Garlic 127

Striped Pickled Peppers 128

Pickled Rosemary Carrots 129

Pickled Asparagus 130

Spicy Pickled Green Beans 132

Michael's Pickled Onions 134

Antipasto Pickles 136

Sweet Spiced Pickled Beets 138

Pickled Cherries with Tarragon 139

Pickled Pears with Honey and
Red Wine 140

Pickles

Many people who have never tried their hand at pickling are astonished how simply and quickly many varieties of pickles can be made. It is possible to complete a batch of pickles in an afternoon, and then reap the mouth-watering benefits for weeks and months to come.

Pickling, the preservation of vegetables or fruits in a vinegar and/or salt solution, is one of the most ancient methods of preserving foods.

There are three basic forms of pickling: long-term brining, short-term brining and quick process (also known as fresh-pack).

The traditional long-term brining process, utilizing controlled fermentation, can take weeks or months to accomplish and requires close supervision. In this method, vegetables are placed into a large crock and covered with a saltwater solution, the brine. As fermentation occurs, lactic acid is produced, increasing the acidity of the solution and controlling the growth of undesirable microorganisms.

Pickles produced by this age-old, natural process have a characteristic, sharp, tangy flavor. Only certain types of vegetables are suitable for fermentation pickling.

A second method, short-term or nonfermentation brining, is a two-step process which involves submerging vegetables in a high salt or salt-vinegar brine for several hours or days, de-salting them, then bottling them in a vinegar pickling liquid.

The main disadvantages of both brining methods are that they are time- and space-consuming.

The recipes here use a speedier, more straightforward procedure called the fresh-pack method. Most modern pickle recipes use this method and it is more appropriate for small quantities.

Some purists argue that fermentation produces a distinct flavor that cannot be duplicated by fresh-packing in vinegar. This may be so, but fresh-packing, done properly, provides the most thorough protection from spoilage. This, combined with the ease and convenience of fresh-packing, makes it the method of choice for most picklers today.

In fresh-packing, vinegar provides the acid necessary to prevent spoilage. It is important to note that you must always follow pickle recipes exactly. Never reduce the amount of vinegar called for in a recipe. If you find a particular pickle too tangy, add a little sugar the next time to offset its tartness, or simply find another recipe that is more suited to your taste.

Many types of pickles made by the fresh-pack method can be completed within an hour or two. In some recipes, the clean vegetables or fruit are simply placed directly into the jars, salt and seasonings added and a hot vinegar solution poured over the food to cover it. Other recipes may call for steeping or simmering the produce in a vinegar solution, while others require short-brining foods with salt for a few hours or overnight. The pickles are then briefly processed in a boiling water bath.

Despite what you may have read or heard, for safety's sake, all pickles must be heat processed, as directed in the recipe. This ensures that any organisms that might cause spoilage have been destroyed. In addition, heat processing is the final step that provides your jars with an airtight seal. Heat processing, if done correctly, will not cause pickles to become soft. As long as top-quality produce is used in properly balanced, well-tested recipes and recommended processing times are followed, you will achieve a superior crisp result.

Virtually any vegetable and many fruits can be pickled successfully, but obviously some will make better pickles than others. Making your own pickles can be a highly personal experience—you can vary spices, herbs and seasonings to suit your own individual taste. No wonder so many old-time pickle recipes are named after their makers! This chapter includes a wide variety of pickles to appeal to many different tastes—I hope that they will inspire you to become an enthusiastic and passionate pickler.

THE ESSENTIALS OF MAKING PICKLES

Vegetables and Fruits

As always, select the finest and freshest vegetables and fruits available. Produce intended for pickling should not be more than 24 hours old—this is especially important with cucumbers, which tend to deteriorate quickly after picking. Choose young, tender vegetables and firm, ripe fruits. Never use any bruised, moldy or overripe produce for pickling—nothing can spoil a batch of pickles faster. Imperfect specimens may be saved for relishes or chutneys as long as the undesirable parts are cut away and discarded.

All foods must be washed thoroughly, in some cases vigorously scrubbed with a vegetable brush, to remove dirt. Rinse in clear water and pat dry.

Vinegar

Use vinegar that contains at least 5 percent acetic acid. This is pretty much any type of vinegar, except homemade. You may find a special pickling vinegar with a 7 percent acidity level. It will give a more astringent flavor and possibly a crisper texture to pickles.

The choice of vinegar really depends on the flavor that you want, although color does play an important part. Cider vinegar, for example, imparts a mellow flavor but will discolor pale vegetables

such as cauliflower or onions. Red wine vinegar does likewise. Only white wine or white distilled vinegar will not affect the color of your pickles.

Sugar

Use white granulated sugar for pickling, unless the recipe specifically calls for brown. Brown sugar tends to darken pickles. An exception would be in pickled beets or onions, where a particular flavor, not color, is the issue. Brown sugar is also commonly used in chutneys and relishes.

Water

Soft water makes the best pickles. Minerals present in hard water may cause pickles to darken or become soft. To soften hard tap water, simply boil it for 15 minutes, then let it stand, covered, for 24 hours. Carefully skim off any scum that has formed on the surface, then pour it slowly out of the container without disturbing any sediment. An easier but more expensive alternative is to buy distilled water.

ABOUT CUCUMBERS

When pickling, cucumbers up to 4 inches (10 cm) long may be used whole, while longer cucumbers, as long as they are firm, can be halved, quartered or sliced. Freshly harvested cucumbers are a must, as older specimens may become shriveled after pickling. Sometimes pickling cucumbers start out hollow. Hollow cucumbers will usually float in water—weed them out while you're washing your cukes and save them for relish. Make sure to cut a ⅛- to ¼-inch (3 to 6 mm) slice from the blossom end of pickling cucumbers. These blossoms contain an enzyme that can cause pickles to soften.

pickles |

ABOUT ALUM

A fine white powder used
in old-time recipes as an aid
in keeping pickles crisp.
Alum may cause bitterness
in pickles, and is no longer
recommended as it may
cause stomach upset in
some people.

Salt

Use coarse pickling salt only. Regular
table salt contains iodine and anti-caking
agents that may darken or cloud pickling
liquids. Sea salt contains minerals that
may cause discoloration of light-colored
foods. Kosher salt is a pure, but somewhat
weak relative of pickling salt and is difficult to measure.

Seasonings

Herbs and spices add immeasurably to the
flavor of your finished product. For finest
quality and taste, always use fresh seasonings. Spices that have been stored too long
tend to deteriorate and lose their pun-
gency. It is a good idea to purchase new
spices at the start of each pickling season.
Buy small quantities and store them away
from heat in airtight containers.

Either fresh or dried herbs may be
used in pickling, but try to avoid powdered seasonings that tend to darken or
cloud pickling liquids. Whole spices may
be added loose to boiling pickling liquids,
then strained out, or a spice bag may be
used for easy removal. Sometimes whole
spices are placed directly into the jars
and left there to add to the visual appeal
of the pickles.

PICKLE PROBLEMS

Because so many factors can affect the
pickling process, things may occasionally
go wrong. If you have any doubts about
the quality of your pickles, it is essential to
determine if they are safe to eat, or if the
pickles are potentially hazardous and must
be discarded.

The following are signs that pickles
are unsafe to eat. If any of these signs are
present, THROW THE PICKLES OUT.
Never taste a questionable food as a test
for spoilage. Destroy the food so it cannot
be eaten by people or animals.

- A broken seal or a bulging or leaking
  lid.
- Mold in the contents of the jar, around
  the rim or on the underside of the lid.
- Pressure inside the jar or liquid that
  spurts from the jar upon opening.
- Fermentation, gassiness or bubbles in
  the contents.
- Sour, yeasty or off odors—any kind of
  unpleasant or musty smell.
- Slimy, mushy or slippery pickles.

Sometimes pickles may not be absolutely perfect, but they are still safe to eat. Here are some examples.

- **Pickles are not crisp and crunchy.** There was not enough salt or vinegar in the recipe.
- **Pickles look bleached or pale.** They were exposed to too much light during storage.
- **Pickles are shriveled.** Cooked pickles were heated too vigorously in a vinegar/sugar solution, the vinegar or salt solution was too strong, the vegetables were not fresh enough or hard water was used.
- **Pickles are hollow.** Raw cucumbers were either poorly developed or too mature, or raw cucumbers were the wrong variety or stored too long before use.
- **Pickles are dark or murky-looking.** Too many spices—or ground spices—were added; iodized table salt was used instead of pickling salt; iron, copper, brass or zinc utensils or cookware were used; a dark vinegar was used; hard water was used; cooked pickles were heated too long.
- **Garlic turns green or blue.** Although unappetizing, this color change is just the result of a chemical reaction and is harmless. It may occur if the garlic is immature, or not fully dry. It may help to blanch the garlic in boiling water before use.
- **Cauliflower or onions turn pink.** Colorless pigments that are naturally present in these foods change color in the presence of an acid—vinegar. As with garlic, this reflects a chemical change and is nothing to worry about.

PICKLE POINTERS

- Read and follow the advice regarding the selection of produce, ingredients and utensils.
- Use reliable, up-to-date pickle recipes.
- Don't start pickling until you have thoroughly read the recipe, assembled all the ingredients, and have your produce prepared and your equipment ready to go.
- Work quickly and follow instructions. Both the jars and the pickling liquid must be good and hot or the pickles may not seal properly. It is especially important to heed recommendations that direct you to pack jars one at a time.
- Don't try to make large batches of pickles. Your pickling adventure will be more successful and enjoyable if you make pickles in small, manageable amounts.
- It is advisable to wait several weeks at least before testing pickles to allow the flavors time to develop and mingle.

ALL CUCUMBERS are not created equal. Long English cucumbers, while superior for eating raw, are not suitable for pickling. Neither are waxed cucumbers from the supermarket; the waxy coating that is used to prolong their shelf life cannot be penetrated by a pickling solution. (However, they may be peeled and used for relishes.)

Simply Good Dill Pickles

MAKES FOUR 1-QUART (1 L) JARS

Crisp and tangy, these pickles can be garlicky or not, spicy or not, to suit your own taste. But be sure to use plenty of nice, fresh dill—both the heads and leaves.

To add an unusual flavor to homemade salad dressing, substitute some strained leftover pickle juice for part of the vinegar in your recipe.

4 lb • 1.8 kg pickling cucumbers

4 cups • 950 mL water

3 cups • 720 mL vinegar

12 heads fresh dill, plus some leaves

8 cloves garlic, peeled (optional)

8 small hot chili peppers (optional)
    (see "Handling Hot Peppers," page 60)

¼ cup • 60 mL pickling salt

4 tsp • 20 mL mixed pickling spice

ABOUT PICKLING SPICE

Indispensable in the flavoring of—guess what?—pickles, pickling spice originated in England. It is a mixture of several whole spices, including cinnamon, bay leaves, peppercorns, mustard seed, mace, cloves, dill seed, chili pepper, coriander seed and allspice. You can certainly blend your own if you like, but pickling spice is easy to find. Pickling spice may either be tied into a cheesecloth bag and removed once pickling is completed or placed loose in the jars of pickles to add flavor and visual appeal.

SCRUB the cucumbers thoroughly. Cut a ¼-inch (6 mm) slice from the blossom end. Slice if necessary (see "About Cucumbers," page 121). Prepare the preserving jars.

Combine the water and vinegar in your preserving pot and bring to a boil. Reduce heat and keep at a simmer.

Working with 1 jar at a time, place 3 dill heads (and some leaves), 2 garlic cloves, 2 hot peppers, 1 Tbsp (15 mL) salt and 1 tsp (5 mL) pickling spice in each jar.

Fill the hot, sterilized jar with cucumbers to within 1 inch (2.5 cm) of the rim, wedging them in so that none can escape and float to the top when the liquid is added. Pour in the hot vinegar solution, leaving a ½-inch (1.2 cm) head space. Release the air bubbles. Top up with liquid, leaving a ¼-inch (6 mm) head space. Wipe the rims clean. Seal according to manufacturer's directions. Repeat with the remaining jars. Process the jars in a boiling water bath for 15 minutes.

LEFT TO RIGHT» Michael's Pickled Onions (page 134), Simply Good Dill Pickles (this page) and Pickled Asparagus (page 130).

pickles

Authentic Bread and Butter Pickles

This classic pickle is a favorite with sliced cold meats and cheeses or any savory sandwich.

4 lb • 1.8 kg medium, unwaxed cucumbers
(about 6–8), unpeeled, cut into ⅛-inch
(3 mm) slices
4 onions, peeled, halved and cut into ⅛-inch
(3 mm) slices
2 red bell peppers, cored, seeded, halved
and cut into ⅛-inch (3 mm) slices
⅓ cup • 80 mL pickling salt
4 cups • 950 mL white vinegar
3 cups • 720 mL sugar
2 tsp • 10 mL celery seed
2 tsp • 10 mL mustard seed
1 tsp • 5 mL ground ginger
1 tsp • 5 mL turmeric

DISCARD the stem and blossom ends of the cucumbers. Combine the prepared vegetables and salt in a large bowl. Cover with ice water. Chill overnight.

The next day, drain the vegetables in a colander. Rinse well. Prepare the preserving jars.

Combine the remaining ingredients in your preserving pot. Bring to a boil over high heat. Add the vegetables and return to a boil. Cook briefly, about 1 minute, or just until the cucumbers change color.

Using a slotted spoon, ladle the pickles into the hot, sterilized jars. Fill the jars up with liquid to within ½ inch (1.2 cm) of the rim. Make sure that the liquid covers all the pickle slices. Release the air bubbles. Wipe the rims clean. Seal according to manufacturer's directions. Process the jars in a boiling water bath for 10 minutes.

Pickled Garlic

MAKES ABOUT FOUR 8 OZ (250 ML) JARS

A real hit at Halloween parties, pickled garlic may be served alongside traditional pickles as a snack or finely chopped to enliven salad dressings or sauces. Use narrow-mouthed preserving jars for these pickles.

2 cups • 475 mL garlic cloves, about
    1½ lb (680 g)
3 cups • 720 mL red or white wine vinegar
¼ cup • 60 mL pickling spice
2 tsp • 10 mL pickling salt

FILL a medium-sized pot with water and bring to a boil over high heat. Add the garlic, stir and simmer for 1 minute. Remove from the heat. Drain the garlic in a colander and rinse in cold water. Slip the skins off the garlic. Set aside.

Prepare the preserving jars.

Combine the remaining ingredients in your preserving pot and bring to a boil over high heat. Turn the heat down, cover and keep hot. Pack the garlic into hot, sterilized jars, leaving a ½-inch (1.2 cm) head space. Pour the hot vinegar solution over the garlic cloves, leaving a ¼-inch (6 mm) head space. Release the air bubbles. Wipe the rims clean. Seal according to manufacturer's directions. Process the jars in a boiling water bath for 5 minutes.

Striped Pickled Peppers

MAKES ABOUT FIVE 1-PINT (500 ML) JARS

A really eye-catching pickle—thanks to the vibrant contrast of the red and yellow peppers. They have a crisp texture with just a whisper of sweetness. Be sure to use wide-mouthed jars—it will be much easier to arrange the peppers.

4 cups • 950 mL white vinegar

2 cups • 475 mL water

4 medium-sized yellow bell peppers, about
     2 lb (900 g) in total, seeded, cored and cut
     lengthwise in ½-inch (1.2 cm) strips

4 medium-sized red bell peppers, about 2 lb
     (900 g) in total, seeded, cored and cut
     lengthwise in ½-inch (1.2 cm) strips

5 cloves garlic, peeled

5 tsp • 25 mL pickling salt

2½ tsp • 12.5 mL sugar

PREPARE the preserving jars.

Combine the vinegar and water in your preserving pot and bring to a boil. Reduce heat and keep at a simmer.

Working with 1 jar at a time, place 1 clove garlic, 1 tsp (5 mL) salt and ½ tsp (2.5 mL) sugar in each jar. Arrange the pepper strips upright in the jar, packing them tightly and alternating red and yellow. Place the most attractive, uniform slices around the perimeter; the shorter peppers can go in the center. Sometimes it helps to place the jar on its side.

Pour the hot vinegar solution over the peppers, leaving a ½-inch (1.2 cm) head space. Release the trapped air bubbles. Add additional liquid if necessary, leaving a ¼-inch (6 mm) head space. Wipe the rims clean. Seal according to manufacturer's directions. Repeat with the remaining jars. Process the jars in a boiling water bath for 10 minutes.

Pickled Rosemary Carrots

MAKES FIVE TO SIX 1-PINT (500 ML) JARS

Carrots are a wonderful addition to your pickle pantry. Their vivid orange color provides a delightful contrast to all that green! Don't attempt these pickles unless you have fresh rosemary—dried rosemary won't do.

Mixed peppercorns are a colorful blend of whole black, white, green and pink peppercorns. If you can't find them, black peppercorns are just fine.

3 cups • 720 mL water

3 cups • 720 mL vinegar

¼ cup • 60 mL each sugar and pickling salt

2 Tbsp • 30 mL mixed peppercorns

6 cloves garlic, peeled

6 hot chili peppers, preferably red

4 lb • 1.8 kg carrots, peeled, cut into sticks about 4 inches (10 cm) long and ½ inch (1.2 cm) wide

six 3-inch (7.5 cm) sprigs fresh rosemary

PREPARE the preserving jars. Combine the water, vinegar, sugar, salt and peppercorns in your preserving pot. Bring to a boil over high heat. Reduce the heat to medium and simmer for 5 minutes.

Working with 1 jar at a time, place 1 clove of garlic and 1 chili pepper in each hot, sterilized jar. Pack the carrot sticks tightly into the jar, standing them upright. Slide 1 sprig of rosemary into the jar. Carefully pour the boiling vinegar solution into the jars, leaving a ¼-inch (6 mm) head space. Release the air bubbles. Wipe the rims clean. Seal according to manufacturer's directions. Repeat with the remaining jars. Process the jars in a boiling water bath for 15 minutes.

Pickled Asparagus

MAKES ABOUT THREE 1-QUART (1 L) JARS

To most of us, the first asparagus is truly a sign of the onset of spring. When you have eaten your fill of fresh asparagus, pickle some to enjoy later on in the year. Asparagus deteriorates quickly, so be sure to preserve it as soon as possible once you get it home. Select firm, straight asparagus with closed dry tips. Try to choose spears that are about the same thickness—about ½ inch (1.2 cm) in diameter is best.

5–6 lb • 2.25–2.75 kg asparagus

3 cups • 720 mL water

3 cups • 720 mL white vinegar

2 small onions, peeled, halved and cut into ¼-inch (6 mm) slices

6 cloves garlic, peeled

3 small hot chili peppers (optional)

3 Tbsp • 45 mL pickling salt

3 Tbsp • 45 mL vinegar

3 Tbsp • 45 mL mustard seeds

2 Tbsp • 30 mL dill seeds

PREPARE the asparagus spears. Trim the spears to jar length. They should stand about 1 inch (2.5 cm) shorter than the rim of the jar. Measure carefully ahead of time as it can be very frustrating to be trimming asparagus as you are trying to pack them into the jars.

You will find that you are cutting off a heartbreaking amount of tender asparagus along with the tough ends. Save the trimmings to make Pickled Asparabits (see facing page) or to use in soups, salads or stir-fries.

Prepare the preserving jars.

Combine the water and vinegar in your preserving pot and bring to a boil. Reduce the heat to keep the liquid at a simmer.

Working with 1 jar at a time, place a third of the onion slices, 2 cloves of garlic, 1 chili pepper, 1 Tbsp (15 mL) each of salt, sugar and mustard seeds, and 2 tsp (10 mL) of dill seeds in each jar. Pack the asparagus into the jar, tips down. It helps to lay the jar on its side, and pack the asparagus first around the perimeter of the jar, then fill in the center. The asparagus must be packed in quite tightly.

Carefully pour the hot vinegar solution into the jars, leaving a ¼-inch (6 mm) head space. Release the air bubbles. Add additional liquid if necessary. Wipe the rims clean. Seal according to manufacturer's directions. Repeat with the remaining jars. Process the jars in a boiling water bath for 20 minutes.

Pickled Asparabits

USE only the tender asparagus trimmings, cut into small pieces no longer than 1 inch (2.5 cm) long. The "bits" need not be in uniform pieces. Use pint (500 mL) jars. Narrow-mouthed jars are best. Prepare the jars and make up a batch of pickling liquid using equal amounts of vinegar and water. You may even have a little liquid left over from the Pickled Asparagus. Heat the liquid to a simmer.

To each jar add:

1½ tsp • 7.5 mL pickling salt

1½ tsp • 7.5 mL sugar

1½ tsp • 7.5 mL mustard seeds

a couple of onion slices

1 clove garlic

½ small hot chili pepper

1 tsp • 5 mL dill seed

Fill up the jars with the asparagus bits to within 1 inch (2.5 cm) of the rim. Pour in the hot pickling liquid, leaving a ¼-inch (6 mm) head space. Wipe the rims clean. Seal according to manufacturer's directions. Process the jars in a boiling water bath for 10 minutes.

Spicy Pickled Green Beans

MAKES FOUR 1-QUART (1 L) JARS

Garden favorites, green beans are plentiful and reasonably priced in late summer. Use the longest, straightest beans you can find. Curved or misshapen beans can be pickled too, but the perfect ones are much more impressive.

4 lb • 1.8 kg green beans

5 cups • 1.2 L water

5 cups • 1.2 L white vinegar

¼ cup • 60 mL mustard seeds

¼ cup • 60 mL dill seeds OR 8–12 stalks of fresh dill

¼ cup • 60 mL pickling salt

8 cloves garlic, peeled

8 small hot chili peppers OR 4 tsp (20 mL) dried chili flakes (optional)

TRIM the stem ends from the beans and cut to jar length if necessary. When standing upright the beans should be about 1 inch (2.5 cm) below the rim of the jar.

Prepare the preserving jars.

Combine the water and vinegar in your preserving pot and bring to a boil. Reduce the heat to keep the liquid at a simmer.

Working with 1 jar at a time, place 1 Tbsp (15 mL) each of mustard seed, dill seed and salt, 2 cloves of garlic, and 2 hot peppers or 1 tsp (5 mL) dried chili flakes in each jar. Pack the beans tightly into the jar. The easiest way to do this is to lay the jar on its side and place the beans inside by small handfuls. As the jar fills up, stand it upright, and add additional beans one by one. It is important to pack the beans tightly to prevent beans from floating when you add the liquid.

Carefully pour the hot vinegar solution over the beans to within ½ inch (1.2 cm) of the rim. Release the air bubbles. Add additional liquid if necessary, leaving a ¼-inch (6 mm) head space. Wipe the rims clean. Seal according to manufacturer's directions. Repeat with the remaining jars. Process the jars in a boiling water bath for 10 minutes.

Michael's Pickled Onions

MAKES FOUR TO FIVE 1-PINT (500 ML) JARS

These are the traditional, pungent pickled onions served in English pubs as part of a ploughman's lunch—a simple meal of crusty bread and good cheese.

4 cups • 950 mL water

½ cup • 120 mL pickling salt

3 lb • 1.4 kg shallots or small white onions,
     up to ¾ inch (2 cm) in diameter, peeled

2 tsp • 10 mL each whole black peppercorns,
     allspice berries and mustard seeds

1 tsp • 5 mL dried chili flakes

two ¼-inch (6 mm) slices of peeled fresh ginger

3 bay leaves

2½ cups • 600 mL malt vinegar

2 cups • 475 mL cider vinegar

¼ cup • 60 mL brown sugar

COMBINE the water and salt in a large bowl. Stir until the salt is dissolved. Add the shallots or onions and mix well. Cover and refrigerate overnight, stirring the mixture 3 or 4 times.

The next day, prepare the preserving jars. Put the peppercorns, allspice, mustard seeds, chili flakes, ginger and bay leaves into a cheesecloth bag and tie the top with string.

Combine the spice bag, vinegars and sugar in your preserving pot. Bring to a boil over medium heat. Simmer gently for 5 minutes; cover and keep hot until you are ready to fill the jars.

Meanwhile, drain the onions in a colander. Cover with cold water and drain again. Do this 3 times; if the onions are not rinsed thoroughly the finished pickle will be too salty. Roll the onions in a clean dish towel to dry them.

Return the pickling liquid to a boil and add the onions. Cook only until the liquid returns to a boil. Quickly remove the onions with a slotted spoon and transfer them to the hot, sterilized jars, filling them to within 1 inch (2.5 cm) of the rims. Discard the spice bag. Carefully pour the hot vinegar solution over the onions to within ½ inch (1.2 cm) of the rim. Release the air bubbles. Add additional liquid if necessary. Wipe the rims clean. Seal according to manufacturer's directions. Process the jars in a boiling water bath for 10 minutes.

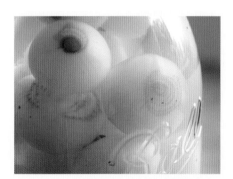

HOW TO PEEL ONIONS (OR SHALLOTS)

Place the onions in a large bowl and add enough boiling water to cover them. Let stand 2 to 3 minutes. Pour off the hot water. Place the bowl in the sink and run cold water into the bowl to cool the onions quickly. Drain in a colander. Using a sharp knife, remove only the minimum at the base and tip of the onions and peel away the outer skin.

Antipasto Pickles

A wonderful way to pickle a variety of fresh vegetables,
this makes an instant appetizer.

4 cups • 950 mL cauliflower florets, cut into 1–1½-inch
   (2.5–3.8 cm) pieces

2 cups • 475 mL unpeeled zucchini, cut into ¼-inch
   (6 mm) rounds

2 cups • 475 mL peeled carrots, cut diagonally into
   ½-inch (1.2 cm) slices

2 cups • 475 mL green beans, cut into 1-inch (2.5 cm) pieces

2 cups • 475 mL celery, cut into 2- × ½-inch (5 × 1.2 cm) sticks

1 cup • 240 mL red bell pepper, cut into 1-inch (2.5 cm) pieces

1 cup • 240 mL yellow bell pepper, cut into 1-inch (2.5 cm) pieces

2 cups • 475 mL pearl onions, peeled (see "How to Peel Onions,"
   page 135)

⅔ cup • 160 mL pickling salt

6 cups • 1.5 L cider vinegar

2 cups • 475 mL water

1¼ cups • 300 mL sugar

3 Tbsp • 45 mL mustard seeds

3 Tbsp • 45 mL celery seeds

1 Tbsp • 15 mL turmeric

2 tsp • 10 mL coriander seeds

2 tsp • 10 mL peppercorns

7–8 bay leaves

7–8 cloves garlic, peeled

7–8 small red chili peppers

COMBINE cauliflower, zucchini, carrots, green beans, celery, bell peppers and pearl onions in a large bowl.

Bring 6 cups (1.5 L) of water to a boil. Add the salt and stir until dissolved. Let cool. Pour the cooled brine over the vegetables. It should cover them completely; add more water if necessary. Place a weighted plate on top of the vegetables to keep them submerged. Cover and let stand overnight.

The next day, drain the vegetables in a colander. Rinse thoroughly in cold water, then drain again. Set aside.

Prepare the preserving jars.

Combine the vinegar, water, sugar, mustard seeds, celery seeds, turmeric, coriander seeds and peppercorns in your preserving pot. Bring to a boil over medium-high heat and boil for 5 minutes. Add the vegetables and return to a boil. Reduce the heat to medium and simmer for another 5 minutes, stirring constantly to mix the vegetables thoroughly.

In each hot, sterilized jar place 1 bay leaf, 1 clove of garlic and 1 chili pepper. Using a slotted spoon, remove the vegetables from the pot, and divide them among the jars. Quickly bring the hot liquid in the pot to a boil and pour over the vegetables, distributing the spices evenly and leaving a $^1/_4$-inch (6 mm) head space. (If you don't have enough liquid, top up with additional vinegar.) Release the air bubbles. Wipe the rims clean. Seal according to manufacturer's directions. Process the jars in a boiling water bath for 10 minutes.

Sweet Spiced Pickled Beets

MAKES FOUR TO FIVE 1-PINT (500 ML) JARS

The pleasant, sweet taste and firm texture of beets makes them a natural for pickling. Small, tender baby beets may be pickled whole, but medium-sized beets up to 2½ inches (6 cm) are better sliced. Avoid large beets—they tend to have tough, woody centers.

two 3-inch (7.5 cm) cinnamon sticks, broken

1 tsp • 5 mL each whole cloves and allspice berries

2 cups • 475 mL red wine vinegar

2 cups • 475 mL water

1½ cups • 360 mL brown sugar

1 tsp • 5 mL salt

4 lb • 1.8 kg beets, cooked, peeled and sliced

2 medium onions, peeled, halved and cut into
    ¼-inch (6 mm) slices

PREPARE the preserving jars. Put the cinnamon sticks, cloves and allspice into a cheesecloth bag and tie the top with string.

Combine the vinegar, water, sugar, salt and the spice bag in your preserving pot. Bring to a boil over medium-high heat and simmer for 5 minutes. Add the beets and onions. Simmer for 5 minutes over medium heat. Discard the spice bag. Leaving the pot on low heat, spoon the beets and onions into hot, sterilized jars. Cover with the hot liquid, leaving a ½-inch (1.2 cm) head space. Release the air bubbles. Add additional liquid, leaving a ¼-inch (6 mm) head space. Wipe the rims clean. Seal according to manufacturer's directions. Process the jars in a boiling water bath for 20 minutes.

NOTE Never peel beets before cooking or their lovely red color will bleed into the water. Scrub them well, then cut off the tops about 2 inches (5 cm) above the crown. Leave the root end intact. Cook the beets in a saucepan, with just enough water to cover. Simmer 20 to 30 minutes, until they are barely tender. Drain, cover with ice water and let cool 3 to 5 minutes. Drain and cut off the tops and root ends. The skins will slip off easily.

Pickled Cherries with Tarragon

MAKES FOUR TO FIVE 1-PINT (500 ML) JARS

A most unusual condiment. Eat them like olives. This is
also delicious made with seedless red grapes.

  3 lb • 1.4 kg firm, ripe, sweet black cherries

  2 cups • 475 mL red wine vinegar

  2 cups • 475 mL water

  4 tsp • 20 mL pickling salt

  4 tsp • 20 mL sugar

  eight 3-inch (7.5 cm) sprigs fresh French
      tarragon

PREPARE the preserving jars.

Trim the stems of the cherries to about 1 inch (2.5 cm). Do not remove the
pits. Prick each cherry several times with a needle so the skins don't burst.

Combine the vinegar and water in your preserving pot and bring to a boil
over high heat. Reduce the heat to keep the liquid at a simmer.

In each hot, sterilized jar place 1 tsp (5 mL) each of salt and sugar and
2 sprigs of tarragon. Fill the jars with cherries to 1 inch (2.5 cm) below the rim.
Pour the hot liquid into the jars, leaving a $^1\!/_2$-inch (1.2 cm) head space. Release
the air bubbles. Add additional liquid if necessary. Wipe the rims clean. Seal
according to manufacturer's directions. Process the jars in a boiling water bath
for 10 minutes.

Pickled Pears with Honey and Red Wine

MAKES ABOUT SIX 1-PINT (500 ML) JARS

A very elegant pickle. Serve it as an accompaniment to roasted meats. Be sure that the pears are firm and not overly ripe.

1½ cups • 360 mL honey

2½ cups • 600 mL red wine vinegar

2½ cups • 600 mL full-bodied red wine

six 3-inch (7.5 cm) cinnamon sticks

1 lemon, zest only, cut in a continuous spiral

5 lb • 2.25 kg small firm but ripe pears

whole cloves

IN your preserving pot, combine the honey, vinegar, red wine, cinnamon sticks and lemon zest. Bring to a boil over medium heat and simmer 10 minutes, stirring occasionally.

Peel, core and halve the pears. Stick 2 cloves into each half. Add the pears to the simmering liquid and poach them gently for about 10 minutes. They should be just barely tender. Turn them frequently. Remove from the heat, cool slightly and cover with a clean dish towel. Leave the pears to stand overnight in the syrup.

The next day, prepare the preserving jars. Using a slotted spoon, remove the pears and cinnamon sticks from the syrup and set aside. Discard the lemon zest.

Bring the syrup quickly to a boil over high heat, and boil rapidly for 10 minutes. Place the pears cut side down in the hot, sterilized jars, overlapping them slightly. Place 1 cinnamon stick in each jar. Pour the boiling syrup over the pears, leaving a ½-inch (1.2 cm) head space. Release the air bubbles. Add additional syrup if necessary. Wipe the rims clean. Seal according to manufacturer's directions. Process the jars in a boiling water bath for 10 minutes.

Relishes

Carrot and Cucumber Relish 145

Chow Chow 146

Beet and Red Cabbage Relish 147

Salsa Fiesta! 148

Old-Time Corn Relish 150

Zesty Zucchini Relish 152

India Relish 155

Ripe Tomato Relish 157

Pepper Relish 158

Cranberry, Pear and Apple Relish 159

Nectarine and Pepper Relish 160

Relishes

The word relish summons up vivid pictures of outdoor summer fun—impromptu barbecues or picnics on the beach. But relishes are much more than just simple sauces for hamburgers and hot dogs. These zesty condiments can add a special zing to grilled lamb chops, a roast pork loin or even fish. You can serve relishes with smoked meats, cheeses or any bland dish that needs a little perking up.

Tangy, spicy medleys of vegetables or sometimes fruit, relishes are basically just a chopped pickle. The ingredients for relish may be sliced, coarsely chopped, shredded or ground, but are all of a uniform size. A food processor makes short work of preparing vegetables for relish. Vegetables with a high water content, such as zucchini, cucumbers and onions, are usually salted beforehand to draw out moisture, which reduces the amount of cooking time required. Salting also helps larger pieces of vegetables to retain their shape and texture.

Relishes are cooked quickly—the vegetables are simmered in a vinegar-based syrup just long enough to ensure that they are heated throughout. Vegetables should be barely tender, retaining some of their original crisp character.

This brief cooking time is one way that relishes are distinguished from chutneys. In chutney-making, a long, slow simmering reduces the ingredients to a soft pulp.

Properly made relish will be moist but not watery. In some recipes, a little cornstarch or flour is added at the end of the cooking period to thicken the relish and lightly bind the ingredients together. Relishes also tend to thicken up slightly in the jar, as the vegetables absorb some of the vinegar syrup.

Relishes can be mild or fiery, sweet or tangy, peppery or pungent. Hot peppers, spices and seasonings can be added or subtracted to suit your own personal tastes.

Savory relishes sharpen the taste buds and surprise the palate. They can heighten our enjoyment of everyday foods or contribute a unique finishing touch to any meal.

Carrot and Cucumber Relish

MAKES ABOUT FIVE TO SIX 8 OZ (250 ML) JARS

A simple, old-fashioned relish perfect with cold sliced meats or barbecued burgers.

- 4 cups • 950 mL finely chopped, unpeeled cucumbers (about 5–6 medium)
- 2 cups • 475 mL grated carrots (about 6–7 medium)
- 1 cup • 240 mL finely chopped onion
- 3 Tbsp • 45 mL pickling salt
- 1½ cups • 360 mL cider vinegar
- 1½ cups • 360 mL sugar
- 2 tsp • 10 mL mustard seeds
- 2 tsp • 10 mL celery seeds
- 1 tsp • 5 mL fennel seeds

IN a large bowl, combine the cucumbers, carrots, onion and salt. Mix well and let stand 3 to 4 hours.

The next day, drain the vegetables in a colander. Rinse them and press out as much water as possible. Set aside.

Prepare the preserving jars.

Combine the remaining ingredients in your preserving pot. Bring to a boil over medium-high heat. Reduce the heat and simmer for 10 minutes. Add the drained vegetables. Increase the heat again and once the mixture has returned to a boil, cook, stirring often, for about 10 minutes, until most of the liquid has been absorbed. Don't worry if the relish seems to be too liquid; it will thicken up a little as it cools.

Remove from the heat. Spoon the relish into hot, sterilized jars, leaving a ½-inch (1.2 cm) head space. Release the air bubbles. Wipe the rims clean. Seal according to manufacturer's directions. Process the jars in a boiling water bath for 10 minutes.

Chow Chow

Many different versions of chow chow can be found in old-time cookbooks. This is a relish type—made with ground vegetables. There is also a chunky vegetable chow chow, which is more like a mixed pickle. You can chop the vegetables by hand or use a food processor if you prefer.

7 lb • 3.2 kg green tomatoes, chopped
  very finely

5 medium green or red bell peppers, cored,
  seeded and chopped very finely

5 medium onions, peeled and chopped
  very finely

¼ cup • 60 mL pickling salt

2½ cups • 600 mL cider vinegar

1½ cups • 360 mL sugar

¼ cup • 60 mL mixed pickling spice, tied
  in a cheesecloth bag (see page 125)

2 tsp • 10 mL dry English mustard

COMBINE the vegetables and salt in a large bowl. Mix well. Cover and let stand overnight.

The next day, drain the vegetables in a colander, pressing out excess moisture. Set aside.

Prepare the preserving jars. Combine the remaining ingredients in your preserving pot. Bring to a boil over medium-high heat. Simmer for 10 minutes. Add the drained vegetables. Once the mixture returns to a boil, reduce the heat to medium and simmer for 15 minutes, stirring often.

Remove from the heat; discard the spice bag. Spoon the relish into hot, sterilized jars, leaving a ½-inch (1.2 cm) head space. Release the air bubbles. Wipe the rims clean. Seal according to manufacturer's directions. Process the jars in a boiling water bath for 15 minutes.

Beet and Red Cabbage Relish

MAKES ABOUT FOUR TO FIVE 1-PINT (500 ML) JARS

For a truly unusual sandwich, blend softened cream cheese with a little horseradish and spread on hearty, preferably homemade bread. Top with sliced, rare roast beef and a dollop of this relish.

15 beets, about 2 inches (5 cm) across, cooked,
    peeled and shredded (about 4 lb/1.8 kg)

½ medium red cabbage, shredded

1½ cups • 360 mL finely chopped celery

1½ cups • 360 mL finely chopped onion

1 cup • 240 mL cranberry or orange juice

1½ cups • 360 mL red wine vinegar

1½ cups • 360 mL brown sugar

2 Tbsp • 30 mL prepared creamed horseradish

1 Tbsp • 15 mL finely grated orange zest

1½ tsp • 7.5 mL salt

½ tsp • 2.5 mL ground cloves

½ tsp • 2.5 mL ground allspice

PREPARE the preserving jars.

Combine all the ingredients in your preserving pot and bring to a boil over medium heat, stirring occasionally. Simmer 20 to 25 minutes, stirring often.

Remove from the heat. Spoon the relish into hot, sterilized jars, leaving a ½-inch (1.2 cm) head space. Release the air bubbles. Wipe the rims clean. Seal according to manufacturer's directions. Process the jars in a boiling water bath for 10 minutes.

Salsa Fiesta!

MAKES ABOUT FIVE TO SIX 1-PINT (500 ML) JARS

How hot is this salsa? It all depends on your tolerance for spicy foods. I consider it medium-hot. If hot peppers make you nervous, cut the amount of jalapeños in half, or leave them out altogether, substituting extra bell peppers instead.

8 cups • 2 L coarsely chopped tomatoes

2 cups • 475 mL coarsely chopped onions

1 cup • 240 mL coarsely chopped green bell peppers

1 cup • 240 mL finely chopped, seeded jalapeño peppers (see "Handling Hot Peppers," page 60)

6 large cloves garlic, finely chopped

¼ cup • 60 mL finely chopped fresh coriander

⅔ cup • 160 mL red wine vinegar or lemon juice

1 Tbsp • 15 mL salt

1 tsp • 5 mL white pepper

PREPARE the preserving jars.

Combine all the ingredients in your preserving pot and bring to a boil over medium-high heat. Reduce the heat to medium and simmer, stirring often, for 20 minutes.

Remove from the heat. Ladle the salsa into hot, sterilized jars, leaving a ½-inch (1.2 cm) head space. Wipe the rims clean. Seal according to manufacturer's directions. Process the jars in a boiling water bath for 20 minutes.

CHUNKY SALSA GUACAMOLE Instead of serving salsa and guacamole separately, use this colorful dip as an all-in-one topping for tacos or a zesty accompaniment for chicken or fish.

Simply toss 1 cup (240 mL) of salsa with 1 peeled, diced avocado. Sprinkle with a little lemon juice, season with salt and freshly ground pepper and garnish with 1 Tbsp (15 mL) finely chopped fresh coriander.

Old-Time Corn Relish

MAKES ABOUT FOUR TO FIVE 1-PINT (500 ML) JARS

Make this classic country relish in September when corn is at its best and sweetest. You can also use drained, canned corn kernels or frozen corn that has been defrosted and drained.

5 cups • 1.2 L fresh corn kernels (about 10 ears)

1 cup • 240 mL finely chopped red bell peppers

½ cup • 120 mL finely chopped green bell peppers

1 cup • 240 mL finely chopped onion

½ cup • 120 mL finely chopped celery

1¾ cups • 420 mL cider vinegar

¾ cup • 180 mL sugar

1½ tsp • 7.5 mL salt

2 tsp • 10 mL celery seed

1½ tsp • 7.5 mL dry English mustard

½ tsp • 2.5 mL turmeric

2 Tbsp • 30 mL flour (optional)

PREPARE the preserving jars.

If you are using fresh corn, husk it and cook the ears for 10 minutes in a pot of boiling water. Drain, then plunge the corn into ice water to cool quickly so it can be handled easily. Standing the ears of corn on end, cut the kernels carefully off the cobs using a very sharp knife. Do not scrape the cobs—the milky juice will make the relish cloudy.

Combine the red and green peppers, onion, celery, vinegar, sugar, salt, celery seed, mustard and turmeric in your preserving pot. Bring to a boil over medium heat and simmer for 10 minutes, stirring occasionally. Add the corn and simmer another 5 minutes, stirring often.

If you desire a slightly thicker relish, combine the flour with ¼ cup (60 mL) cold water in a small measuring cup. Mix until smooth, then add to the relish when you add the corn. Take care to stir the relish often, as the thickened relish may tend to stick to the bottom of the pot.

Remove from the heat. Spoon the relish into hot, sterilized jars, leaving a ½-inch (1.2 cm) head space. Release the air bubbles. Wipe the rims clean. Seal according to manufacturer's directions. Process the jars in a boiling water bath for 15 minutes.

CURRIED CORN RELISH Add 2 tsp (10 mL) curry powder and 1 tsp (5 mL) liquid hot pepper seasoning along with the other spices.

Zesty Zucchini Relish

MAKES ABOUT FIVE TO SIX 8 OZ (250 ML) JARS

Nothing like it with burgers, European wieners or grilled
Italian sausages on crusty French rolls. You can use a
food processor to shred the vegetables.

6 cups • 1.5 L grated, unpeeled zucchini

1 cup • 240 mL grated carrot

2 cups • 475 mL finely chopped onion

1 cup • 240 mL finely chopped red bell pepper

1 cup • 240 mL finely chopped green bell
  pepper

2–3 jalapeño peppers, seeded and finely
  chopped

¼ cup • 60 mL pickling salt

2 cups • 475 mL sugar

2 cups • 475 mL herb vinegar, divided

2 tsp • 10 mL celery seed

1 tsp • 5 mL red chili flakes

½ tsp • 2.5 mL each ground cinnamon, nutmeg,
  turmeric and freshly ground black pepper

2 tsp • 10 mL cornstarch

1½ tsp • 7.5 mL dry English mustard

COMBINE the vegetables and pickling salt in a large bowl. Mix well. Cover with
ice and refrigerate overnight.

The next day, prepare the preserving jars. Drain the vegetables in a colander; rinse well and squeeze out excess moisture. (An efficient way to do this is
to line the colander with cheesecloth before rinsing the vegetables under running water; then you can gather up the corners of the cloth and squeeze out
the moisture.)

(continued on page 154)

well preserved

FRONT TO BACK» Zesty Zucchini Relish, Old-Time Corn Relish (page 150) and Cranberry, Pear and Apple Relish (page 159).

Zesty Zucchini Relish (continued)

Combine the sugar, 1½ cups (360 mL) of the vinegar, and the celery seed, chili flakes and spices in your preserving pot. Bring to a boil over high heat, stirring until the sugar is dissolved. Stir in the drained vegetables. Reduce the heat to medium and simmer about 30 minutes, stirring often, until the mixture begins to thicken and a lot of the liquid has been absorbed.

In a measuring cup or small bowl, stir the cornstarch and mustard together with a fork. Gradually pour in the remaining ½ cup (120 mL) vinegar, stirring to form a smooth paste. Stir into the relish. Cook another 5 minutes, stirring constantly, until the liquid clears and thickens.

Remove from the heat. Spoon the relish into hot, sterilized jars, leaving a ½-inch (1.2 cm) head space. Release the air bubbles. Wipe the rims clean. Seal according to manufacturer's directions. Process the jars in a boiling water bath for 10 minutes.

India Relish

MAKES ABOUT FIVE TO SIX 1-PINT (500 ML) JARS

This classic mixed vegetable relish was traditionally made in the autumn to use up garden surpluses. The quickest and easiest way to prepare the vegetables is to shred them in a food processor. India Relish is an excellent accompaniment to lamb or pork.

4 cups • 950 mL chopped green cabbage

1 cup • 240 mL chopped green bell pepper

1 cup • 240 mL chopped red bell pepper

2 cups • 475 mL chopped onions

6 cups • 1.5 L grated zucchini

2 cups • 475 mL grated carrots

¼ cup • 60 mL pickling salt

1½ cups • 360 mL brown sugar

3 cups • 720 mL cider vinegar

1 tsp • 5 mL each ground ginger, ground coriander and curry powder

½ tsp • 2.5 mL each turmeric and ground cumin

4 tsp • 20 mL dry English mustard

IN a large bowl, combine the cabbage, green and red peppers, onion, zucchini, carrots and salt. Cover and let stand 3 to 4 hours. Drain the vegetables in a colander, pressing out excess liquid. Return the drained vegetables to the bowl.

Combine the remaining ingredients in your preserving pot. Bring to a boil over high heat and boil rapidly for 5 minutes. Pour the mixture over the vegetables in the bowl, and stir to combine. Let stand, uncovered, at room temperature until cool, about 2 hours.

Prepare the preserving jars.

Drain the liquid from the vegetables into your preserving pot. Bring to a full boil over high heat and stir in the vegetables. Once the mixture returns to a boil,

(continued next page)

India Relish (continued)

reduce the heat to medium and simmer for 10 to 15 minutes, until the vegetables are thoroughly hot, stirring constantly.

Remove from the heat. Spoon the relish into hot, sterilized jars, leaving a $1/2$-inch (1.2 cm) head space. Release the air bubbles. Wipe the rims clean. Seal according to manufacturer's directions. Process the jars in a boiling water bath for 15 minutes.

Ripe Tomato Relish

MAKES ABOUT FOUR TO FIVE 1-PINT (500 ML) JARS

Take advantage of a bountiful tomato crop and cook up a batch of this hearty relish. Serve it alongside homemade macaroni and cheese or meat loaf.

12 cups • 3 L chopped tomatoes, preferably
    plum or Roma

2 cups • 475 mL chopped onions

1 cup • 240 mL chopped red bell pepper

1 cup • 240 mL chopped celery

3 Tbsp • 45 mL pickling salt

1 cup • 240 mL red wine vinegar

2 cups • 475 mL brown sugar

3 Tbsp • 45 mL mustard seeds

1 Tbsp • 15 mL dried chili flakes

1 tsp • 5 mL each ground cloves, cinnamon
    and nutmeg

PREPARE the preserving jars. Combine the tomatoes, onion, pepper and celery in a large bowl. Sprinkle with the salt and stir well. Let stand for 15 minutes. Drain well in a colander, pressing to remove as much liquid as possible. Do not rinse.

Combine the remaining ingredients in your preserving pot and bring to a boil over medium heat. Add the drained vegetables. Simmer, stirring often, for 30 to 50 minutes, or until the relish is slightly thickened. If the tomatoes are especially juicy, the cooking time will be longer.

Remove from the heat. Ladle the relish into hot, sterilized jars, leaving a ½-inch (1.2 cm) head space. Release the air bubbles. Wipe the rims clean. Seal according to manufacturer's directions. Process the jars in a boiling water bath for 15 minutes.

SPICY RIPE TOMATO RELISH Add 3 jalapeño peppers, seeded and finely chopped, to the vegetables during the salting stage, and ¼ cup (60 mL) prepared creamed horseradish when the vegetables are added to the boiling liquid.

Pepper Relish

Use any combination of red, green, yellow or orange peppers for this relish, or substitute some hot peppers if you like. Just be sure that the total amount matches the recipe. Don't use all green peppers or you'll end up with relish that is an unattractive muddy color.

3 cups • 720 mL finely chopped red bell
    peppers

3 cups • 720 mL finely chopped green
    bell peppers

2 cups • 475 mL finely chopped onion

2 cups • 475 mL cider vinegar

1 cup • 240 mL sugar

2 Tbsp • 30 mL mixed pickling spice, tied
    in a cheesecloth bag (see page 125)

2 tsp • 10 mL crushed red chili flakes

2 tsp • 10 mL salt

PREPARE the preserving jars.

Combine the peppers and onions in a large bowl. Add enough boiling water to cover them. Let stand 5 minutes. Drain thoroughly in a colander, pressing to remove excess moisture.

Combine the remaining ingredients in your preserving pot and bring to a boil over high heat. Add the drained vegetables. Reduce the heat to medium and simmer, stirring occasionally, for 25 to 30 minutes.

Remove from the heat; discard the spice bag. Spoon the relish into hot, sterilized jars, leaving a ½-inch (1.2 cm) head space. Release the air bubbles. Wipe the rims clean. Seal according to manufacturer's directions. Process the jars in a boiling water bath for 10 minutes.

Cranberry, Pear and Apple Relish

MAKES ABOUT SIX TO SEVEN 8 OZ (250 ML) JARS

Use Granny Smith or any type of crisp, tart apple that
will not disintegrate during cooking. This is a fresh,
exciting alternative to traditional cranberry sauce.

1 cup • 240 mL cranberry or apple juice

1½ cups • 360 mL sugar

¾ cup • 180 mL cider vinegar

½ tsp • 2.5 mL salt

½ tsp • 2.5 mL ground cloves

½ tsp • 2.5 mL ground allspice

one 3-inch (7.5 cm) cinnamon stick

3 cups • 720 mL cranberries

3 firm-ripe pears, peeled, cored and chopped

3 Granny Smith apples, peeled, cored and chopped

½ cup • 120 mL finely chopped red onion

PREPARE the preserving jars.

In your preserving pot, combine the cranberry or apple juice, sugar, vinegar, salt, cloves, allspice and cinnamon stick. Bring to a boil over medium-high heat. Stir in the remaining ingredients. Reduce the heat to medium and simmer, stirring often, for 20 to 25 minutes, until the mixture begins to thicken.

Remove from the heat. Discard the cinnamon stick. Spoon the relish into hot, sterilized jars, leaving a ½-inch (1.2 cm) head space. Release the air bubbles. Wipe the rims clean. Seal according to manufacturer's directions. Process the jars in a boiling water bath for 10 minutes.

ZESTY CRANBERRY RELISH Omit the cloves, allspice and cinnamon and add ¼ cup (60 mL) creamed prepared horseradish.

Nectarine and Pepper Relish

MAKES ABOUT SIX TO SEVEN 8 OZ (250 ML) JARS

A sweet and spicy relish that is delectable with roast pork, roast chicken or baked ham. You can substitute peaches or pears for the nectarines, but be sure to use fruit that is quite firm or it will turn to mush during cooking.

6 cups • 1.5 L coarsely chopped firm but ripe
    nectarines
2 cups • 475 mL coarsely chopped red bell
    peppers
1 cup • 240 mL finely chopped onions
¼ cup • 60 mL pickling salt
1½ cups • 360 mL brown sugar
¾ cup • 180 mL cider vinegar
1 cup • 240 mL dark raisins
2 tsp • 10 mL mustard seeds
1 tsp • 5 mL cinnamon
1 tsp • 5 mL ground nutmeg
½ tsp • 2.5 mL ground cloves
½ tsp • 2.5 mL ground ginger

COMBINE the nectarines, peppers, onions and salt in a large bowl. Let stand at room temperature for 3 hours. Drain well in a colander, rinse thoroughly and drain again, pressing to remove as much liquid as possible.

Prepare the preserving jars.

In your preserving pot, combine the remaining ingredients and bring to a boil over medium-high heat. Stir in the fruit and vegetable mixture. Simmer, stirring often, for about 30 minutes, or until the mixture starts to thicken.

Remove from the heat. Spoon the relish into hot, sterilized jars, leaving a ½-inch (1.2 cm) head space. Release the air bubbles. Wipe the rims clean. Seal according to manufacturer's directions. Process the jars in a boiling water bath for 15 minutes.

Chutneys

Mango Chutney 165

Pear Chutney 166

Pineapple and Papaya Chutney 168

Plum Chutney with Cinnamon
and Coriander 169

Blueberry Chutney 170

Fig and Lemon Chutney 171

Cranberry, Orange and Apricot
Chutney 172

Ripe Tomato Chutney 173

Green Tomato and Apple Chutney 174

Banana and Date Chutney 175

Carrot and Coconut Chutney 176

Curried Apple Chutney 178

Blackberry and Apple Chutney 179

Rhubarb and Ginger Chutney 180

Chutneys

distinctive, pungent condiment of Indian origin, chutney has a characteristic sweet-and-sour flavor and a soft jam-like texture; it is usually much smoother and slightly sweeter than traditional pickle relishes.

In India, chutneys are commonly made fresh before each meal, with a considerable amount of toasting, grinding and blending of whole spices.

Western-style chutneys, whether store-bought or homemade, are quite different from their authentic Indian counterparts. Fruits or vegetables, sugar, vinegar and spices are gently simmered to form a thick, soft pulp, somewhat like a chunky ketchup. A rich, mellow flavor is achieved by long, slow cooking, and additional complexity develops as chutney matures in the jar.

Chutney can be made from virtually any mixture of fruits, and an endless variety of spices can be used to enhance the taste. Exotic and intriguing, chutneys exhibit great diversity in flavor—from mild and sweet to fiery and piquant. You can turn up the heat by adding one or two finely chopped chili peppers or reduce it by omitting or cutting back on peppers and hot spices.

Be enthusiastic with spices. Chutney is supposed to be aromatic, exotic and flavorful—a bland, boring chutney is a waste of time. Once you have gained some confidence, experiment with new combinations of fruit, vegetables and spices. Tried and true recipes will always be classics, but part of the fun and creativity of making chutney is going beyond the recipe and trying something new. Just keep in mind the ratios of fruit, vinegar and sugar.

Making chutney affords an excellent opportunity to use up less than perfect produce. Provided that the bruised or damaged portions are removed, you can safely use slightly blemished or mis-shapen fruit.

Another advantage of chutney is that it is not necessarily a seasonal preserve, but may be made from fresh or dried fruit and vegetables that are available throughout the year. Combinations can vary depending on personal taste and ingredients at hand.

A crucial stage of chutney-making is the storage and maturation of the finished product. Don't be tempted to taste your chutney too soon, but give the flavors a chance to mingle and mellow. Like a fine wine, your chutney will develop as it ages; you'll be amazed at how much the flavor intensifies with time.

Traditionally served with curried dishes, chutney has a myriad uses—in appetizers, salads, main courses, even desserts. It is superb with any kind of hot or cold roasted meat or poultry and great for a nibble with cheese and crackers, especially robust cheeses like Stilton or Gorgonzola. Chutney brings sparkle to everyday foods such as burgers, meat loaf or chops. Add a dollop to a stir-fry, or spread a little on a sandwich in place of

mayonnaise. Illuminate vegetarian meals by spooning chutney over baked potatoes, squash or steamed vegetables, or add it to an omelette. Enjoy a delicious snack of a toasted bagel spread with cream cheese and topped with chutney. Mix it into your homemade stuffing for roast turkey or chicken.

Creative cooks can incorporate chutney as an ingredient in dips, salad dressings and sauces. It can even be made into sorbet.

Chutney is terrific!

Mango Chutney

Mango chutney is what most often comes to mind when chutney is mentioned, but this recipe works equally well with peaches or papayas. Mango chutney is a traditional accompaniment for curried dishes.

5 large mangoes, barely ripe

1½ cups • 360 mL cider vinegar

1 cup • 240 mL demerara sugar

½ cup • 120 mL finely chopped onion

½ cup • 120 mL finely chopped red bell pepper

½ cup • 120 mL finely chopped green bell
    pepper

¼ cup • 60 mL fresh ginger, minced

½ cup • 120 mL lime juice

2 tsp • 10 mL salt

1 Tbsp • 15 mL mustard seeds

1 Tbsp • 15 mL dried chili flakes

½ cup • 120 mL chopped dried apricots

PREPARE the preserving jars. Peel the mangoes and slice the pulp away from the pit. Cut into chunks.

Combine all the ingredients in your preserving pot and bring to a boil over medium heat. Simmer, stirring often, for 45 to 60 minutes, until the mixture starts to thicken. Reduce the heat to low. If there is a lot of liquid on the surface of the chutney, skim off as much as possible and place it in a small saucepan. Boil hard until the liquid is reduced by half, then stir it back into the chutney. Bring the chutney back to a boil.

Remove from the heat. Ladle into hot, sterilized jars, leaving a ½-inch (1.2 cm) head space. Wipe the rims clean. Seal according to manufacturer's directions. Process the jars in a boiling water bath for 10 minutes.

BANANGO CHUTNEY Replace the 5 mangoes with 3 mangoes and 4 bananas, sliced.

Pear Chutney

MAKES ABOUT FIVE TO SIX 8 OZ (250 ML) JARS

Try this intriguing chutney spooned over baked squash or sweet potato.

6 cups • 1.5 L chopped pears

1 cup • 240 mL chopped apple

½ cup • 120 mL finely chopped onion

½ cup • 120 mL finely chopped red bell pepper

¾ cup • 180 mL dark raisins

½ cup • 120 mL chopped candied ginger

2 cups • 475 mL brown sugar

¾ cup • 180 mL cider vinegar

1 lemon, juice and finely grated zest

1 Tbsp • 15 mL mustard seeds

2 tsp • 10 mL dried chili flakes

1 tsp • 5 mL salt

½ tsp • 2.5 mL ground nutmeg

½ tsp • 2.5 mL ground cloves

PREPARE the preserving jars.

Combine all the ingredients in your preserving pot. Bring to a boil over medium heat, stirring occasionally. Simmer, stirring often, until the pears are tender and the mixture has thickened, about 1 hour.

Remove from the heat. Ladle the chutney into hot, sterilized jars, leaving a ½-inch (1.2 cm) head space. Wipe the rims clean. Seal according to manufacturer's directions. Process the jars in a boiling water bath for 10 minutes.

FRONT TO BACK» **Pear Chutney and Mango Chutney (page 165).**

Pineapple and Papaya Chutney

MAKES ABOUT FOUR TO FIVE 8 OZ (250 ML) JARS

A sweet, succulent chutney redolent of the flavors of the tropics. For a new twist on chicken salad, mix a spoonful or two of this chutney in with the mayonnaise.

3 cups • 720 mL pineapple, cut into ½-inch (1.2 cm) dice

2 cups • 475 mL papaya, cut into ½-inch (1.2 cm) dice

1 cup • 240 mL finely chopped onion

2 small chili peppers, seeded and minced

2 cups • 475 mL brown sugar

1½ cups • 360 mL cider vinegar

½ cup • 120 mL chopped dates

2 Tbsp • 30 mL grated fresh ginger

1 lime, juice and finely grated zest

1 tsp • 5 mL cinnamon

½ tsp • 2.5 mL salt

½ tsp • 2.5 mL ground allspice

PREPARE the preserving jars.

Combine all the ingredients in your preserving pot. Bring to a boil over medium-high heat. Reduce the heat to medium and simmer, stirring often, for 45 to 60 minutes, or until the chutney is thick enough to mound on a spoon.

Remove from the heat. Spoon the chutney into hot, sterilized jars, leaving a ½-inch (1.2 cm) head space. Wipe the rims clean. Seal according to manufacturer's directions. Process the jars in a boiling water bath for 10 minutes.

Plum Chutney with Cinnamon and Coriander

MAKES ABOUT SIX TO SEVEN 8 OZ (250 ML) JARS

A dark and delicious chutney with an assertive flavor, this is especially good with barbecued pork, lamb or chicken.

- 6 cups • 1.5 L chopped purple or red plums
- 1 cup • 240 mL finely chopped apple
- 1 cup • 240 mL finely chopped onion
- 2 cups • 475 mL brown sugar
- 1½ cups • 360 mL red wine vinegar
- ½ cup • 120 mL chopped prunes
- 1 Tbsp • 15 mL mustard seeds
- 2 tsp • 10 mL dried chili flakes
- 2 tsp • 10 mL salt
- 2 tsp • 10 mL cinnamon
- 2 tsp • 10 mL ground coriander seeds

ABOUT CORIANDER

A member of the parsley family, coriander seeds have a sweet, orangey aroma and a fresh flavor that is somewhat mild compared to other spices. Coriander is available powdered or as whole seeds; it is an ingredient in pickling spice and in many spice mixtures used in Indian cooking. Fresh coriander leaves (also called cilantro) are popular in Asian and Mexican cooking.

PREPARE the preserving jars.

Combine all the ingredients in your preserving pot. Bring to a boil over medium-high heat, stirring occasionally. Reduce the heat to medium and simmer, stirring often, for 45 to 60 minutes, until the chutney is thick enough to mound on a spoon.

Remove from the heat. Ladle the chutney into hot, sterilized jars, leaving a ½-inch (1.2 cm) head space. Wipe the rims clean. Seal according to manufacturer's directions. Process the jars in a boiling water bath for 10 minutes.

Blueberry Chutney

MAKES ABOUT FOUR TO FIVE 8 OZ (250 ML) JARS

Surprise the palate with the intriguing combination of flavors in this scrumptious chutney. Blend it half and half with plain yogurt and spoon it over a fresh fruit salad, or try it with grilled salmon.

5 cups • 1.2 L blueberries

1 medium tart apple, peeled, cored and grated

1 cup • 240 mL finely chopped onion

1½ cups • 360 mL red wine vinegar

1 cup • 240 mL brown sugar

⅔ cup • 160 mL maple syrup

½ cup • 120 mL dark raisins

1 Tbsp • 15 mL finely grated lemon zest

2 tsp • 10 mL mustard seeds

½ tsp • 2.5 mL salt

½ tsp • 2.5 mL ginger

½ tsp • 2.5 mL cinnamon

¼ tsp • 1.2 mL ground cloves

¼ tsp • 1.2 mL ground nutmeg

¼ tsp • 1.2 mL cayenne pepper

PREPARE the preserving jars.

Place the blueberries in your preserving pot and crush them with a potato masher. Add the remaining ingredients. Bring to a boil over medium-high heat. Reduce the heat to medium and simmer, stirring often, for 45 to 60 minutes, or until the chutney is thick enough to mound on a spoon.

Remove from the heat. Ladle the chutney into hot, sterilized jars, leaving a ½-inch (1.2 cm) head space. Wipe the rims clean. Seal according to manufacturer's directions. Process the jars in a boiling water bath for 10 minutes.

Fig and Lemon Chutney

MAKES ABOUT FOUR TO FIVE 8 OZ (250 ML) JARS

A memorable chutney with an exotic twist. The tart flavor
goes particularly well with game.

3–4 medium lemons

1 tsp • 5 mL whole allspice

1 tsp • 5 mL whole cloves

one 3-inch (7.5 cm) stick cinnamon, broken

1 lb • 454 g dried figs, cut into ½-inch
    (1.2 cm) pieces

½ cup • 120 mL finely chopped onion

1½ cups • 360 mL cider vinegar

¾ cup • 180 mL sugar

½ cup • 120 mL honey

¼ cup • 60 mL chopped candied ginger

1 tsp • 5 mL salt

SLICE the lemons in half lengthwise. Place the cut side down and slice the lemons
very thinly, discarding the ends and seeds. You will need 2 cups (475 mL) of
sliced lemon. Place the lemon slices in a small bowl and add enough water to
cover them. Cover the bowl and let stand overnight at room temperature.

The next day, prepare the preserving jars.

Put the allspice, cloves and cinnamon stick in a cheesecloth bag and tie the
top with string.

Drain the lemons in a colander. Combine the lemons and the remaining
ingredients in your preserving pot and bring to a boil over medium-high heat.
Reduce the heat to medium and simmer, stirring often, for 1 to 1½ hours, or
until the chutney is thick enough to mound on a spoon. You may need to add a
little water if the mixture gets too thick before the figs are plump.

Remove from the heat. Discard the spice bag. Spoon the chutney into hot,
sterilized jars, leaving a ½-inch (1.2 cm) head space. Wipe the rims clean. Seal
according to manufacturer's directions. Process the jars in a boiling water bath
for 10 minutes.

Cranberry, Orange and Apricot Chutney

MAKES ABOUT FOUR TO FIVE 8 OZ (250 ML) JARS

Dress up curry, poultry or ham with this flavorful chutney. It's also delicious with cold meats—try some on a chicken or turkey sandwich.

1 orange

4 cups • 950 mL cranberries

½ cup • 120 mL finely chopped onion

1 cup • 240 mL chopped dried apricots

¾ cup • 180 mL cider vinegar

¾ cup • 180 mL orange juice

½ cup • 120 mL water

2 cups • 475 mL brown sugar

½ tsp • 2.5 mL each ground cloves, ginger and allspice

PREPARE the preserving jars.

Slice the orange very thinly, discarding the ends and seeds. Chop very finely.

Combine all the ingredients in your preserving pot and bring to a boil over medium heat. Simmer, stirring often, for about 20 minutes, or until the mixture thickens.

Remove from the heat. Ladle into hot, sterilized jars, leaving a ½-inch (1.2 cm) head space. Wipe the rims clean. Seal according to manufacturer's directions. Process the jars in a boiling water bath for 10 minutes.

Ripe Tomato Chutney

MAKES ABOUT SEVEN TO EIGHT 8 OZ
(250 ML) JARS

A sweet, spicy accompaniment for any type of meat
or a pasta, rice or vegetable casserole. You can even
serve it for breakfast, with bacon and eggs.

8 cups • 2 L chopped tomatoes

6 cups • 1.5 L chopped apples

1 cup • 240 mL chopped onion

1 cup • 240 mL chopped red bell pepper

2 cloves garlic, peeled and minced

1 cup • 240 mL red wine vinegar

2 cups • 475 mL brown sugar

1 Tbsp • 15 mL mustard seeds

1½ tsp • 7.5 mL salt

1 tsp • 5 mL each ground cumin, coriander,
    cinnamon and chili powder

PREPARE the preserving jars.

Combine the tomatoes, apples, onion, red pepper, garlic and vinegar in your
preserving pot. Bring to a boil over high heat. Reduce the heat to medium and
simmer for 30 minutes, stirring occasionally. Stir in the remaining ingredients
and simmer for another 30 to 40 minutes, or until thickened, stirring often.

Remove from the heat. Ladle the chutney into hot, sterilized jars, leaving a
½-inch (1.2 cm) head space. Wipe the rims clean. Seal according to manufacturer's directions. Process the jars in a boiling water bath for 10 minutes.

ABOUT CUMIN

One of the major components of curry powder, cumin is used in chili powder as well.
Cumin is available as seeds or powder and
has a distinctive warm, sweet flavor that is
quite powerful and lasting. Cumin is often
paired with coriander.

chutneys |

Green Tomato and Apple Chutney

MAKES ABOUT SIX TO SEVEN 8 OZ (250 ML) JARS

A traditional English condiment, this chutney is excellent in a sandwich with any type of meat or cheese. It is a great accompaniment to beef dishes such as meat loaf, scrambled eggs or macaroni and cheese.

1 lemon

5 cups • 1.2 L finely chopped green tomatoes

2 cups • 475 mL finely chopped apples

1 cup • 240 mL finely chopped onions

2 cloves garlic, peeled and minced

1 cup • 240 mL currants

1 cup • 240 mL brown sugar

1 cup • 240 mL cider vinegar

1 Tbsp • 15 mL mustard seeds

1½ tsp • 7.5 mL dried chili flakes

1 tsp • 5 mL salt

1 tsp • 5 mL ground ginger

PREPARE the preserving jars.

Slice the lemon very thinly, discarding the ends and seeds. Chop very finely.

Combine all the ingredients in your preserving pot. Simmer over medium heat for 25 to 30 minutes, or until thickened. Stir often to prevent sticking, especially during the last 10 minutes of cooking time.

Remove from the heat. Spoon the chutney into hot, sterilized jars, leaving a ½-inch (1.2 cm) head space. Wipe the rims clean. Seal according to manufacturer's directions. Process the jars in a boiling water bath for 10 minutes.

Banana and Date Chutney

MAKES ABOUT FIVE TO SIX 8 OZ (250 ML) JARS

Spread a little cream cheese on a toasted bagel. Top with
banana chutney and crumbled crisp bacon. Mmm . . .

1 cup • 240 mL chopped apple

½ cup • 120 mL finely chopped onion

1½ cups • 360 mL cider vinegar

¼ cup • 60 mL lime juice

7 medium bananas, ripe but not mushy

1 cup • 240 mL chopped dates

¼ cup • 60 mL chopped candied ginger

½ cup • 120 mL brown sugar

¼ cup • 60 mL molasses

1 tsp • 5 mL salt

½ tsp • 2.5 mL each curry powder, cayenne
     pepper, ground allspice and coriander

PREPARE the preserving jars.

Combine the apples, onion, vinegar and lime juice in your preserving pot.
Bring to a boil over medium heat and simmer for 10 minutes.

Peel the bananas and chop them into ½-inch (1.2 cm) pieces; add them to
the pot. Stir in the remaining ingredients. Reduce the heat to medium-low and
simmer for about 20 minutes, stirring often, until the mixture is thick and pulpy.

Note: The chutney can become very thick and sticky. You may need to add
¼ to ⅓ cup (60 to 80 mL) water to prevent the chutney from sticking and to
make it easier to fill the jars. Just be sure that the chutney is uniformly hot and
bubbling before removing it from the heat. (If you have a suitable nonstick pot,
use it for making this chutney.)

Remove from the heat. Spoon the chutney into hot, sterilized jars, leaving a
½-inch (1.2 cm) head space. Wipe the rims clean. Seal according to manufacturer's directions. Process the jars in a boiling water bath for 10 minutes.

chutneys |

175

Carrot and Coconut Chutney

The slightly larger yield of this recipe will give you some
extra jars for gift-giving. This piquant and colorful chutney
can be made at any time of the year. You can make
an interesting spread for celery or crackers by blending
½ cup (120 mL) chutney with 1 cup (240 mL) cream cheese.

> 4 lb • 1.8 kg carrots (about 24 medium)
>
> 2 oranges
>
> 1 lemon
>
> 2½ cups • 600 mL brown sugar
>
> 1½ cups • 360 mL cider vinegar
>
> 1 cup • 240 mL flaked coconut
>
> ½ cup • 120 mL chopped dried apricots
>
> 2 Tbsp • 30 mL grated fresh ginger
>
> 1 Tbsp • 15 mL mustard seeds
>
> 1 Tbsp • 15 mL dried chili flakes
>
> 1 tsp • 5 mL salt
>
> one 3-inch (7.5 cm) cinnamon stick, broken

PEEL and slice the carrots. Cook them in boiling water until soft, about 35 to
40 minutes. Drain, then mash or purée the carrots until they are quite smooth.
Measure the mashed carrots; you should have about 5 cups (1.2 L).

Using a sharp knife, peel the zest from the oranges and lemon, including as
little of the white pith as possible. Cut the peel into very thin shreds. Set aside.
Trim away any excess pith from the oranges and lemon. Slice the fruit, then
chop it finely, discarding the seeds.

Combine the sugar, vinegar and orange and lemon zest in your preserving pot. Bring the mixture to a boil over medium heat. Reduce the heat to low,
cover and simmer for 5 minutes.

Prepare the preserving jars.

Add the carrots, chopped oranges and lemon and the remaining ingredients to the preserving pot. Increase the heat to medium and simmer for 30 to 40 minutes, stirring often, until the chutney has thickened. Stir the chutney almost constantly during the last 10 to 15 minutes of cooking to prevent scorching.

Remove from the heat. Ladle the chutney into hot, sterilized jars, leaving a ½-inch (1.2 cm) head space. Wipe the rims clean. Seal according to manufacturer's directions. Process the jars in a boiling water bath for 10 minutes.

ABOUT FRESH GINGER

What we often refer to as ginger root is actually not a root at all, but a rhizome—a tuber-like stem. When purchasing fresh ginger, look for firm, fresh "hands" with smooth, unblemished skin. Try to select ginger that has as few knobs as possible—it will be easier to peel. Avoid shriveled or moldy-looking ginger that is definitely past its prime.

If you will be using the ginger right away, just store it unwrapped in the crisper drawer of your refrigerator. For longer storage—up to about 3 weeks—wrap it first in a paper towel and then in a plastic bag. Old ginger dries out and loses its flavor.

To peel ginger, remove the tough outer skin by peeling it away with a sharp paring knife or a vegetable peeler, exposing the flesh. Most recipes call for finely chopped or grated fresh ginger, which are essentially the same thing. The quickest way to chop ginger is using a food processor fitted with the steel blade. Simply drop the ginger in through the feed tube while the motor is running. To chop ginger using a French knife, slice the peeled ginger very thinly, then mince. To grate, use the finest surface of a stainless steel box grater.

Curried Apple Chutney

MAKES ABOUT SEVEN TO EIGHT 8 OZ (250 ML) JARS

The ultimate chutney with cheese and crackers and a perfect partner for the Cheddar Cheese Ball with Port and Dijon Mustard (page 228).

9 cups • 2.2 L peeled, cored, chopped apples
    (about 3 lb/1.4 kg)
2 cups • 475 mL finely chopped onion
2 cups • 475 mL golden raisins
2 cups • 475 mL brown sugar
1½ cups • 360 mL cider vinegar
1 Tbsp • 15 mL mustard seeds
1½ tsp • 7.5 mL salt
1 tsp • 5 mL dried chili flakes
1 tsp • 5 mL curry powder
½ tsp • 2.5 mL each ground turmeric, cumin,
    coriander, cardamom and ginger

PREPARE the preserving jars.

    Combine all the ingredients in your preserving pot. Bring to a boil over medium-high heat, stirring occasionally. Reduce the heat to medium and simmer for 1 to 1½ hours, or until thickened, stirring often. Stir almost constantly during the last 15 to 20 minutes of cooking time to prevent scorching.

    Remove from the heat. Ladle the chutney into hot, sterilized jars, leaving a ½-inch (1.2 cm) head space. Wipe the rims clean. Seal according to manufacturer's directions. Process the jars in a boiling water bath for 10 minutes.

Blackberry and Apple Chutney

MAKES ABOUT FOUR TO FIVE 8 OZ (250 ML) JARS

An elegant preserve brimming with the flavor of ripe blackberries. The perfect complement to pâtés, roast poultry or game.

1 orange, juice and grated zest

½ cup • 120 mL finely chopped onion

1 cup • 240 mL brown sugar

½ cup • 120 mL honey

½ cup • 120 mL red wine vinegar

2 cups • 475 mL blackberries

3 cups • 720 mL peeled, cored,
   chopped apples

½ cup • 120 mL golden raisins

1 tsp • 5 mL salt

½ tsp • 2.5 mL each ground cloves and
   allspice

ABOUT ALLSPICE

The small round, dried fruit of an evergreen tree of the myrtle family, allspice berries look like large peppercorns. This aptly named spice combines the flavors of cinnamon, nutmeg and cloves, with the flavor of cloves predominating. This complex spice blends well with other spices and complements a wide variety of foods, particularly apples, tomatoes and pumpkins. Ground allspice does not store well, as the flavor tends to deteriorate, so buy it whole and grind it right before using.

PREPARE the preserving jars.

In your preserving pot, combine the orange juice and zest, onion, sugar, honey and red wine vinegar. Bring to a boil over medium heat and simmer for 5 minutes, stirring occasionally. Add the remaining ingredients and simmer for 30 to 35 minutes, stirring often, until the chutney has thickened slightly.

Remove from the heat. Ladle the chutney into hot, sterilized jars, leaving a ½-inch (1.2 cm) head space. Wipe the rims clean. Seal according to manufacturer's directions. Process the jars in a boiling water bath for 10 minutes.

Rhubarb and Ginger Chutney

MAKES ABOUT SEVEN TO EIGHT 8 OZ (250 ML) JARS

For ginger lovers only! This unusual chutney adds zest to any curried main dish, or for that matter, to a simple snack of bread and cheese.

8 cups • 2 L rhubarb cut into ½-inch (1.2 cm) dice

2 cups • 475 mL finely chopped onion

2 cloves garlic, peeled and minced

4 cups • 950 mL dark brown sugar

2 cups • 475 mL cider vinegar

1 cup • 240 mL golden raisins

⅔ cup • 160 mL grated fresh ginger

2 tsp • 10 mL salt

2 tsp • 10 mL mustard seeds

1 tsp • 5 mL dried chili flakes

1 tsp • 5 mL ground allspice

1 tsp • 5 mL ground coriander

½ tsp • 2.5 mL cinnamon

½ tsp • 2.5 mL ground cloves

PREPARE the preserving jars.

Combine all the ingredients in your preserving pot and bring to a boil over medium-high heat, stirring occasionally. Reduce the heat to medium and simmer, stirring often, for 35 to 45 minutes, until thickened.

Remove from the heat. Ladle the chutney into hot, sterilized jars, leaving a ½-inch (1.2 cm) head space. Wipe the rims clean. Seal according to manufacturer's directions. Process the jars in a boiling water bath for 10 minutes.

Ketchups

Old-Fashioned Tomato Ketchup 185

Country Style Chili Sauce 186

Five-Fruit Ketchup 188

Cranberry Ketchup 189

Feisty Red Pepper Ketchup 191

Ketchups

Subtly sweet and richly flavored, homemade ketchups are versatile sauces that every home preserver should have in his or her repertoire. You'll be forgiven should your mind stray to a grungy bottle of tomato sauce atop a table in a seedy, all-night diner, or perhaps to a sticky bottle lurking in the depths of your own refrigerator. Yes, that may be ketchup to some people, but homemade ketchup encompasses so much more. You don't have to limit yourself to tomatoes—although homemade tomato ketchup is glorious. Simmer up a batch of fruity cranberry or five-fruit ketchup to serve with roast pork, chicken or grilled fish. A robust vegetable ketchup is de rigueur with grilled burgers, of course, but why not try some with rare roast beef, hearty pork or veal chops, or a sizzling steak?

Ketchups bear close resemblance to a couple of characters you are already familiar with—chutneys and fruit butters. Usually highly seasoned, ketchups are made of ingredients similar to those in chutney, but are generally smooth and of a thinner consistency. Juicy, fully ripe fruits are used. The actual preparation of ketchup is more like that of a fruit butter. The fruit and/or vegetables are prepared, aromatic seasonings added and the concoction simmered for about an hour. This evaporation process reduces the sauce to the desired thickness. The ketchup is most often sieved or puréed to velvety smoothness before being bottled. Half-pint (250 mL) jars are recommended, as ketchup is usually used in small quantities.

Ketchup is ready when it has thickened to a—well, a ketchup-like consistency. To test for doneness, simply spoon a little ketchup on a cold plate and chill in the freezer for 2 minutes. Draw your finger through the center; if a clear track remains, the ketchup is done. Should the ketchup become too thick, either during cooking or afterwards in the jar, it can be diluted with a little water, vinegar or both.

Old-Fashioned Tomato Ketchup

MAKES ABOUT FIVE TO SIX 8 OZ (250 ML) JARS

This hearty, homemade version beats store-bought any day.
Stir a little into gravy or savory sauces for an extra zing.

two 3-inch (7.5 cm) cinnamon sticks, broken

1 tsp • 5 mL whole cloves

1 tsp • 5 mL whole allspice

2 Tbsp • 30 mL mustard seeds

1 tsp • 5 mL celery seeds

10 lb • 4.5 kg ripe tomatoes, preferably
plum or Roma

1 cup • 240 mL chopped onion

1 cup • 240 mL chopped red or green bell
peppers

1½ cups • 360 mL cider vinegar

1 cup • 240 mL brown sugar

1½ Tbsp • 22.5 mL salt

COARSELY chop the tomatoes. Combine the tomatoes, onion and peppers in your preserving pot. Bring to a boil over medium heat and simmer for 30 minutes, stirring occasionally. Remove from the heat. Press the pulp through a sieve or food mill.

Put the cinnamon sticks, cloves, allspice, mustard and celery seeds into a cheesecloth bag and tie the top with string.

Return the pulp to the pot and add the remaining ingredients. Prepare the preserving jars. Simmer the sauce about 1 hour, until thickened, stirring often. (Stir constantly during the last 15 to 20 minutes to prevent scorching.)

Remove from the heat. Discard the spice bag. Pour the ketchup into hot, sterilized jars, leaving a ½-inch (1.2 cm) head space. Wipe the rims clean. Seal according to manufacturer's directions. Process the jars in a boiling water bath for 15 minutes.

CERTAIN MODERN varieties of tomatoes can vary considerably in acidity. In order to safely process tomato-based foods such as salsa, chili sauce or ketchup in a boiling water bath, it is essential to add lemon juice or vinegar to compensate for any lack of natural acid.

ketchups |

185

ABOUT PEELING AND SEEDING TOMATOES

There are two schools of thought on the subject of peeling tomatoes. Many cooks shudder at the very idea of using unpeeled tomatoes. Others believe that tomato skins contribute a stronger, richer flavor to their recipes.

I don't mind eating tomato skins, and I can't say that I've ever noticed a difference in taste one way or the other. To me, peeling tomatoes is not a necessity. But for those times when you want to peel and seed your tomatoes, here's how to do it.

Bring a large pot of water to a boil. Using a sharp paring knife, remove the cores from the tomatoes and make a small X at the base of each one.

Working with just a few tomatoes at a time, carefully place the tomatoes in the boiling water and leave them there for 30 to 60 seconds.

Remove the tomatoes with a slotted spoon, and transfer them to a big bowl of cold water. After a few minutes, they will be cool enough to handle, and the skins will slide right off.

Cut the tomatoes in half crosswise, gently squeeze out the seeds and the juice, then chop them for your recipes.

Country Style Chili Sauce

MAKES ABOUT FIVE TO SIX 1-PINT (500 ML) JARS

Chili sauce is a lot like ketchup, only chunkier. It is highly compatible with barbecued meats or poultry and terrific with savory meat pies.

10 cups • 2.4 L chopped tomatoes, preferably plum or Roma

3 cups • 720 mL chopped onions

2 cups • 475 mL chopped red bell peppers

1½ cups • 360 mL chopped celery

3 small chili peppers, seeded and minced

2 cloves garlic, minced

1½ cups • 360 mL cider vinegar

1 cup • 240 mL brown sugar

2½ tsp • 12.5 mL salt

½ tsp • 2.5 mL ground black pepper

½ tsp • 2.5 mL dry English mustard

½ tsp • 2.5 mL celery seed

½ tsp • 2.5 mL each ground cloves, allspice, cinnamon and ginger

PREPARE the preserving jars.

Combine all the ingredients except the spices in your preserving pot. Bring to a boil over medium-high heat. Reduce the heat to medium and simmer, stirring often, for 1 hour. Stir in the spices, and continue to cook the sauce until it reaches a consistency that is slightly thicker than ketchup. This may take 1 to 1½ hours. You can test for doneness by placing a little sauce on a cold plate. When the plate is tilted, very little liquid should ooze away from the solids. Once the cooking is complete, taste the sauce and adjust the seasoning to suit your taste, adding a little more vinegar, sugar, spices or some liquid hot sauce, if desired. You may need to cook the sauce a little longer if you add additional vinegar.

Remove from the heat. Ladle the sauce into hot, sterilized jars, leaving a ½-inch (1.2 cm) head space. Wipe the rims clean. Seal according to manufacturer's directions. Process the jars in a boiling water bath for 15 minutes.

Five-Fruit Ketchup

MAKES ABOUT SIX TO SEVEN 8 OZ (250 ML) JARS

Savor summer's finest fruits in this mellow, richly flavored ketchup. Serve with pâtés, cold sliced meats or cheese and crackers.

two 3-inch (7.5 cm) cinnamon sticks

1 tsp • 5 mL whole cloves

1 tsp • 5 mL whole allspice berries

1 tsp • 5 mL black peppercorns

1 tsp • 5 mL mustard seeds

6 cups • 1.5 L chopped tomatoes

2 cups • 475 mL each chopped peaches,
   apples, pears and plums

1 cup • 240 mL chopped onion

2 cloves garlic, minced

2 jalapeño peppers, seeded and finely chopped

2 cups • 475 mL cider vinegar

2 cups • 475 mL brown sugar

2 tsp • 10 mL salt

PUT the cinnamon sticks, cloves, allspice, peppercorns and mustard seeds in a cheesecloth bag and tie the top with string.

Combine all the ingredients in your preserving pot. Bring to a boil over medium-high heat. Reduce the heat to medium and simmer for about 1 hour, stirring frequently. Remove from the heat. Discard the spice bag. Press the mixture through a sieve or food mill, then return it to the pot. Return to a boil and when the ketchup is uniformly hot and bubbling, remove from the heat.

Pour the sauce into hot, sterilized jars, leaving a ½-inch (1.2 cm) head space. Wipe the rims clean. Seal according to manufacturer's directions. Process the jars in a boiling water bath for 15 minutes.

Cranberry Ketchup

MAKES ABOUT SIX TO SEVEN 8 OZ (250 ML) JARS

A gorgeous, ruby-red sauce with a lively flavor, this is an excellent companion to rich entrées such as roast duck, goose or venison. Cranberries are very rich in pectin, so the ketchup may thicken up faster than you expect. If it should become too thick, add a little water or orange juice to thin it down. Be careful not to add too much; start with about ¼ cup (60 mL).

- 2 cups • 475 mL chopped red onion
- 2 oranges, juice and finely grated zest
- 3 cups • 720 mL water
- 8 cups • 2 L fresh cranberries (about 2 lb/900 g)
- 1 cup • 240 mL red wine vinegar
- 2 cups • 475 mL brown sugar
- 1 tsp • 5 mL each ground cloves, cinnamon, allspice and ginger
- 1 tsp • 5 mL salt
- ½ tsp • 2.5 mL pepper

PREPARE the preserving jars.

Combine the onion, orange juice and zest, and water in your preserving pot. Bring to a boil over medium heat and simmer, covered, for about 10 minutes, until the onion is tender. Add the cranberries, cover and cook for another 10 to 15 minutes, stirring occasionally, until the cranberries burst.

Remove from the heat and pass the mixture through a sieve or food mill. Return the puréed mixture to the pot and stir in the remaining ingredients. Bring to a boil, stirring constantly. As soon as the mixture is bubbling and heated through, remove from the heat and immediately pour into hot, sterilized jars, leaving a ¼-inch (6 mm) head space. Wipe the rims clean. Seal according to manufacturer's directions. Process the jars in a boiling water bath for 15 minutes.

Feisty Red Pepper Ketchup

MAKES ABOUT FIVE TO SIX 8 OZ (250 ML) JARS

You can also use brightly colored yellow or orange peppers for this stylish sauce, but stay away from green ones—they do not produce an attractive ketchup. This ketchup will not be perfectly smooth. If you would like it that way, pass it through a sieve or food mill after it is removed from the heat. Return the ketchup to the pot, heat to boiling and fill the jars as usual.

2 Tbsp • 30 mL mustard seeds

1 Tbsp • 15 mL black peppercorns

1 Tbsp • 15 mL whole coriander seeds

1 tsp • 5 mL whole cloves

3 lb • 1.4 kg red bell peppers, cored and seeded

3 onions, peeled

2 apples, peeled and cored

3 small hot red chili peppers

2 cups • 475 mL red wine vinegar

¾ cup • 180 mL brown sugar

2 Tbsp • 30 mL prepared creamed horseradish

2 tsp • 10 mL pickling salt

1 lemon, zest only, cut off in a continuous spiral

PUT the mustard seeds, black peppercorns, coriander seeds and cloves in a cheesecloth bag and tie the top with string.

Cut the peppers, onions and apples into chunks. Place in the bowl of a food processor along with the chilies. Process until very finely puréed. Transfer to your preserving pot.

Prepare the preserving jars.

(continued next page)

Feisty Red Pepper Ketchup (continued)

Add the remaining ingredients and the cheesecloth bag of spices to the preserving pot and bring to a boil over high heat. Reduce the heat to medium and simmer, stirring occasionally, for 45 to 60 minutes, until thickened.

Remove from the heat. Discard the lemon zest and spice bag. Pour into hot, sterilized jars, leaving a ½-inch (1.2 cm) head space. Wipe the rims clean. Seal according to manufacturer's directions. Process the jars in a boiling water bath for 15 minutes.

Infused Vinegars

Lovely Lavender Vinegar 201

Opal Basil Vinegar 202

Scarborough Fair Vinegar 203

French Tarragon Vinegar 204

Cranberry Christmas Vinegar 206

Raspberry Vinegar 208

Hot Chili Pepper Vinegar 209

Spiced Plum Vinegar 210

Infused Vinegars

Specialty food shops often have gorgeous displays of imported herb and fruit vinegars. If you've ever longed to purchase such vinegars but have found them to be too expensive, you will be delighted to discover how easily and inexpensively they can be made at home.

No specialized equipment is required, just a little time and patience. Any recycled or purchased bottles will do, as long as they are properly prepared and can be sealed with plastic caps or corks.

Flavored vinegars are known as infused vinegars. An infused vinegar is a vinegar that has been steeped with a flavoring such as herbs, spices, fruit or flowers for a period of time, allowing the vinegar to take on the flavors of the other ingredients.

Do not confuse infusing vinegars with actually making vinegar. Vinegar is a solution of acetic acid and water. Making vinegar is a natural process that occurs if you allow a sweet liquid to undergo fermentation. The sugar in the liquid is first converted to alcohol by yeasts, and then the alcohol is eventually converted to acetic acid by bacteria. Certain conditions must exist to allow fermentation to occur.

Infusing vinegar is a much simpler process that begins with good-quality ready-made white or red wine vinegar. Mellow-flavored cider vinegar is also a good choice, especially for fruit vinegars, where color is not an issue. Do not be tempted to use regular white distilled vinegar; it is a little too harsh for this purpose. Mild wine or cider

BLENDING FLAVORS

The flavors of infused vinegars mellow and blend in the bottle, so you can use virtually any combination of flavorings and get a good result. Infused vinegars offer plenty of room for creativity and experimentation. Satisfy your urge to be innovative by blending finished vinegars together like wines to create new and unexpected combinations that are definitely not garden-variety.

vinegars readily absorb delicate herb and fruit flavors.

As an acid, vinegar reacts with metal ions from the surface of aluminum, copper, iron or zinc-lined vessels. Never steep vinegar in metal containers—the chemical reaction will cause undesirable flavors to develop. You can also discolor your pots. Use glass or ceramic containers to steep vinegars, and heat them only in stainless steel or enamel-lined pots.

Old or new, bottles for vinegar must be absolutely clean. Put them through the dishwasher, then boil them for 15 minutes to sterilize them. Dry the bottles on their sides on a baking sheet in a warm oven, about 150°F (65°C), until there is no sign of moisture inside.

STOPPERING THE BOTTLES

Seal bottles of vinegar using either plastic screw-top caps or corks. Metal screw-tops are fine for short-term storage but may corrode if the vinegar is kept for long periods.

Corks are a practical and aesthetically pleasing choice for stoppering bottled vinegars. Never use recycled corks, which can lead to spoilage. New corks are inexpensive and are usually available from cookware or wine-making supply stores. Try to find tapered corks if you can; they are much easier to work with.

Simmer the corks in a covered pot for 15 minutes just prior to use. The heat will kill any microorganisms that might be

present and will also soften the corks, making it easier to insert them into the bottles.

Push the cork into the bottle as far as you can manually, then use a wooden mallet or similar tool to gently tap the cork in as far as it will go. Any cork protruding over the rim of the bottle can be trimmed neatly off with a sharp knife, if desired.

Infused vinegars are not heat processed, as the vinegar itself is a preservative. The acidity of full-strength vinegar is too high to allow the growth of microorganisms, as long as proper sanitary procedures have been followed.

SEALING BOTTLES WITH WAX

The final step is to seal and protect the bottles with wax, to keep them airtight.

The hard, glossy coating that you see on fancy, gourmet bottles sold in shops is proper sealing wax. It is rather expensive and difficult to come by, and is really better saved for decorative applications only (see the last chapter, Gifts from the Pantry).

Simple paraffin wax can be purchased from grocery or hardware stores and will do a very satisfactory job. It can be colored by melting an old candle stub (unscented) or crayon along with the paraffin.

I like to use a mixture of paraffin and beeswax, about half and half. This is primarily for aesthetic reasons—beeswax has a delightful scent and a lovely golden color that is most attractive. Beeswax can often be found at craft stores, but I buy mine from a shop that sells honey and beekeeping supplies.

You need an old pot or a small metal container in which to melt the wax. Once used, this container is pretty much dedicated to the purpose of melting wax. I use a small pot that I bought at a garage sale. I leave the wax to harden after each use, then just wrap the whole thing in a plastic bag and it's ready for next time. A clean tin can works well too.

Chop up the wax and place it in the metal container, then place the container in a pot of water that is simmering (not boiling) over low heat. The melted wax needs to be deep enough so that it will cover part of the neck of the bottle. The bottles and corks must be completely dry. Dip the top of the bottle repeatedly into the melted wax, allowing the wax to set between applications. (Setting only takes a minute or two, if that.) Several coats of wax are needed to give an attractive and effective seal.

BASIC HERB VINEGAR

1. Rinse the herbs briefly under running water or swish them in a sinkful of water. Do not soak the herbs for a long time.
2. Drain the herbs in a colander, then gently roll them in a towel to blot up moisture or spin them in a salad spinner.

SUGGESTED USES FOR HERB VINEGARS

Aromatic herb vinegars can be used almost anywhere you would use regular vinegar.
- Use it in vinaigrettes—to dress salads of greens, vegetables, pasta, grains, poultry or fish.
- Splash it on steamed vegetables to liven them up.
- Try it in potato salad—it's terrific!
- Use it in any kind of marinade to tenderize and add interesting flavors.
- Make a delicately flavored herb mayonnaise.
- Add a dash to give flavor and interest to reduced-salt recipes.
- Make quick "pickled" vegetables by marinating cucumber, tomato or carrot slices or mushrooms in herb vinegars.

3. Leave the herbs to air-dry for at least an hour. There must be no water clinging to the leaves.
4. Trim the herbs if necessary, removing coarse stem ends, flower buds and any withered or insect-eaten leaves.
5. Place the herbs in a clean, dry, sterilized jar. A wide-mouthed glass jar that narrows slightly at the top is best—that is, a jar that has shoulders, not one that is straight up and down. This will help keep the herbs covered with the vinegar.
6. The herbs should fill the jar two-thirds to three-quarters full. The basic ratio is about 1 cup (240 mL) of loosely packed herbs to about 2 cups

(475 mL) of vinegar, but this is not a hard and fast rule.

7. Fill the jar with vinegar to a maximum of 1 inch (2.5 cm) below the rim of the jar. The herbs must be completely immersed in the vinegar—you may need to trim longer sprigs or poke the herbs down below the surface. Mold can develop if the herbs are exposed.

8. Cover the vinegar tightly. If the jar has a metal lid, cover the mouth of the jar with plastic wrap first.

9. Place the vinegar in a sunny spot where you will remember to shake or stir it once or twice a week. The warmth will speed up the decomposition of the herbs, drawing out the aromatic oils more quickly.

10. Let the vinegar steep for 2 to 4 weeks. Some vinegars will be ready more quickly than others. You can sniff and taste the vinegar after 10 days or so to see if the flavor has developed to your liking. If it has, proceed to the next step. If not, let it steep for a longer period. The flavors will intensify with time, but after about 4 weeks the flavors will pretty much have been extracted from the herbs.

11. Strain the vinegar through a sieve lined with a double thickness of dampened cheesecloth. The cheesecloth is dampened first so it doesn't absorb a lot of the vinegar.

12. In a nonreactive pot, gently heat the vinegar just to a simmer.

13. Remove from the heat and strain a second time through clean cheesecloth.

14. Using a funnel, carefully pour the vinegar into clean, dry, sterilized bottles.

15. Place clean, dry fresh herb sprigs in the bottles if desired, for decoration and identification.

16. Cover loosely with cheesecloth and leave the vinegar to cool.

17. Seal the bottles by capping with plastic screw-tops or corks. Complete the seal by dipping the tops of the bottles in melted wax.

18. Label the bottles, listing the types of herbs and the date, and store them in a cool, dark place. Herb vinegars will keep almost indefinitely but are at their best if used within 6 months— a year at the most.

19. Once the vinegar is opened, remove and discard the herbs. They may become moldy once they are exposed to the air.

Some Suggested Flavorings for Herb Vinegars

- thyme, savory and marjoram with red wine vinegar
- rosemary, garlic and hot chili pepper with red wine vinegar
- rosemary and orange zest with red wine vinegar

- oregano, shallot and hot chili pepper with red wine vinegar
- mint and grapefruit zest with white wine vinegar
- mint, dill and lime zest with white wine vinegar
- dill, lemon zest and fennel seeds with white wine vinegar

BASIC FRUIT VINEGAR

1. Allow 3 to 4 lb (1.4 to 1.8 kg) of fruit for every 4 cups (950 mL) of vinegar. Use fruit that is fully ripe.

2. Rinse or wash the fruit briefly. Do not allow it to soak in water for a long time.

3. Drain the fruit thoroughly in a colander, then gently blot it dry using paper towels.

4. Sort the fruit, discarding any that is damaged or moldy. (It is fine to use bruised fruit as long as the bruises are completely cut away.)

5. It is not necessary to stem currants, hull strawberries or pit cherries. Likewise, you do not need to peel or pit peaches or plums, but larger fruit should be cut into approximately ½-inch (1.2 cm) pieces.

6. Place the fruit in a bowl and crush with a potato masher to release the juices.

7. In a nonreactive pot, heat the vinegar gently, just to a simmer. Remove from the heat, let it cool slightly, then stir in the prepared fruit.

8. Cover the pot loosely with a clean dish towel and let stand until it is completely cool.

9. Transfer the mixture to a clean, dry, sterilized jar, and cover tightly. A wide-mouthed jar that narrows slightly at the top is best. This will help keep the fruit covered with the vinegar. If the jar has a metal lid, cover the mouth of the jar with plastic wrap first.

10. Store in a cool, dark place for at least 1 month. Stir the vinegar 3 or 4 times a week. Taste the vinegar after 1 month—it should have a rich, full, fruit flavor. If you are not satisfied with the intensity of the flavor, leave it to steep for another 2 weeks.

11. When the vinegar is ready, pour it into a dampened jelly bag suspended over a bowl and allow it to drip through overnight. (You can also use a sieve lined with a double thickness of cheesecloth.) Discard the drained fruit.

12. Pour the vinegar into a large, non-reactive pot. The wider the pot is, the better. The vinegar should be no more than 4 inches (10 cm) deep to allow it to come to a boil very quickly. The rapid boiling preserves the rich color of the vinegar. If necessary, boil the vinegar in several batches.

13. If desired, the vinegar can be sweetened slightly with sugar. Add 1 to

USING GARLIC OR SHALLOTS FOR ADDITIONAL FLAVOR

Garlic or shallots can be added to any herb vinegar for additional flavor. This is done at the time the vinegar is heated, just prior to bottling.

Select small cloves of garlic and/or the tiniest shallots. Shallots will need to be halved or quartered to fit through the opening of the bottle. Add the garlic or shallots to the vinegar in the pot, heat gently to simmering, then strain. Place the garlic or shallots in the bottle, then proceed as usual.

You can also thread the garlic or shallots onto a bamboo skewer for a decorative look. The skewer should be about three-quarters the length of the bottle you are using. Soak the skewer in water beforehand; otherwise it will float to the top of the bottle.

- Team fruit vinegars with delicate salad oils in vinaigrette dressings. Fruit vinegars are especially delightful with nut-flavored oils such as hazelnut or pistachio.
- Replace the lemon juice in many recipes with fruit vinegar—for example, in dressings for fruit salads.
- Use fruit vinegar to deglaze the pan when preparing sautéed veal or chicken to make a tart, fruity sauce.
- Use fruit vinegars in marinades to tenderize and add flavor to pork, veal or poultry.
- Sprinkle fruit vinegar and sugar over fresh berries.
- Mix fruit vinegar with an equal amount of honey to make a tart sauce for fresh fruit.
- Use it to add a sweet-tart flavor to preserves, stewed fruit or fruit sauces and purées.
- Make a refreshing, old-fashioned fruit drink known as a shrub—stir fruit vinegar into club soda, and add ice and sugar to taste.

often develop a fine sediment, which, though unattractive, is harmless. Simply decant the vinegar through a dampened coffee filter or cheesecloth into another bottle.

18. Fruit vinegars will keep almost indefinitely if they are properly prepared and stored, but it is recommended to use them within 6 months, or a year at the most.

Some Suggested Flavorings for Fruit Vinegars

Many fruits can be used to make fruit vinegars, including strawberries, blackberries, raspberries, blueberries, cherries, currants, peaches, apricots, pears and plums. You can also combine fruits with herbs, spices or citrus zests for extra-special flavors.

- blueberry and mint with red wine vinegar
- cranberry and orange zest with red wine vinegar
- blackberry and lemon balm with red wine vinegar
- peach and ginger with white wine vinegar
- strawberry and lime zest with white wine vinegar
- pear and rosemary with red wine vinegar

1½ Tbsp (15 to 22.5 mL) for 1 cup (240 mL) of vinegar.

14. Quickly bring the vinegar to a boil over high heat. Boil for 3 minutes.

15. Skim off any foam and allow the vinegar to cool. Strain the vinegar a second time, discarding any sediment. Bottle and seal as for herb vinegar.

16. Label the sealed bottles with the type of fruit and the date and store the vinegar in a cool, dark place.

17. Although the flavor of fruit vinegar improves with age, colors may eventually fade or darken. Fruit vinegars

Lovely Lavender Vinegar

MAKES 2 CUPS (475 ML)

Delectably different in a vinaigrette, or try a splash over
fresh strawberries or ripe melon.

8 large-headed stalks of fresh lavender

2 cups • 475 mL white wine vinegar

BRIEFLY swish the lavender in a bowl of salted water to get rid of any insects.
Rinse in clear water, shake dry, then blot with paper towels. Trim the stalks
if necessary to fit your bottle—the lavender should stand about three-quarters
as high.

Place the lavender in a clean, dry, sterilized, wide-mouthed jar.

Heat the vinegar just to a simmer, then remove from the heat and let it
cool slightly. Pour the vinegar into the jar, ensuring the lavender is completely
covered. Cover and leave it to stand in a sunny spot for 2 to 3 weeks, giving the
bottle a slight shake occasionally.

Strain the vinegar through a sieve lined with dampened cheesecloth. In a
nonreactive pot, gently heat the vinegar just to a simmer, then strain it a second time. Cover loosely with cheesecloth and allow the vinegar to cool to room
temperature. Carefully pour vinegar into 1 or 2 clean, dry, sterilized bottles. If
you like, place 1 or 2 stalks of fresh lavender in the bottles before sealing. Cap or
stop the bottles with corks. Seal with wax.

Opal Basil Vinegar

MAKES 4 CUPS (950 ML)

A tender annual, aromatic basil may well be the most popular of culinary herbs. Basil is available in many varieties, including anise basil, lemon basil, cinnamon basil and the star of this recipe, opal basil. Opal basil has a warm, spicy fragrance and slightly peppery flavor with overtones of clove and nutmeg. Its beautiful dark purple leaves give the vinegar a rich jewel-toned hue.

2 cups • 475 mL rinsed and dried opal basil, lightly packed

4 cups • 950 mL white wine vinegar

GENTLY bruise the basil in your hands to release the fragrant oils. Place the basil into a dry, sterilized wide-mouthed jar. Pour the vinegar over the herbs, making sure they are completely covered. Cover and steep for 2 to 3 weeks, stirring once or twice a week.

Strain the vinegar through a sieve lined with dampened cheesecloth.

In a nonreactive pot, gently heat the vinegar just to a simmer, then strain it a second time. Cover loosely with cheesecloth and allow the vinegar to cool to room temperature.

Carefully pour the vinegar into clean, dry, sterilized bottles, using a funnel. If you like, add some fresh basil to each bottle before sealing. Cap or stop the bottles with corks. Seal with wax.

Scarborough Fair Vinegar

MAKES 4 CUPS (950 ML)

This pungent blend of gardeners' favorite herbs and red
wine vinegar is an excellent multipurpose vinegar to have
on hand in the pantry for vinaigrettes and marinades.

- 2 cups • 475 mL equal amounts of rinsed and
  dried fresh parsley, sage, rosemary and
  thyme, lightly packed
- 4 cups • 950 mL red wine vinegar

PLACE the herbs in a clean, dry, sterilized wide-mouthed jar. Pour the vinegar
over the herbs, making sure they are completely covered. Cover and steep for
2 to 3 weeks, stirring once or twice a week.

Strain the vinegar through a sieve lined with dampened cheesecloth.

In a nonreactive pot, gently heat the vinegar just to a simmer, then strain it
a second time. Cover loosely with cheesecloth and allow the vinegar to cool to
room temperature.

Carefully pour the vinegar into clean, dry, sterilized bottles, using a funnel.
If you like, add a couple of sprigs of fresh herbs to each bottle before sealing.
Cap or stop the bottles with corks. Seal with wax.

FLAVORING VINEGARS WITH FRESH GINGER

Fresh ginger adds an exciting
dimension to infused vinegars
and can complement a variety
of herbs or fruits.

Simply add about 2 oz
(57 g) of peeled fresh ginger,
cut into 1/4-inch (6 mm) slices,
to every 4 cups (950 mL)
of vinegar, during the initial
steeping process. Strain the
ginger out before bottling.

French Tarragon Vinegar

MAKES ABOUT 4 CUPS (950 ML)

Tarragon has a pronounced aroma and flavor slightly suggestive of licorice. Nothing can match the flavor of true French tarragon. Other varieties are considerably inferior in flavor. French tarragon is only propagated by root division or from cuttings taken in early summer. Accept no imitations!

2 cups • 475 mL rinsed and dried French tarragon, lightly packed
4 cups • 950 mL white wine vinegar

PLACE the tarragon into a dry, sterilized, wide-mouthed jar. Pour the vinegar over the herbs, making sure they are completely covered.

Cover and steep for 3 to 4 weeks, stirring once or twice a week.

Strain the vinegar through a sieve lined with dampened cheesecloth.

In a nonreactive pot, gently heat the vinegar just to a simmer, then strain it a second time. Cover loosely with cheesecloth and allow the vinegar to cool to room temperature.

Carefully pour the vinegar into clean, dry, sterilized bottles, using a funnel. If you like, add a couple of sprigs of fresh tarragon to each bottle before sealing. Cap or stop the bottles with corks. Seal with wax.

LEFT TO RIGHT» Cranberry Christmas Vinegar (page 206), French Tarragon Vinegar (this page) and Raspberry Vinegar (page 208).

Cranberry Christmas Vinegar

MAKES 1½ TO 2 CUPS (360 TO 475 ML)

In this recipe, the fruit, spices and vinegar are steeped in the bottle. The result is a festive-looking, intriguingly flavored infused vinegar, perfect for Christmas gift-giving. The recipe is for one 12 to 16 oz (360 to 500 mL) bottle of vinegar. Simply multiply to make a larger quantity.

½–¾ cup • 120–180 mL cranberries*

1 tsp • 5 mL whole cloves

one 3-inch (7.5 cm) cinnamon stick

1½–2 cups • 360–475 mL cider vinegar*

6 dried apricots

1 orange, zest only

one 6–8-inch (15–20 cm) sprig fresh mint, rinsed
    and dried

* Use the smaller amounts of cranberries and vinegar for smaller bottles.

FOR each jar soak 1 bamboo skewer in water. Measure the skewers against your bottles—the skewers should be about three-quarters as long as the bottles. Break a little off if necessary.

Rinse the cranberries and pat dry with paper towels.

In a nonreactive pot, combine the cranberries, cloves, cinnamon stick and vinegar and heat gently until just barely simmering. Do not boil. Remove from the heat and let cool completely.

Strain the mixture through a sieve, reserving the vinegar. Place the berries and spices in a clean, dry sterilized bottle. If you are making more than 1 bottle, divide the berries and spices evenly between them.

Carefully thread the apricots onto the skewer. Remember, the apricots have to fit through the opening of the bottle—if they are too big you may need to trim them. Make sure that you don't choose a bottle with a neck that's really narrow—you'll go crazy trying to get the apricots inside.

Place the skewer of apricots, the orange zest and a sprig of mint in the bottle. Using a funnel, pour the vinegar into the bottle, ensuring that all the ingredients are covered. Cap or seal with a cork. Let steep 2 to 3 weeks before using. This vinegar should be used within 3 to 4 months once the bottle has been opened. Remove and discard the fruit and spices as they will mold if exposed to air.

Raspberry Vinegar
MAKES ABOUT 6 CUPS (1.5 L)

This blush-red vinegar is the most popular of all fruit vinegars. Its slightly sweet flavor and divine color make it indispensable for all kinds of recipes.

3–4 lb • 1.4–1.8 kg fresh raspberries, fully ripe
4 cups • 950 mL white wine vinegar

RINSE and sort the raspberries. Pat them dry with paper towels. Place them in a large bowl and crush gently with a potato masher.

In a nonreactive pot, gently heat the vinegar just to a simmer. Remove from the heat and let it cool slightly. Stir in the raspberries. Cover the pot with a clean dish towel and let stand until completely cool.

Transfer the mixture to a clean, dry, sterilized jar. Cover tightly and store in a cool, dark place for about a month.

When the vinegar is ready, pour it into a dampened jelly bag suspended over a bowl and let it drip through overnight. (You can also use a sieve lined with a double thickness of cheesecloth.)

The next day, discard the berries and place the vinegar in a large, non-reactive pot. Quickly bring it to a boil over high heat. Boil for 3 minutes. Remove from the heat. Skim off any foam that may have occurred. Strain the vinegar a second time. Cover loosely with cheesecloth. When the vinegar has cooled, pour it into clean, dry, sterilized bottles. Cap or stop the bottles with a cork. Seal with wax.

Hot Chili Pepper Vinegar

MAKES ABOUT 4 CUPS (950 ML)

I like to find a really gorgeous bottle and pack it full of hot chili peppers. For an even more flavorful vinegar, add a big bushy sprig of rosemary and some juicy cloves of fresh garlic. The peppers can be chopped up and used in cooking, if desired.

3–4 hot chili peppers, preferably red
   (see "Handling Hot Peppers," page 60)
4 cups • 950 mL cider vinegar

USING a paring knife, make 2 or 3 small slits in each pepper. In a nonreactive pot, gently heat the vinegar just to a simmer.

Remove from the heat. Add the peppers and let cool slightly.

Transfer the peppers to clean, dry, sterilized bottles. Using a funnel, pour in the vinegar. Cover loosely and allow the vinegar to cool to room temperature. Cap or stop with a cork. Seal with wax.

ABOUT CHILIES

Chilies originated in Latin America, and are members of the capsicum family. There are a vast variety of chili types—more than 100 varieties in Mexico alone. Chilies differ in size, shape, color and strength; the most commonly available to North Americans are small, thin, green or red chilies from 1 to 4 inches (2.5 to 10 cm) long. As a very general rule of thumb, the smaller, thinner and darker the chili, the more fiery it will be. Fresh green chilies are usually milder than dried ones. Many types of seasonings are made from chilies; among them are chili powder, cayenne pepper, paprika, dried chili flakes and prepared chili sauces. Chilies may be used whole, either fresh or dried, to spice up many types of pickles or chopped fresh into relishes or chutneys. Dried chili flakes are an excellent substitute for fresh chilies.

Spiced Plum Vinegar

MAKES ABOUT 6 CUPS (1.5 L)

This vinegar adds a spicy, fruity tartness to vinaigrette dressings for green salads, fruit salads or sauces for chicken or veal.

3 lb • 1.4 kg plums, any kind

5 cups • 1.2 L red wine vinegar

¼–⅓ cup • 60–80 mL mixed whole spices
   (broken cinnamon sticks, allspice, cloves,
   juniper berries, peppercorns, mustard seeds,
   star anise), tied in a cheesecloth bag

CUT the plums into ½-inch (1.2 cm) pieces, discard the pits and place the plums in a large bowl. Crush with a potato masher.

In a nonreactive pot, gently heat the vinegar and spice bag just to a simmer. Remove from the heat. Let it cool slightly, then stir in the plums. Cover the pot loosely with a clean dish towel and allow to cool completely. Transfer the mixture to a clean, dry, sterilized jar. Cover the jar tightly and store it in a cool, dark place for at least a month. Stir the mixture 3 or 4 times a week.

When the flavor has developed to your satisfaction, transfer the mixture to a dampened jelly bag suspended over a bowl and let it drip through overnight. (You can also use a sieve lined with a double thickness of cheesecloth.)

The next day, discard the plums and place the vinegar in a large nonreactive pot. Quickly bring it to a boil over high heat. Boil for 3 minutes. Remove from the heat. Skim off any foam that may have occurred. Strain the vinegar a second time. Cover loosely with cheesecloth and allow to cool to room temperature. Pour into clean, dry, sterilized bottles. Cap or stop the bottles with a cork. Seal with wax.

Cooking with Preserves

Basic Fruit Vinaigrette 216

Mayonnaise Flavored with Fruit Vinegar 217

Creamy Herb and Garlic Dip or
Salad Dressing 218

Curried Chutney Dip 219

Cucumber and Dill Pickle Dip 220

Fresh Fruit Salsa 221

Guacamole 222

Blackberry, Rosemary and Red Wine
Marinade 223

Gingered Orange Spread 224

Sesame Plum Sauce 225

Tartar Sauce 226

Cumberland Sauce 227

Cheddar Cheese Ball with Port and Dijon
Mustard 228

Baked Brie with Chutney and
Toasted Nuts 229

Prosciutto Asparagus Roll-ups 230

Wonton Crisps with Gorgonzola and Grape
Salsa 231

Little Crab Cakes with Fresh Fruit Salsa 232

Sweet Potato Fries with Feisty Red Pepper
Ketchup 233

Pork Satay with Pineapple 234

Chicken Breasts with Blueberries
and Tarragon 236

Duck Breasts with Blackberry
Cassis Sauce 237

Mexican Chicken Lasagne 238

Old-Fashioned Glazed Baked Ham 240

Marvelous Meat Loaf with Chili Sauce 242

Salmon Fillets with Citrus Beurre Blanc 243

Lamb Chops with Mint Vinaigrette 244

Green Beans Mexicana 245

Baked Banana Squash with Orange
Marmalade 246

Apple Glazed Carrots 247

Sweet and Sour Red Cabbage 248

Rhubarb Ginger Chutney and
Walnut Loaf 249

Applesauce Spice Cake with Cream Cheese
Icing 250

Marmalade Oatmeal Muffins 252

Gingerbread with Spiced Pear Sauce 253

Apricot Coconut Drops 254

Jim Jams 255

Triple Apple Galette 256

Lemon Cheesecake 258

Jam-Filled Buttery Layer Cake 260

Black Forest Trifle 262

Brandied Cherries 265

Raspberry Vinegar Sorbet 266

Cooking with Preserves

When you preserve fruits and vegetables in season you are establishing a well-stocked larder of ready-made condiments fit to embellish any meal, from the simplest to the most elegant.

Preserves can also be used as ingredients in a variety of recipes from appetizers to desserts. They can be the inspiration for exotic sauces and glazes or intriguing salad dressings. Relishes and chutneys can be made into dips; and jams, butters and jellies can turn up in muffins, cookies and cakes. Fruit sauces, preserves and conserves can be indispensable in creating elaborate desserts like cheesecakes, trifles or crêpes.

What follows are some imaginative suggestions to start you thinking about your preserves in a whole new way. Think of them as homemade convenience foods! Once you put your mind to it, you will be bursting with ideas for incorporating them into tried and true recipes or using them to invent new ones.

The word *vinaigrette* is derived from the French word for vinegar—*vinaigre*. Vinaigrettes are simply oil and vinegar dressings. They can be used to dress fresh greens or salads of cold vegetables, grains or fish. Many vinaigrettes make terrific marinades for grilled meats, poultry, fish or vegetables.

Vinaigrettes can be a lifesaver to have on hand in the refrigerator, where they will easily keep for months. You can also make them up fresh in just a few minutes using your own infused vinegars and a good-quality salad oil. Experiment with the proportions of oil and vinegar until you find one that is right for you. Plan on about 2 Tbsp (30 mL) of vinaigrette per serving on salads.

Basic Fruit Vinaigrette

MAKES ABOUT 1½ CUPS (360 ML)

Fruit vinaigrette is delightful on a summer salad of fresh mixed greens, such as endive, spinach, radicchio and red leaf lettuce. Toss in some sliced fresh fruit or berries just before serving. I like to add a little crumbled fresh goat's cheese.

½ cup • 120 mL fruit vinegar of your choice
½ cup • 120 mL olive oil
½ cup • 120 mL canola oil
1 Tbsp • 15 mL sugar
salt and freshly ground black pepper to taste

WHISK all ingredients together in a small bowl. Refrigerate until ready to use. Whisk again before pouring over the salad greens. This will keep for weeks in the refrigerator.

Mayonnaise Flavored with Fruit Vinegar

MAKES ABOUT 2½ CUPS (600 ML)

Fruit-flavored mayonnaise may be used as a dressing for chicken, turkey or fruit salads. Thinned with additional vinegar, it makes a delightful sauce for poached chicken breasts or grilled salmon served cold.

    1 egg
    2 egg yolks
    2 tsp • 10 mL Dijon mustard
    ¼ cup • 60 mL fruit vinegar of your choice
    2 cups • 475 mL canola oil
    salt and freshly ground black pepper to taste

BEAT the egg, egg yolks, mustard and vinegar to combine, using a whisk, food processor or blender.

Gradually add the oil, drop by drop at first, then in a slow, steady stream, beating all the while. Season with salt and pepper.

Creamy Herb and Garlic Dip or Salad Dressing

MAKES ABOUT 1 CUP (240 ML)

Serve this with raw vegetables as a dip or thin with a little milk to use as a salad dressing. You can use a large, hollowed-out red bell pepper to hold the dip. Trim a thin slice from the bottom of the pepper, if necessary, to even it out and make it stand upright.

½ cup • 120 mL mayonnaise

½ cup • 120 mL sour cream or yogurt

2 Tbsp • 30 mL herbal vinegar of your choice

2 Tbsp • 30 mL finely chopped fresh herbs of your choice

½ tsp • 2.5 mL sugar

salt and freshly ground black pepper to taste

WHISK all the ingredients together in a small bowl. Refrigerate for 3 to 4 hours to blend the flavors.

Curried Chutney Dip

MAKES ABOUT 1¼ CUPS (300 ML)

Serve this fast and fabulous dip with sliced unpeeled red apples and pears. Sprinkle the fruit with a little lemon juice to prevent browning. Any kind of chutney may be used; Pineapple and Papaya Chutney (page 168) is especially nice.

1 cup • 240 mL sour cream or yogurt

3 Tbsp • 45 mL chutney (pages 165–180)

2 Tbsp • 30 mL finely chopped candied ginger

2 Tbsp • 30 mL curry powder

COMBINE all the ingredients in a small bowl. Cover and refrigerate for at least 1 hour to blend the flavors. Serve in a small crock or decorative serving dish.

Cucumber and Dill Pickle Dip

MAKES ABOUT 2½ CUPS (600 ML)

Sounds weird, but tastes great! A dandy appetizer dip—
serve it with a rainbow of fresh, crisp vegetables.

1 cup • 240 mL finely diced, peeled cucumbers

2 Simply Good Dill Pickles (page 125), finely
   chopped

¼ cup • 60 mL finely chopped green onions

1 Tbsp • 15 mL red wine herb vinegar, such as
   Scarborough Fair Vinegar (page 203)

½ cup • 120 mL sour cream or yogurt

½ cup • 120 mL mayonnaise

1 Tbsp • 15 mL chopped fresh dill (optional)

DISCARD the cucumber seeds if the cucumber is especially seedy; if you're using
English cucumbers, don't worry about it.

Mix all the ingredients together until well combined. Transfer into a small
decorative serving dish. Refrigerate at least 1 hour to blend the flavors.

Fresh Fruit Salsa

MAKES ABOUT 3 CUPS (720 ML)

You can make a quick, fresh fruit salsa using homemade tomato salsa as a base. The contrasting flavors and textures of fruit salsa complement fried foods, like crab cakes, as well as grilled or barbecued meats or fish.

3 cups • 720 mL peeled, finely chopped fruit
(such as apples, pears, papaya, mangos,
peaches or pineapple)

½–⅔ cup • 120–160 mL Salsa Fiesta! (page 148)

½ lime, juice only

¼ cup • 60 mL finely chopped coriander

STIR all the ingredients together in a large mixing bowl. Cover and let stand at room temperature for at least half an hour before serving.

Guacamole

MAKES ABOUT 3 CUPS (720 ML)

Serve with salsa as a dip for tortilla chips or alongside any Mexican food.

4 large avocados, peeled and pitted

½ lime or small lemon, juice only

½ cup • 120 mL finely chopped green
   bell peppers

½ cup • 120 mL finely chopped onion

½ cup • 120 mL finely chopped tomatoes

¼ cup • 60 mL finely chopped celery

¼ cup • 60 mL finely chopped fresh coriander

3 cloves garlic, minced

3 Tbsp • 45 mL Salsa Fiesta! (page 148)

½ tsp • 2.5 mL salt

¼ tsp • 1.2 mL freshly ground black pepper, or
   to taste

MASH the avocados with a potato masher and squeeze the lime or lemon juice overtop. Add the remaining ingredients and mix well. Transfer the guacamole to a serving dish. Cover with plastic wrap, pressing the plastic onto the surface of the guacamole. Refrigerate for at least 30 minutes before serving.

Blackberry, Rosemary and Red Wine Marinade

MAKES ABOUT 1 CUP (240 ML)

Absolutely fabulous with lamb. If you have fresh rosemary on hand, you can use a sprig as a brush to baste the meat while it is grilling.

- ½ cup • 120 mL Blackberry Jam (page 22)
- ¼ cup • 60 mL red wine rosemary vinegar (pages 197–199)
- ¼ cup • 60 mL red wine
- 2 Tbsp • 30 mL grainy Dijon mustard
- 2 Tbsp • 30 mL finely chopped fresh rosemary

SIEVE the blackberry jam to remove the seeds. In a small bowl, combine the jam with the remaining ingredients. Place lamb chops, kebabs or whatever you wish to marinate in a shallow pan and pour two-thirds of the marinade overtop. Cover and refrigerate for at least 2 to 3 hours, or overnight. Use the reserved marinade to baste the meat during grilling.

Gingered Orange Spread

MAKES ABOUT 1¼ CUPS (300 ML)

Perfect with Marmalade Oatmeal Muffins (page 252),
English muffins or just plain toast.

1 cup • 240 mL cream cheese, softened

3 Tbsp • 45 mL Traditional English Marmalade
(page 65) or Orange Marmalade (page 66)

2 Tbsp • 30 mL orange juice

2 tsp • 10 mL honey

2 tsp • 10 mL chopped candied ginger
OR ½ tsp • 2.5 mL ground ginger

1 tsp • 5 mL finely grated orange zest

BLEND all the ingredients in a food processor for 1 minute. Place in a small crock
or decorative serving dish. Chill until ready to use. Serve at room temperature.

Sesame Plum Sauce

MAKES ABOUT 1¼ CUPS (300 ML)

A delightful balance of sweet, sour and spice. Keep on hand to use as a glaze for chicken, duck or pork. Serve slightly warmed as a dipping sauce for meatballs, samosas, wontons or spring rolls.

one 8 oz (250 mL) jar Plum Jam (page 36)

2 Tbsp • 30 mL soy sauce

2 Tbsp • 30 mL lime juice

1 Tbsp • 15 mL chili paste (see sidebar)

1 tsp • 5 mL minced fresh ginger

½ tsp • 2.5 mL sesame oil

IN a small saucepan, combine all ingredients. Heat gently over medium low heat until just bubbling. Remove from the heat and use as desired.

CHILI PASTE, also known as *Sambal Oelek*, is a mixture of hot chilies and vinegar. It is available in the Asian section of most supermarkets.

Tartar Sauce

MAKES ABOUT 1½ CUPS (360 ML)

Tartar sauce is a cinch to make with store-bought mayonnaise and your own homemade relish. It will keep for several weeks in the refrigerator.

1 cup • 240 mL mayonnaise

3 Tbsp • 45 mL Pepper Relish (page 158)

2 Tbsp • 30 mL finely chopped onion

1 Tbsp • 15 mL finely chopped parsley

1 Tbsp • 15 mL finely chopped capers

1 Tbsp • 15 mL finely chopped fresh tarragon
     or ½ tsp (2.5 mL) dried

IN a small bowl, combine all of the ingredients and mix well. Chill for at least 1 hour to blend the flavors. Serve with grilled or fried fish or shellfish.

Cumberland Sauce

MAKES ABOUT 1½ CUPS (360 ML)

Named for a county in England famous for hunting,
Cumberland Sauce is a sweet cold sauce for game. Made
with red currant jelly, port, orange juice and other good
things, it is a natural with venison, goose or duck.

½ cup • 120 mL ruby port

½ cup • 120 mL orange juice

¼ cup • 60 mL lemon juice

1 shallot, minced

1 cup • 240 mL Red Currant Jelly (page 55)

2 tsp • 10 mL finely grated orange zest

1 tsp • 5 mL finely grated lemon zest

¼ tsp • 1.2 mL cayenne pepper

¼ tsp • 1.2 mL ground ginger

IN a small pot, combine the port, orange juice and lemon juice. Bring to a
boil over medium heat and simmer until reduced by half. Stir in the remaining ingredients and cook for another 15 minutes, until the mixture is slightly
thickened. Remove from the heat. Let stand until cool, then refrigerate.
Serve chilled.

Cumberland Sauce will keep for months in the refrigerator.

Cheddar Cheese Ball with Port and Dijon Mustard

SERVES 12 TO 16 AS AN APPETIZER

A terrific make-ahead or take-along appetizer for a party. Serve with your favorite chutney and crackers. Curried Apple Chutney (page 178) is highly recommended.

> two 8 oz (225 g) packages cream cheese, softened
> 3 cups • 720 mL shredded aged Cheddar cheese
> ¼ cup • 60 mL port
> 3 Tbsp • 45 mL very finely minced onion
> 1 Tbsp • 15 mL Dijon mustard
> ½ tsp • 2.5 mL paprika
> parsley or chopped toasted walnuts or pecans

USING a food processor, combine all the ingredients, except the nuts or parsley, until smooth. Refrigerate the mixture until it is firm enough to handle, about 1 hour. Shape into a ball. Wrap in plastic wrap and refrigerate at least 1 hour, or until ready to serve.

Remove from the refrigerator about 30 minutes before serving. Roll the ball in the chopped nuts or parsley to coat it. Place the cheese ball in the center of a platter and surround it with crackers. Pass the chutney.

Baked Brie with Chutney and Toasted Nuts

SERVES 6 TO 8 AS AN APPETIZER

An irresistible appetizer. Serve it with crackers, crusty bread, bagel chips or slices of red apples and green pears that have been tossed with lemon juice to prevent browning. You can use any chutney that you have on hand. Mango Chutney (page 165) and Pear Chutney (page 166) are favorites.

one 4–5-inch (10–12.5 cm) wheel Brie cheese

½ cup • 120 mL chutney (pages 165–180)

½ cup • 120 mL coarsely chopped hazelnuts, walnuts or almonds

PREHEAT the oven to 350°F (175°C). Unwrap the cheese and place it in a shallow, ovenproof dish. Bake the cheese for about 10 minutes. Spoon the chutney over the cheese, sprinkle with the nuts and bake for another 10 minutes, until the cheese is heated through but not melted open. Remove from the oven and serve immediately.

Prosciutto Asparagus Roll-ups

MAKES 24

Be sure to use top quality prosciutto, sliced very thinly.
If you like, you can substitute a jar of Striped Pickled
Peppers (page 128) for the asparagus.

12 slices prosciutto

½ cup • 120 mL goat cheese or Boursin

1 quart (1 L) jar Pickled Asparagus, well drained
   (page 130)

SEPARATE the prosciutto slices. Cut each slice in half crosswise, to make approximately 4-inch (10 cm) sections. Carefully spread each half slice of prosciutto with a thin layer of cheese, about ½ tsp (2.5 mL).

Pat the asparagus dry with paper towels. Select 12 spears of fairly uniform thickness and cut them in half. If you prefer to use only asparagus tips, you may have to open another jar, but in that case, save the ends for snacking.

Tightly wrap the prosciutto around each asparagus spear. Repeat until the prosciutto is all used. Small wooden picks may be used to secure the rolls, but are usually not necessary.

Wonton Crisps with Gorgonzola and Grape Salsa

MAKES 48

This lively combination of robust Gorgonzola, tangy salsa and crunchy pecans may inspire gluttony!

1 Tbsp • 15 mL vegetable oil

twelve 3-inch (7.5 cm) square wonton wrappers

4 oz • 113 g Gorgonzola cheese, softened

4 oz • 113 g cream cheese, softened

1 green onion, minced

freshly ground black pepper

1 cup • 240 mL Pickled Grapes with Tarragon (page 139), drained

½ cup • 120 mL Grape Pecan Conserve (page 80)

½ cup • 120 mL pecans, toasted and coarsely chopped

PREHEAT the oven to 350°F (175°C).

Lightly brush a baking sheet with the oil. Cut the wonton wrappers into quarters. Arrange on the baking sheet. Bake 8 to 10 minutes until golden brown.

In a small bowl, break up the Gorgonzola. Add the cream cheese, onion and pepper. Mix together until thoroughly combined. In a separate bowl, stir together the grape halves, conserve and pecans.

To assemble, spoon ½ tsp (2.5 mL) of the cheese mixture on each wonton crisp. Top with a spoonful of the grape mixture.

Little Crab Cakes with Fresh Fruit Salsa

MAKES 20

Crab cakes are usually the first things to be devoured on an appetizer tray! These oven-baked bites are much easier to prepare than the typical fried version.

1 lb • 454 g crab meat

¼ cup • 60 mL mayonnaise

¼ cup • 60 mL dry breadcrumbs

1 egg

1 Tbsp • 15 mL Dijon mustard

½ bunch green onions, minced

1 Tbsp • 15 mL chopped fresh coriander

2 tsp • 10 mL minced fresh ginger

¼ tsp • 1.2 mL hot pepper sauce

¼ tsp • 1.2 mL salt

¼ tsp • 1.2 mL freshly ground black pepper

Fresh Fruit Salsa (page 221)

PREHEAT the oven to 350°F (175°C).

Spread the crab meat on a baking sheet and examine closely for shell fragments. In a medium bowl, combine the crab meat with the remaining ingredients except the salsa and mix thoroughly.

Divide the crab mixture into 20 portions and shape into little cakes. Place the cakes on a parchment lined baking sheet and bake 10 to 15 minutes or until golden brown.

Serve with Fresh Fruit Salsa.

Sweet Potato Fries with Feisty Red Pepper Ketchup

MAKES ABOUT 50 FRIES

Chinese 5-spice powder is a ready-made blend of cinnamon, cloves, fennel, anise and black pepper. It is available in Asian markets and many regular grocery stores.

    1½ lb • 680 g sweet potatoes
    2 Tbsp • 30 mL olive oil
    ¼ tsp • 1.2 mL Chinese 5-spice powder
    ½ tsp • 2.5 mL coarse salt
    ¼ tsp • 1.2 mL red pepper flakes

PREHEAT the oven 400°F (200°C).

Peel the sweet potatoes and cut them into 3-inch (7.5 cm) lengths, about ½ inch (1.2 cm) thick.

In a large bowl, toss the sweet potatoes with the remaining ingredients. Place on a foil lined baking sheet, and bake until tender, about 20 to 25 minutes.

Serve immediately with Feisty Red Pepper Ketchup (page 191).

Pork Satay with Pineapple

SERVES 4 TO 6

Satays are spicy Indonesian bite-size pieces of meat cooked on bamboo skewers. They make wonderful appetizers or main courses for entertaining because they can be made ahead of time and then grilled just prior to serving.

1¼ lb • 565 g boneless pork loin

1 small onion, finely chopped

2 cloves garlic, minced

¼ cup • 60 mL soy sauce

2 Tbsp • 30 mL Pineapple and Papaya Chutney (page 168)

2 Tbsp • 30 mL Hot Chili Pepper Vinegar (page 209)

2 Tbsp • 30 mL demerara sugar

1 tsp • 5 mL ground cumin

1 tsp • 5 mL ground coriander

1 tsp • 5 mL turmeric

finely grated zest of ½ lemon

one 8 oz (227 mL) can pineapple chunks, drained

Sauce

¾ cup • 180 mL canned coconut milk

⅓ cup • 80 mL crunchy peanut butter

¼ cup • 60 mL Pineapple and Papaya Chutney (page 168), puréed in blender until smooth

1 Tbsp • 15 mL soy sauce

2 cloves garlic, minced

TRIM any fat from the pork and cut into 1-inch (2.5 cm) cubes. Place the meat in a large bowl. Using a food processor or blender, combine the onion, garlic, soy sauce, chutney, vinegar, sugar, cumin, coriander, turmeric and lemon zest. Mix well. Add to the cubed pork, tossing thoroughly. Cover and refrigerate for 30 minutes.

Meanwhile, make the sauce. In a small saucepan, whisk together the coconut milk and peanut butter. Stir in the remaining ingredients. Cook gently over medium-low heat, stirring until the mixture is smooth and heated through. Cover and keep warm.

Preheat the barbecue to medium-high. Thread the pork cubes onto bamboo skewers* alternately with pineapple chunks. Barbecue 8 to 10 minutes, turning occasionally. To serve as an appetizer, pile satays onto a serving platter. Place a small bowl of sauce on the side for dipping. To serve as a main course, place several satays on a bed of rice and spoon sauce overtop.

* Soak the skewers for at least 20 minutes prior to use to prevent scorching.

Chicken Breasts with Blueberries and Tarragon

SERVES 4 TO 6

Serve with buttered noodles or a mixture of brown and white rice. Crisp green asparagus or snow peas make a lovely accompaniment.

2 Tbsp • 30 mL each olive oil and butter

2 boneless skinless chicken breasts, halved

salt and freshly ground black pepper to taste

¼ cup • 60 mL flour

½ cup • 120 mL red wine

¼ cup • 60 mL French Tarragon Vinegar (page 204)

⅔ cup • 160 mL chicken stock

3 Tbsp • 45 mL finely chopped fresh tarragon

½ cup • 120 mL Blueberry Chutney (page 170)

⅔ cup • 160 mL cream

1 egg yolk

⅔ cup • 160 mL fresh blueberries

fresh tarragon sprigs

PREHEAT the oven to 350°F (175°C).

In a large frying pan, heat the olive oil and butter until sizzling. Season the chicken with salt and pepper and cook for 2 to 3 minutes on each side to seal in the juices. Transfer the chicken to a greased, ovenproof casserole dish with a lid.

Stir the flour into the pan, scraping up any browned bits. Whisk in the wine, vinegar and chicken stock and bring to a boil. Stir in the tarragon and chutney. Pour the sauce over the chicken. Cover and bake for 30 to 40 minutes.

In a small bowl, whisk the cream and egg yolk together. Remove the casserole from the oven. Remove the chicken and set aside. Pour off about ½ cup (120 mL) liquid and add it to the egg mixture. Mix well, then pour this back into the casserole dish. Replace the chicken and add about ½ cup (120 mL) of the blueberries, reserving the rest for garnish. Cover and cook for another 10 to 15 minutes. Garnish with the remaining blueberries and the tarragon.

Duck Breasts with Blackberry Cassis Sauce

SERVES 4

An impressive way to enjoy blackberries as an accompaniment to a main-course dish. The rich flavor of the duck is nicely balanced by the tartness of the berries.

  4 duck breasts
  olive oil
  salt and freshly ground black pepper to taste
  1 recipe Blackberry Cassis Sauce

LIGHTLY brush the duck breasts with a little olive oil. Season with salt and pepper. Grill for 8 to 10 minutes on both sides. Remove to a serving plate. Spoon the warm Blackberry Cassis Sauce over the duck and serve immediately.

Blackberry Cassis Sauce

Prepare the sauce before you grill the duck, and keep it warm.

  1 cup • 240 mL Blackberry and Apple Chutney
    (page 179)
  ½ cup • 120 mL dry red wine
  2 cups • 475 mL beef broth
  ¼–½ cup • 60–120 mL crème de cassis liqueur
  2 Tbsp • 30 mL butter
  1 cup • 240 mL fresh blackberries

COMBINE the chutney, red wine and beef broth. Bring to a boil over medium heat. Reduce the heat to medium-low and simmer gently until the mixture is reduced by half, stirring occasionally. Add the crème de cassis to taste. Just prior to serving, whisk in the butter and add the blackberries.

Mexican Chicken Lasagne

SERVES 8 TO 10

Coriander, also known as cilantro, is a herb that you either love or hate. If you're not a fan, you can substitute chopped fresh parsley instead.

12 lasagne noodles

2 Tbsp • 30 mL olive oil

1 onion, finely chopped

1 red pepper, finely chopped

2 cloves garlic, minced

one 16 oz (500 mL) jar Salsa Fiesta! (page 148)

1 cup • 240 mL tomato sauce

1 tsp • 5 mL chili powder

1 tsp • 5 mL ground cumin

½ tsp • 2.5 mL salt

freshly ground pepper

2 eggs

1 lb • 454 g ricotta cheese, drained, if necessary

½ cup • 120 mL coarsely chopped fresh
     coriander

1 jalapeño pepper, seeded and finely chopped

1½ cups • 360 mL grated Mozzarella cheese

1½ cups • 360 mL grated Monterey Jack
     cheese

4 cups • 950 g diced, cooked chicken breast

IN a large pot of boiling, salted water, cook the lasagne noodles until *al dente* (tender but firm to the bite), about 10 minutes. Drain the noodles, rinse and set aside.

Meanwhile, in a large frying pan, heat the olive oil over medium heat. Add the onions, red pepper and garlic, and cook about 10 minutes, until the onions are soft. Stir in the salsa, tomato sauce, chili powder, cumin, and salt and pepper. Bring the mixture to a boil, then reduce the heat and simmer, covered, for about 10 minutes.

In a large bowl, using an electric mixer, beat the eggs, then mix in the ricotta, coriander and jalapeño.

In a separate bowl, combine the Mozzarella and Monterey Jack cheeses.

Preheat the oven to 375°F (190°C). Spray a 13- × 9-inch (33 × 23 cm) pan with vegetable oil cooking spray.

Spread about ⅔ cup (160 mL) of sauce over the bottom of the pan. Completely cover the sauce with a layer of lasagne noodles. Cover the noodles with another layer of sauce, then spoon on about half of the ricotta mixture, then half of the chicken cubes. Over that, sprinkle half of the cheese mixture. Add another layer of noodles and repeat layering, ending with the remaining cheese.

Bake 45 minutes to 1 hour, until golden brown and bubbling around the edges.

Old-Fashioned Glazed Baked Ham

SERVES 8 TO 10

These days most hams we buy at the grocery store are
fully cooked and ready to serve. They are available either
boneless or bone-in.

    one 5 lb (2.25 kg) bone-in ham

    1 recipe Jelly Glaze, Marmalade Glaze or

        Cranberry, Orange and Port Glaze (recipes on

        facing page)

PREHEAT the oven to 350°F (175°C).

    Remove the rind from the outside of the ham and trim the fat if necessary,
leaving about a ¼-inch (6 mm) layer to protect the meat. Score the fat in a diamond pattern, cutting only about ¼-inch (6 mm) deep.

    Place the ham, fat side up, on a wire rack in a shallow roasting pan. Bake
the ham for 1 hour at 350°F (175°C). Remove from the oven. Increase the heat
to 400°F (200°C). Spoon your choice of glaze over the ham. If desired, insert
a whole clove in the center of each diamond. Bake another 15 to 20 minutes,
basting often.

Jelly Glaze

IN a small saucepan, heat 1 cup (240 mL) Red Currant Jelly (page 55) or Basic Apple Jelly (page 44) until melted.

Marmalade Glaze

- 1 cup • 240 mL Traditional English Marmalade (page 65), Orange Marmalade (page 66), or Amber Marmalade (page 70)
- ¼ cup • 60 mL orange juice
- ¼ cup • 60 mL brown sugar

MIX all ingredients together.

Cranberry, Orange and Port Glaze

- ¾ cup • 180 mL Cranberry, Orange and Apricot Chutney (page 172)
- ½ cup • 120 mL brown sugar
- ¼ cup • 60 mL port

USING a food processor or blender, purée the chutney until smooth. Blend in the sugar and port.

Marvelous Meat Loaf with Chili Sauce

SERVES 6 TO 8

A hearty mixture of ground beef, pork and vegetables spiked with your own homemade Chili Sauce. Not like Mom used to make!

1 cup • 240 mL milk

2 cups • 475 mL soft breadcrumbs

1 lb • 454 g each ground beef and ground pork

½ cup • 120 mL finely chopped onion

½ cup • 120 mL grated carrot

¼ cup • 60 mL chopped parsley

1 cup • 240 mL Country Style Chili Sauce
(page 186), divided

2 eggs, well beaten

2 Tbsp • 30 mL prepared creamed horseradish
or Dijon mustard

2 tsp • 10 mL salt

½ tsp • 2.5 mL freshly ground black pepper

PREHEAT the oven to 350°F (175°C).

Combine the milk and breadcrumbs in a large bowl. Let stand for 5 minutes. Add the remaining ingredients, reserving ½ cup (120 mL) of the chili sauce. Mix thoroughly. Shape the mixture into a loaf and place on a lightly greased baking sheet. Spread the remaining ½ cup (120 mL) chili sauce over the top of the meat loaf. Bake for 1 hour.

Salmon Fillets with Citrus Beurre Blanc

SERVES 4

Serve this salmon with rice that has been cooked in chicken broth and orange juice (half and half) instead of water.

½ grapefruit

½ cup • 120 mL dry white wine

½ cup • 120 mL citrus vinegar (pages 199–200)

1 Tbsp • 15 mL finely chopped onion

1 Tbsp • 15 mL heavy cream

1 cup • 240 mL butter, softened

1 Tbsp • 15 mL finely chopped fresh
    lemon balm leaves

2 Tbsp • 30 mL olive oil

four 6–7 oz (175–200 g) salmon fillets

salt and freshly ground pepper

REMOVE the pulp from the grapefruit, working over a small bowl to catch the juice. Discard the seeds. Purée the pulp in a blender or food processor.

In a small saucepan, combine the wine, vinegar and onion, and bring to a boil over medium heat. Reduce the heat to low and simmer gently until the mixture is syrupy and the liquid is almost all evaporated. Whisk in the cream. Whisk in the butter, ½ cup (120 mL) at a time. Do not allow the mixture to boil. Stir in the grapefruit purée and lemon balm. Keep warm.

In a large heavy frying pan, heat the olive oil over medium-high heat until very hot.

Season the salmon with salt and pepper. Place the salmon in the pan and cook 3 to 5 minutes on each side or until the salmon is opaque and flakes easily when tested with the tip of a sharp knife.

Transfer the salmon to warmed serving plates and pour the sauce over it.

Lamb Chops with Mint Vinaigrette

SERVES 4

Lamb and mint are an irresistible combination. This delectable sauce gives a special touch to easy-to-prepare lamb chops.

3 Tbsp • 45 mL mint vinegar (pages 197–199)

1 Tbsp • 15 mL Apple Mint Jelly (page 46), melted

1 tsp • 5 mL honey

1 clove garlic, minced

¼ cup • 60 mL olive oil

½ cup • 120 mL fresh mint leaves, finely chopped

1 tomato, seeded and finely chopped

salt and freshly ground black pepper, more for seasoning lamb

8 lamb loin chops

IN a small bowl, whisk together the vinegar, jelly, honey and garlic. Slowly whisk in the olive oil, then add the tomatoes and mint. Season with salt and pepper. Set aside.

Trim any excess fat from the lamb chops. Heat a heavy, nonstick frying pan over high heat for about 2 minutes. Season the lamb on both sides with pepper, then place in the hot pan. Reduce the heat to medium and cook for 3 minutes on each side for medium rare, 1 to 2 minutes more for medium. Remove the chops from the pan and keep warm.

Add the vinaigrette to the juices that are left in the pan. Heat gently for about 2 minutes, then spoon over the lamb chops to serve.

Green Beans Mexicana

SERVES 8

This versatile dish is equally good hot, cold or at room temperature.

2 lb • 900 g green beans, trimmed

2 Tbsp • 30 mL olive oil

1 cup • 240 mL Salsa Fiesta! (page 148)

salt and freshly ground black pepper to taste

fresh lemon juice

1 Tbsp • 15 mL finely chopped fresh coriander

BRING a large pot of water to a boil and blanch the beans for 3 to 4 minutes. Do not overcook—they must be very crisp. Drain the beans in a colander, then plunge them into ice water to cool quickly. Drain again and blot them dry with paper towels.

Heat the olive oil in a large frying pan over high heat until it sizzles. Add the salsa and stir until hot, about 2 minutes. Add the beans and cook for about 5 minutes, until the beans are hot but still crisp. Season with salt and pepper. Squeeze a little lemon juice over (just a quick squeeze!). Transfer the beans to a serving platter and sprinkle with chopped coriander.

Baked Banana Squash with Orange Marmalade

SERVES 4 TO 6

The tartness of the marmalade and the sweetness of the maple syrup give a wonderful complex flavor to the humble squash.

3 lb • 1.4 kg banana squash

salt and freshly ground black pepper to taste

¼ cup • 60 mL Orange Marmalade (page 66)

¼ cup • 60 mL maple syrup

PREHEAT the oven to 350°F (175°C).

Cut the squash into serving-size pieces and put it in an ungreased baking dish. Sprinkle with a little salt and pepper. Pour water into the dish to a depth of about ¼ inch (6 mm). Cover the dish with foil and bake for about 30 minutes until the squash is tender.

Stir the marmalade and maple syrup together over medium-low heat until melted.

Remove the squash from the oven and drain. Spoon the marmalade-syrup mixture over the squash and bake for another 10 to 15 minutes.

Apple Glazed Carrots

SERVES 4

This is an easy dish to prepare when you are cooking a
big dinner and don't have time to babysit your vegetables.
It can easily be doubled or tripled.

2 cups • 475 mL peeled, sliced carrots

¼ cup • 60 mL Apple Butter (page 110) or
Honeyed Applesauce (page 98)

3 Tbsp • 45 mL brown sugar

2 Tbsp • 30 mL butter

PREHEAT the oven to 350°F (175°C).

Cook the carrots in boiling water until just tender. Drain and set aside.

In the same saucepan, heat the apple butter or applesauce, brown sugar and
butter together until the sugar dissolves, about 5 minutes.

Place the carrots in a greased, shallow baking dish. Pour the apple mixture
over the carrots. Bake for 15 minutes.

Sweet and Sour Red Cabbage

SERVES 6 TO 8

A robust, colorful accompaniment to serve with roast
pork or poultry.

1 large red cabbage, about 1½–2 lb (680–900 g)

3 Tbsp • 45 mL butter

2 onions, finely chopped

3 unpeeled apples, diced

¼ cup • 60 mL apple juice

¼ cup • 60 mL Spiced Plum Vinegar (page 210)
   or Raspberry Vinegar (page 208)

¼ cup • 60 mL Red Currant Jelly (page 55)

2 Tbsp • 30 mL brown sugar

¼ tsp • 1.2 mL cinnamon

salt and freshly ground pepper

TO prepare the cabbage, discard the tough outer leaves, then quarter, core and
cut the cabbage into thin slices. In a large, heavy pot, melt the butter, add the
onions and cook over medium heat until the onions are soft, about 10 minutes.
Stir in the cabbage, cover and cook 5 to 10 minutes, until the cabbage is somewhat wilted.

Add the apples, apple juice, vinegar, jelly, sugar and cinnamon. Stir well.

Cover the pot and cook for 10 to 15 minutes, until the cabbage is tender.
Season with salt and pepper to taste.

Rhubarb Ginger Chutney and Walnut Loaf

MAKES 1 LOAF

A favorite for breakfast, at teatime or even as a simple dessert, this is terrific toasted.

2¼ cups • 535 mL flour

1 Tbsp • 15 mL baking powder

½ tsp • 2.5 mL salt

½ tsp • 2.5 mL cinnamon

1 cup • 240 mL chopped walnuts

3 Tbsp • 45 mL butter, softened

½ cup • 120 mL honey

3 eggs

1 cup • 240 mL Rhubarb and Ginger Chutney
(page 180)

PREHEAT the oven to 350°F (175°C). Grease a 9- × 5- × 3-inch (23 × 13 × 7.5 cm) loaf pan.

In a small bowl, mix together the flour, baking powder, salt, cinnamon and walnuts. Set aside.

In a large bowl, cream the butter and honey until smooth. Beat in the eggs, one at a time. Stir in the chutney. Add the dry ingredients, stirring just until blended.

Turn into the prepared pan. Bake for 50 to 60 minutes. When done, the bread should be quite moist-looking, but will not be wet in the center. Cool on a rack. This bread is at its best when it is sliced and served the next day.

Applesauce Spice Cake with Cream Cheese Icing

MAKES A 13- × 9-INCH (33 × 23 CM) CAKE

This old-fashioned favorite was adapted from a family recipe. Instead of the frosting you can simply dust the cake with icing sugar, or leave it plain.

2½ cups • 600 mL flour

2 cups • 475 mL sugar

1½ tsp • 7.5 mL baking soda

1 tsp • 5 mL salt

½ tsp • 2.5 mL baking powder

1 tsp • 5 mL cinnamon

½ tsp • 2.5 mL each ground cloves, nutmeg, ginger and cardamom

2 eggs

1½ cups • 360 mL Honeyed Applesauce (page 98)

½ cup • 120 mL water

½ cup • 120 mL shortening

1 recipe Cream Cheese Icing (facing page)

PREHEAT the oven to 350°F (175°C). Grease and flour one 13- × 9- × 2-inch (33 × 23 × 5 cm) oblong pan.

In a large mixing bowl, combine all the ingredients. Using an electric mixer, beat at low speed for about 1 minute, scraping the sides of the bowl often. Beat another 2 minutes at high speed, scraping the bowl occasionally.

Scrape the batter into the pan, spreading it evenly. Bake about 1 hour, or until a toothpick inserted in the center of the cake comes out clean. Cool on a rack. When it is completely cool, frost with Cream Cheese Icing.

Cream Cheese Icing

    1 cup • 240 mL cream cheese, softened

    ½ cup • 120 mL icing sugar

    1 Tbsp • 15 mL orange juice

    2 tsp • 10 mL finely grated orange zest

IN a small bowl, beat the cream cheese with an electric mixer on low speed. Gradually blend in the icing sugar with the orange juice and zest.

Marmalade Oatmeal Muffins

MAKES 16 TO 18 MUFFINS

Serve with Gingered Orange Spread (page 224). These
are best served warm.

2 cups • 475 mL old-fashioned rolled oats

2 cups • 475 mL whole wheat flour

5 tsp • 25 mL baking powder

1 tsp • 5 mL salt

1 cup • 240 mL golden raisins

½ cup • 120 mL chopped walnuts

2 eggs

¾ cup • 180 mL Traditional English Marmalade
(page 65), Orange Marmalade (page 66) or
Amber Marmalade (page 70)

½ cup • 120 mL orange juice

½ cup • 120 mL vegetable oil

1 cup • 240 mL milk

2 tsp • 10 mL finely grated orange zest

PREHEAT the oven to 400°F (200°C). Grease the muffin tins.

In a large mixing bowl, stir together the rolled oats, flour, baking powder,
salt, raisins and walnuts.

In a smaller bowl, beat the eggs lightly, then beat in the remaining ingredients. Make a well in the center of the dry ingredients. Pour in the egg mixture,
stirring only enough to moisten the dry ingredients.

Spoon the batter into the greased muffin tins, filling them about two-thirds
full. Bake for 20 to 25 minutes.

Gingerbread with Spiced Pear Sauce

SERVES 6 TO 8

If you don't have sour milk or buttermilk on hand, you
can make your own by adding 2 tsp (10 mL) lemon juice
to regular milk.

½ cup • 120 mL shortening

½ cup • 120 mL brown sugar

1 egg

1 cup • 240 mL molasses

2¼ cups • 535 mL flour

1 tsp • 5 mL baking soda

1½ tsp • 7.5 mL ground ginger

1 tsp • 5 mL cinnamon

½ tsp • 2.5 mL ground cloves

½ tsp • 2.5 mL salt

¾ cup • 180 mL sour milk or buttermilk

¼ cup • 60 mL finely chopped candied ginger

2 Tbsp • 30 mL lemon juice

Spiced Pear Sauce (page 102)

PREHEAT the oven to 350°F (175°C). Grease and flour a 9-inch (23 cm) square pan.

In a large mixing bowl, using an electric mixer, cream the shortening and
brown sugar. Blend in the egg and molasses, beating until light and fluffy, about
3 minutes.

In a separate bowl, sift together the flour, soda, spices and salt. Add the dry
ingredients to the creamed mixture alternately with the sour milk. Make 3 dry
and 2 milk additions, combining lightly after each. Start and finish with the
dry ingredients. Stir in the chopped ginger. Pour the batter into the pan.

Bake 45 to 50 minutes, or until the cake springs back when touched lightly
at the center. Cool in the pan for about 5 minutes. Cut into squares.

Serve the gingerbread while still warm with a large spoonful of Spiced Pear
Sauce and a dollop of whipped or ice cream.

Apricot Coconut Drops

MAKES ABOUT 36 COOKIES

These cookies are quick and easy to make. Check the cookies while baking to ensure that they are not getting overdone on the bottom, especially if you're using a dark-colored cookie sheet.

½ cup • 120 mL cream cheese, softened

½ cup • 120 mL butter, softened

¼ cup • 60 mL sugar

½ cup • 120 mL Apricot Jam (page 28)

¼ tsp • 1.2 mL almond extract

1½ cups • 360 mL flour

1½ tsp • 7.5 mL baking powder

¼ tsp • 1.2 mL salt

½ cup • 120 mL flaked coconut

PREHEAT the oven to 350°F (175°C).

In a large bowl, beat the cream cheese, butter and sugar with an electric mixer until combined. Mix in the jam and almond extract. Stir in the remaining ingredients until well mixed.

Using a teaspoon, drop small spoonfuls of the dough onto a cookie sheet, spacing them 2 inches (5 cm) apart.

Bake for 15 to 20 minutes until lightly browned. Remove from the cookie sheet and cool on wire racks.

Jim Jams

Use any flavor of jam, marmalade or conserve to make
this cookie. Just be sure to choose one that is rather thick.

1 cup • 240 mL jam of your choice

½ cup • 120 mL raisins, chopped

½ cup • 120 mL chopped pecans

1 cup • 240 mL butter

1 cup • 240 mL brown sugar

2 eggs

2 cups • 475 mL flour

2 tsp • 10 mL baking powder

½ tsp • 2.5 mL salt

1 tsp • 5 mL cinnamon

½ tsp • 2.5 mL ground cloves

½ cup • 120 mL milk

2 cups • 475 mL oatmeal

PREHEAT the oven to 350°F (175°C).

Mix together the jam, raisins and pecans. Set aside.

In a large bowl, cream the butter and sugar until fluffy. Beat in the eggs.

In a third bowl, combine the flour, baking powder, salt, cinnamon and
cloves. Add the dry mixture alternately with the milk to the creamed mixture.
Stir in the oatmeal.

Reserve about ¾ cup (180 mL) of the dough.

Drop the remainder of the dough by teaspoonfuls onto a greased cookie
sheet, spacing them about 2 inches (5 cm) apart. Make an indentation in the
center of each cookie, spoon in a little of the jam mixture, then place a dab
of reserved dough on top.

Bake for 10 to 15 minutes. Remove from the cookie sheet and cool on
wire racks.

Triple Apple Galette

SERVES 10 TO 12

A rustic French apple tart, this galette may be served
warm or chilled. Calvados is a French apple brandy.
Another brandy may be substituted, or it may be omitted
altogether.

Pastry

2 cups • 475 mL flour

2 Tbsp • 30 mL sugar

½ tsp • 2.5 mL salt

⅓ cup • 80 mL butter, chilled

⅓ cup • 80 mL shortening, chilled

1 egg yolk

¼ cup • 60 mL ice water (approximately)

IN a large bowl, combine the flour, sugar and salt. Using a pastry blender or
2 knives, cut in the butter and shortening until the mixture resembles fine
crumbs.

In a separate bowl, beat the egg yolk with a fork. Add just enough ice water
to make ½ cup (120 mL) of liquid. Gradually add the liquid to the flour mixture,
adding just enough to result in a dough that can be gathered into a ball. Scrape
the dough from the bowl, flatten the ball slightly, wrap in plastic and chill for
at least 30 minutes. Remove the dough from the refrigerator and let stand for
about 15 minutes before rolling.

Meanwhile, gather the ingredients for the topping.

Topping

¾ cup • 180 mL Apple Butter (page 110)

4 medium apples, peeled and thinly sliced

¼ cup • 60 mL sugar

2 Tbsp • 30 mL lemon juice

1 Tbsp • 15 mL finely grated lemon zest

1 tsp • 5 mL vanilla extract

½ tsp • 2.5 mL cinnamon

2 tsp • 10 mL butter

1 Tbsp • 15 mL milk

sugar

3 Tbsp • 45 mL Basic Apple Jelly, melted
   (page 44)

1 Tbsp • 15 mL Calvados

TO ASSEMBLE Preheat the oven to 425°F (220°C).

On a lightly floured surface, roll the dough into a circle 12 to 14 inches (30 to 36 cm) in diameter, about ¼ inch (6 mm) thick. Leave the edges untrimmed. Transfer to a baking sheet.

Gently spread the apple butter over the center of the dough in a large circle, leaving about a 2-inch (5 cm) border.

In a medium bowl, combine the apple slices, sugar, lemon juice and zest, vanilla and cinnamon. Toss together to coat the apples. Arrange the apples on top of the apple butter. Dot the apples with the butter.

Fold the rough edges of the dough over the apples. Brush the milk over the dough edges using a pastry brush. Sprinkle the edges lightly with sugar.

Bake for 15 minutes, then reduce the heat to 375°F (190°C) and bake for another 30 minutes, or until the pastry is golden and the center is bubbly. It may be necessary to cover the galette with foil during the last 15 minutes to prevent excess browning.

After the galette is removed from the oven, let it cool, then brush the apples with a mixture of the melted jelly and Calvados.

Lemon Cheesecake

SERVES 12 TO 14

Serve this elegant, subtly flavored cheesecake with Black-berry Orange Sauce with Port (page 104), Honeyed Peach and Blueberry Compote (page 101), Pineapple, Straw-berry and Rhubarb Dessert Sauce (page 100) or Spirited Cherry and Raspberry Compote (page 103).

Crust

1¾ cups • 420 mL finely crushed graham
    wafer crumbs

¼ cup • 60 mL very finely chopped walnuts

½ cup • 120 mL melted butter

2 Tbsp • 30 mL sugar

PREHEAT the oven to 350°F (175°C). Mix all the ingredients together until crumbly. Press the crumbs into the bottom and up about two-thirds of the sides of a 9-inch (23 cm) springform pan. Bake for 10 minutes. Set aside while you make the filling.

Filling

1 lb • 454 g cream cheese, softened

¾ cup • 180 mL sugar

3 eggs

½ cup • 120 mL sour cream

2 Tbsp • 30 mL lemon juice

2 tsp • 10 mL finely grated lemon zest

BEAT the cream cheese until it is light and fluffy, using an electric mixer. Gradu-ally beat in the sugar. Beat in the eggs 1 at a time. Scrape down the sides of the bowl occasionally. Mix in the sour cream, lemon juice and zest.

Pour the mixture over the crust. Bake at 350°F (175°C) for 40 to 45 minutes, or until set. Remove from the oven.

Topping

    1 cup • 240 mL sour cream

    ¼ cup • 60 mL sugar

    2 Tbsp • 30 mL lemon juice

MIX the sour cream, sugar and lemon juice together. Spread over the hot cheese-cake. Return to the oven to bake for an additional 10 minutes.

TO ASSEMBLE Remove the cheesecake from the oven. Cool for 30 minutes. Loosen the sides of the springform pan, but leave them in place. When the cheesecake has cooled thoroughly, refrigerate it for at least 6 hours, preferably overnight.

TO SERVE Remove the cake from the pan. Transfer it to a serving platter. Spoon over any of your homemade fruit sauces or preserves. You may also use any jam or conserve thinned to spreading consistency (if necessary) with a little fruit juice, fruit liqueur or brandy.

Jam-Filled Buttery Layer Cake

SERVES 12

Your mom will be proud.

1¾ cups • 420 mL sugar

⅔ cup • 160 mL butter

2 eggs

2 tsp • 10 mL vanilla extract

2¾ cups • 660 mL flour

2½ tsp • 12.5 mL baking powder

½ tsp • 2.5 mL salt

1¼ cups • 300 mL milk

½ cup • 120 mL jam of your choice
(pages 21–36)

¼ cup • 60 mL superfine or berry sugar

PREHEAT the oven to 350°F (175°C). Grease and flour two 9-inch (23 cm) round cake pans.

In a large bowl, combine the sugar and butter. Using an electric mixer, at high speed, beat well for about 3 minutes. Add the eggs and vanilla, and beat for another 2 to 3 minutes, until the mixture is light and fluffy. Scrape the sides of the bowl occasionally.

In a small bowl, stir together the flour, baking powder and salt.

Reducing the mixer speed to low, beat in the flour mixture alternately with the milk, starting and finishing with the dry ingredients, until the batter is smooth.

To ensure easy cake removal, use a pastry brush to lightly coat the bottom and sides of the cake pans with melted shortening or butter. Sprinkle a little flour into the pan. Tilt and tap the pan to coat all the surfaces with flour. Tap out the excess flour. Divide the batter evenly between the prepared cake pans and level the surface with a knife. Bake 30 to 35 minutes. Test for doneness by inserting a toothpick into the center of the cake. If the toothpick comes out clean, the cake is done.

Remove the cakes from the oven. Cool for about 5 minutes in the pans, then invert onto wire racks to cool completely.

Invert 1 cake layer onto a serving plate and spread with the jam. Place the other layer on top and sprinkle with the superfine sugar.

Serve the cake alone or with fresh berries or sliced fresh fruit and whipped cream, if desired.

ICED CITRUS CAKE Add the finely grated zest of 2 limes or 1 lemon when preparing the cake batter. Use ½ cup (120 mL) Lemon-Lime Marmalade (page 68) for the filling. As a glaze for the top of the cake, mix 1 cup (240 mL) icing sugar with enough lemon or lime juice to give a creamy, but slightly runny consistency. Spoon and spread over the cake.

ABOUT BERRY SUGAR

Superfine or berry sugar is more finely granulated than regular white sugar. If you can't find it at the supermarket, you can make your own by whirling regular sugar in your blender or food processor for a couple of minutes.

Black Forest Trifle

SERVES 10 TO 12

Trifle is a classic English dessert consisting of layers of sponge cake, jam, fruit, and custard. This show-off version combines the elements of a traditional trifle with another all-time favorite, Black Forest Cake. This recipe requires Brandied Cherries, for which a separate recipe has been included at the end. In the event that you have not made your own Brandied Cherries ahead of time, commercially canned sweet cherries may be substituted very successfully.

Chocolate Sponge

6 eggs

1 cup • 240 mL sugar

1 tsp • 5 mL vanilla extract

½ cup • 120 mL flour

½ cup • 120 mL cocoa

⅔ cup • 160 mL butter, melted and
cooled slightly

one 8 oz (250 mL) jar Spirited Cherry and
Raspberry Compote (page 103)

½ cup • 120 mL Kirsch

one 16 oz (500 mL) jar Brandied Cherries
(page 265)

OR 14 oz (398 mL) can sweet cherries
in syrup*

* If using canned cherries, drain the cherries, then prick each one several times with a sharp needle. Place into a small bowl and marinate with the Kirsch for several hours or overnight.

PREHEAT the oven to 350°F (175°C). Grease and flour two 9-inch (23 cm) cake pans.

In a large bowl, using an electric mixer at high speed, whip the eggs for about 10 minutes, until they are very light and fluffy. Very gradually beat in the sugar and vanilla.

In a separate bowl, mix together the flour and cocoa, then sift gradually into the eggs, folding in gently. Fold in the melted butter, about 2 Tbsp (30 mL) at a time. Carefully pour the batter into the prepared pans, spreading evenly with a knife.

Bake for 15 to 20 minutes, or until the cake springs back when lightly touched at the center.

Remove the cakes from the oven. Cool in their pans for 5 minutes, then invert onto wire racks to cool completely.

Chocolate Custard

Custard powder is available in a tin in the bakery section of most grocery stores.

7 oz • 200 g good quality chocolate, such as
    Valrhona or Callebaut, chopped into pieces

2 Tbsp • 30 mL custard powder

2 Tbsp • 30 mL sugar

2 egg yolks

¾ cup • 180 mL milk

1 cup • 240 mL mascarpone cheese

IN a small heatproof bowl, melt the chocolate over hot water.

In a separate bowl, combine the custard powder, sugar and egg yolks. Mix into a smooth paste.

(continued next page)

cooking with preserves

263

Black Forest Trifle (continued)

In a small saucepan, over medium-low heat, heat the milk until very hot, but not boiling, then pour into the custard mixture, stirring constantly. Pour the mixture back into the saucepan, and stir constantly over low heat until it is smooth and thickened.

Remove from the heat. Stir in the mascarpone until blended, then add the melted chocolate, mixing well. Cool.

TO ASSEMBLE THE TRIFLE Slice each layer of cake in 2 horizontally, and spread 2 of the 4 layers with the compote. Sandwich 1 plain layer and 1 covered layer together. Repeat with the other layers. Using a serrated knife, slice the cakes into pieces, about 2 inches (5 cm) in size. Cover the bottom of a deep 3- to 4-quart (3 to 4 L) glass bowl with a layer of cake pieces. Arrange more pieces standing up around the sides. Drain the cherries reserving the juice. Drizzle half the juice over the cake pieces in the bowl. Place half the cherries over the cake. Cover with half of the Chocolate Custard. Place the remaining cake pieces on top. Drizzle with the remaining juice and cover with the remaining cherries and custard. Cover and refrigerate until shortly before serving.

TO SERVE Using an electric mixer, whip 1 cup (240 mL) heavy cream until very stiff and sweeten it with 1 Tbsp (15 mL) icing sugar. Spread the whipped cream on top of the trifle. Garnish with shaved or grated bittersweet chocolate.

Brandied Cherries

MAKES FOUR 1-PINT (500 ML) JARS

Because alcohol is a natural preservative, Brandied Cherries do not have to be processed in a boiling water bath.

  2½ lb • 1.1 kg sweet black cherries
  ¾ cup • 180 mL sugar
  3½–4 cups • 840–950 mL brandy

PREPARE the preserving jars.

Wash the cherries. Pat dry with paper towel. Using a cherry pitter, remove the pits. Prick each cherry several times with a large needle.

Divide the cherries amongst the cold sterilized jars. Sprinkle 3 Tbsp (45 mL) sugar in each jar, then fill the jars with brandy.

Close the jars tightly. Shake slightly to help dissolve the sugar.

Leave the jars in a cool dark place, turning the jars over from time to time, for 8 to 10 weeks.

Raspberry Vinegar Sorbet

MAKES ABOUT 5 CUPS (1.2 L)

A piquant ice that makes a delightful finale or a palate refresher between courses.

    4 cups • 950 mL fresh raspberries
    1 cup • 240 mL water
    ¾ cup • 180 mL sugar
    1 Tbsp • 15 mL lemon juice
    1 envelope unflavored gelatin
    3 Tbsp • 45 mL Raspberry Vinegar
       (page 208)
    lemon zest
    fresh mint sprigs

IN a large saucepan, over medium heat, combine the raspberries, water, sugar and lemon juice. Bring to a boil, then simmer, stirring frequently, for about 5 minutes or until the berries have softened and the sugar is completely dissolved.

Press the mixture through a fine sieve and discard the seeds and pulp. Return the raspberry mixture to the clean saucepan.

Sprinkle the gelatin over the raspberry mixture and let stand 5 minutes. Mix well until the gelatin is completely dissolved. If necessary, the mixture may be reheated slightly. Remove from the heat. Stir in the raspberry vinegar.

Pour into a stainless steel bowl and place in the freezer for about 1½ hours or until partially firm. Remove from the freezer.

Using an electric mixer, beat thoroughly until smooth. Cover and freeze 2 to 3 hours or until set.

Prior to serving, remove the sorbet from the freezer for 15 to 20 minutes to soften slightly. Serve in small scoops, garnished with lemon zest and fresh mint.

Gifts from the Pantry

Gifts from the Pantry

The art of giving presents is to give something which others cannot buy for themselves.
—A. A. Milne

ike cooking for the ones you love, giving gifts to family and friends is one of life's simple pleasures. This is especially true when they are gifts that you have made yourself.

At harvest time, in the midst of the busiest preserving season of all, it is easy to forget that another, even busier season is just around the corner. When our kitchens are full of steam and we are up to our elbows in peaches or tomatoes, visions of sugar plums couldn't be further from our minds.

But be assured, Christmas is closer than you think. And so are a host of other eagerly anticipated or totally unexpected occasions that will require giving a gift of one kind of another.

The farsighted home preserver has it made—literally. Like an industrious squirrel hiding away a supply of nuts for the winter, the prudent home preserver will prepare extra jars of favorite condiments for the gift-giving season that looms so near.

If you make a little extra, here and there, when fruits and vegetables are in season, you can stockpile an impressive supply of food to give as gifts for any occasion throughout the year.

Virtually everyone appreciates a gift of good food, and homemade preserves have a universal appeal. They can even be tailor-made to suit the individual preferences of the recipient, if you know their tastes.

When you give preserves as gifts, you are giving a gift of your time and creativity. The hours you spend making homemade preserves cannot be duplicated by simply running out and picking something up from a store. The thoughtfulness of a homemade gift makes the recipient feel very special.

Preserves are ideal to take along to any social gathering when a little token for the host or hostess would be appropriate. A beautifully presented bottle of infused vinegar can be a worthy substitute for the customary bottle of wine, especially if your hosts do not drink alcohol. A tangy jar of pickled beans would be a hit at a cocktail party, a savory relish or chutney perfect for an invitation to a barbecue. And, of course, a fruity jam or jelly is just the thing for a brunch or an afternoon tea.

I almost hate to mention it, but giving preserves as gifts can be very economical too. Last-minute gifts almost always cost more money, since we don't have the time to shop shrewdly. With a good selection of preserves on hand, you will have delicious, useful gifts appropriate for practically anyone—and they will cost pennies instead of the earth.

There is an old saying that "the man who chops his own wood warms himself twice." And you will feel the warmth of pride and satisfaction twice if you give homemade gifts from your pantry—once in the making and once again in the giving.

PACKAGING AND PRESENTATION

Part of the joy of giving is the originality and creativity of the packaging. Since your gift is already made, you can spend a little extra time on the finishing touches that will make it truly one of a kind.

Any present can be enhanced by its wrapping. An attractively wrapped gift is a feast for the eyes.

Packaging and presentation involves a little planning ahead on your part. Always be on the lookout for items that might serve as attractive containers in which to present your preserves. Save and recycle pretty boxes, tins, paper and bags. You can wrap or cover uninteresting containers with fabric or beautiful paper. Some containers lend themselves to being painted. Save baskets of all shapes and sizes. An assortment of preserves can be a visually striking gift. An antique soup tureen from a garage sale (or your attic), a terracotta pot from the florist, a charming wicker basket from Chinatown—any of these can attractively display a selection of preserves. Just wrap it with cellophane and add a festive bow. Kitchenware, either new or vintage, can double as interesting containers to hold just one or several jars of preserves. Try a colander, a handmade pottery bowl, a delicate china cup and saucer, a wok or an Oriental bamboo steamer.

Check out thrift stores, rummage sales or garage sales for unusual jars or elegant decanters. You may even find antique canning jars, old-fashioned bail-type jars (glass-lidded jars with curved wire fasteners) or hinged, clamp-type jars from Europe. Preserves can be transferred to these decorative containers as long as the container is thoroughly washed and sterilized first, but once transferred, the foods must be kept refrigerated. If you choose to give preserves packaged in containers that have not been heat-sealed, make sure to include instructions for refrigerator storage with your gift. Small jars and bottles can also be purchased from cookware shops, hardware stores, even discount and dollar stores.

Give your bottles and jars an expensive "gourmet shop" look by adding inexpensive decorative touches. Everyone has seen pretty jars of jam or jelly done up with little paper or fabric "hats," or lid covers, secured with a bow. This is very easy to do.

Covers can be made from many different types of fabric. Make sure the fabric is not too heavy, stiff or bulky to smoothly fit over the top of the jar. The best choices are cottons or cotton blends. Choose a fabric that doesn't fray too much and that can be cut easily with pinking shears. Avoid thin, sheer or see-through fabrics unless you want to double them. Small-scale prints are best, in keeping with the size of the jar.

Paper can also be used successfully. It should be pliable enough to go over the jar, but not so thin that it will tear. Brown paper, gift wrap, some wallpapers and other similar-weight papers are appropriate. Tissue paper is not. A neat craft product called "paper twist" can be unraveled and cut to fit.

To make lid covers, measure the top of your jar and add about 3½ inches (10 cm) for a nice frill. Now find a small plate or lid or anything round that is approximately that size to use as a template. (I find that a side plate is the perfect size to cover a standard-sized preserving jar lid, while one of my salad plates fits the wide-mouthed lid to a T.)

Using the plate as a guide, draw as many circles as you need to cover your jars. If you are using fabric, use pinking shears to cut the circles so the fabric will not fray. For paper, use the shears for a decorative edge or regular scissors for a plain one.

You can affix the fabric or paper to the jar lid using a glue gun or white craft glue, or you can simply center the decorative top on the lid and secure it around the neck of the jar with an elastic band.

If you are using paper, be extra careful to avoid tearing it. Sometimes you need to do a little adjusting at the neck to get the proper ruffled effect.

Tie a bow around the neck of the jar to decorate it and to hide the elastic band. You can use a matching or contrasting ribbon, raffia, jute twine, string, thick strands of wool—whatever works for you.

Fabric stores have wonderful materials printed with fruits and vegetables that are really fun. At Christmas, you can use seasonal fabrics with Santas or snowmen and decorate them with glued-on pinecones or holly.

Other decorative accessories can be glued on as well. Bits of dried flowers, seed pods, whole spices such as cinnamon sticks or star anise, dried chili peppers or dried orange or apple slices are good ideas. But don't overdo it. Too much will detract from the overall presentation.

Another attractive look is to swathe bottles of vinegar or jars with white tissue, gauze or tulle, secure around the neck with French wired ribbon, then tie on a single full-blown artificial rose. (A nice one, not a cheap one.) Red fruit vinegars look festive with clumps of imitation berries or greenery tied at the neck with a flowing ribbon or raffia.

A bright strip of grosgrain ribbon firmly fastened with sealing wax adds a professional touch to gifts. Sealing wax sticks and decorative metal seals are avail-able at many craft stores and specialty stationery shops. All you have to do is wrap the ribbon around the jar and anchor it in place temporarily, using masking tape. Light the stick of sealing wax following the package directions and hold it about 1 inch (2.5 cm) above the spot to be sealed. Allow the wax to drip continuously until you have a blob about 1 inch (2.5 cm) in diameter. Press the metal seal down firmly onto the melted wax. Wait a couple of seconds before lifting the seal to ensure that a clear impression has been made. Remove the masking tape. You might like to practice the technique a little before you try it on your jars of preserves, just to be sure that you've got the hang of it.

A really beautiful look for extra-special gifts is to cover the jar lids with leaves that have been soaked in glycerine. Glycerine, available at most drugstores, preserves the leaves, keeping them moist and supple.

Wash and dry large leaves, such as maple, and brush both sides with the glycerine. Place the leaves over the top of the jar, overlapping them slightly if necessary. Wrap the lid in plastic wrap and fasten with an elastic band. Place a weight on top and refrigerate overnight. Carefully unwrap the jar and blot up any excess glycerine. Tie a length of raffia around the neck of the jar and finish with a bow.

A gift of food can be as simple as a prettily decorated jar of jam or as elaborate as an elegant basket chock-full of vinegars and exotic condiments.

The most appreciated gifts are often those that people took the time and the effort to make themselves. Spend just a bit more time and make your gifts of home preserves even more special.

LABELS AND TAGS

Most brands of preserving jars have adhesive-backed labels included in the package, but if you are recycling jars, you won't have this option. And while adequate for identification purposes, these labels are rather ordinary—you can produce more attractive, unusual labels with a little time and effort.

Packaged labels with appealing designs especially made for preserving jars are available and often come preprinted with "Contents" or "From the Kitchen of . . ." These can usually be found at cookbook or cookware stores and some stationery shops.

Office supply stores are a good source for plain, gummed mailing labels. These can be dressed up with pretty fruit and vegetable stickers or stamps. Some stores carry unique labels with old-fashioned drawings.

Tie-on tags can be elegant or rustic looking. Gift enclosure cards make good tags; cut-up Christmas cards or trimmed-down cards from birthdays or other special occasions also work well. You can even buy special scissors to give these tags a scalloped or decorative edge.

Beautiful tags can be made by covering one side of heavy cardstock with gift wrap, adhesive-backed paper or fabric.

To attach the tags, punch a hole in one corner using a paper punch, then thread raffia, ribbon or whatever you like through the hole and around the neck of the jar.

Use plain brown baggage tags or heavy brown paper for a rustic, country look. And, of course, you can print labels or tags using your home computer. Don't go for anything too high-tech—you want a simple design to complement your preserves.

Enclose serving suggestions or recipes with your gifts of homemade preserves, so that your friends will know how to use them. And don't forget to note that refrigerator storage is required for all preserves (except vinegar) once they have been opened.

Index

A

acid
    high-acid foods, 4
    in jam, 19
    low-acid foods, 4
    in tomatoes, 185
air bubbles, 9
alcohol, 79
allspice, about, 179
altitude, 11
alum, 122
Amber Marmalade, 70
Antipasto Pickles, 136
apples
    adding to jam, 25
    Apple Basil Jelly, 47
    Apple Butter, 110
    Apple Glazed Carrots, 247
    Apple Lemon Balm Jelly, 47
    Apple Mint Jelly, 46
    Apple Rose Geranium Jelly, 47
    Applesauce Spice Cake with Cream Cheese Icing, 250
    Basic Apple Jelly, 44
    Blackberry and Apple Chutney, 179
    Chunky Apple Marmalade with Ginger, 71
    Cranberry, Pear and Apple Relish, 159
    Cranberry and Apple Jelly, 45
    Curried Apple Chutney, 178
    Gingered Apple Preserves, 93
    Green Tomato and Apple Chutney, 174
    Honeyed Applesauce, 98
    Plum Apple Jam, 36
    Spiced Apple Jelly, 44
    Spiced Blackberry and Apple Jam, 25
    Triple Apple Galette, 256
applesauce
    about applesauce, 98
    Applesauce Spice Cake with Cream Cheese Icing, 250
    Honeyed Applesauce, 98
apricots
    Apricot Coconut Drops, 254
    Apricot Jam, 28
    Cranberry, Orange and Apricot Chutney, 172
    pits and kernels, 28

asparagus
    Pickled Asparabits, 131
    Pickled Asparagus, 130
    Prosciutto Asparagus Roll-ups, 230
Authentic Bread and Butter Pickles, 126

B

Baked Banana Squash with Orange Marmalade, 246
Baked Brie with Chutney and Toasted Nuts, 229
bananas
    Banana and Date Chutney, 175
    Banango Chutney, 165
Basic Apple Jelly, 44
Basic Fruit Vinaigrette, 216
basil
    Apple Basil Jelly, 47
    Opal Basil Vinegar, 202
beans
    Green Beans Mexicana, 245
    Spicy Pickled Green Beans, 132
beeswax, sealing bottles with, 196
beets
    Beet and Red Cabbage Relish, 147
    Sweet Spiced Pickled Beets, 138
blackberries
    Black and Blue Jam, 26
    Blackberry, Rosemary and Red Wine Marinade, 223
    Blackberry and Apple Chutney, 179
    Blackberry Cassis Sauce, 237
    Blackberry Jam, 22
    Blackberry Jelly, 53
    Blackberry Orange Sauce with Port, 104
    Duck Breasts with Blackberry Cassis Sauce, 237
    Jumbleberry Jam, 24
    Spiced Blackberry and Apple Jam, 25
    Wild Blackberry Butter, 111
Black Forest Trifle, 262
blueberries
    about blueberries, 26
    Black and Blue Jam, 26
    Blueberry Chutney, 170
    Chicken Breasts with Blueberries and Tarragon, 236
    Jumbleberry Jam, 24
    True Blueberry Jam, 26

boiling water bath, 7, 10–12

botulism, 4

Brandied Cherries, 265

Brandied Peach Preserves, 94

burns, avoiding, 20

butter

adding to reduce foam, 41

fruit "butters," 64

Butterscotch Peach Jam, 29

C

cakes

Applesauce Spice Cake with Cream Cheese Icing, 250

Jam-Filled Buttery Layer Cake, 260

Lemon Cheesecake, 258

canning. See preserving

carrots

Apple Glazed Carrots, 247

Carrot and Coconut Chutney, 176

Carrot and Cucumber Relish, 145

Carrot Marmalade, 73

Pickled Rosemary Carrots, 129

Rhubarb and Carrot Jam, 32

Cheddar Cheese Ball with Port and Dijon Mustard, 228

cherries

Black Forest Trifle, 262

Brandied Cherries, 265

Pickled Cherries with Tarragon, 139

pitting, 103

Spirited Cherry and Raspberry Compote, 103

Summer Berry Jelly, 51

Sweet Cherry Preserves in Almond Syrup, 91

Chicken Breasts with Blueberries and Tarragon, 236

chilies

about chilies, 209

about chili paste, 225

handling hot peppers, 60

Hot Chili Pepper Vinegar, 209

Chow Chow, 146

Chunky Apple Marmalade with Ginger, 71

Chunky Salsa Guacamole, 148

chutneys

Banana and Date Chutney, 175

Banango Chutney, 165

Blackberry and Apple Chutney, 179

Blueberry Chutney, 170

Carrot and Coconut Chutney, 176

Cranberry, Orange and Apricot Chutney, 172

Curried Apple Chutney, 178

Fig and Lemon Chutney, 171

Green Tomato and Apple Chutney, 174

Mango Chutney, 165

Pear Chutney, 166

Pineapple and Papaya Chutney, 168

Plum Chutney with Cinnamon and Coriander, 169

Rhubarb and Ginger Chutney, 180

Ripe Tomato Chutney, 173

cilantro, about, 169

cinnamon, about, 93

Classic Strawberry Preserves, 89

cloves, about, 81

compotes. See fruit sauces

conserves

Cranberry, Rum and Raisin Conserve, 84

Grape Pecan Conserve, 80

Papaya Nectarine Conserve, 83

Plum Orange Conserve with Figs, 82

Spiced Pear, Peach and Citrus Conserve, 81

cookies

Apricot Coconut Drops, 254

Jim Jams, 255

cooking with preserves

Apple Glazed Carrots, 247

Applesauce Spice Cake with Cream Cheese Icing, 250

Apricot Coconut Drops, 254

Baked Banana Squash with Orange Marmalade, 246

Baked Brie with Chutney and Toasted Nuts, 229

Basic Fruit Vinaigrette, 216

Blackberry, Rosemary and Red Wine Marinade, 223

Black Forest Trifle, 262

Cheddar Cheese Ball with Port and Dijon Mustard, 228

Chicken Breasts with Blueberries and Tarragon, 236

Creamy Herb and Garlic Dip or Salad Dressing, 218

Cucumber and Dill Pickle Dip, 220

Cumberland Sauce, 227

Curried Chutney Dip, 219

Duck Breasts with Blackberry Cassis Sauce, 237

Fresh Fruit Salsa, 221

Gingerbread with Spiced Pear Sauce, 253

Gingered Orange Spread, 224

Green Beans Mexicana, 245

Guacamole, 222

Jam-Filled Buttery Layer Cake, 260

Jim Jams, 255

Lamb Chops with Mint Vinaigrette, 244
Lemon Cheesecake, 258
Little Crab Cakes with Fresh Fruit Salsa, 232
Marmalade Oatmeal Muffins, 252
Marvelous Meat Loaf with Chili Sauce, 242
Mayonnaise Flavored with Fruit Vinegar, 217
Mexican Chicken Lasagne, 238
Old-Fashioned Glazed Baked Ham, 240
Pork Satay with Pineapple, 234
Prosciutto Asparagus Roll-ups, 230
Raspberry Vinegar Sorbet, 266
Rhubarb Ginger Chutney and Walnut Loaf, 249
Salmon Fillets with Citrus Beurre Blanc, 243
Sesame Plum Sauce, 225
Sweet and Sour Red Cabbage, 248
Sweet Potato Fries with Feisty Red Pepper Ketchup, 233
Tartar Sauce, 226
Triple Apple Galette, 256
Wonton Crisps with Gorgonzola and Grape Salsa, 231
coriander, about, 169
corn
    Curried Corn Relish, 151
    Old-Time Corn Relish, 150
Country Style Chili Sauce, 186
Crabapple Jelly, 44
cranberries
    Cranberry, Orange and Apricot Chutney, 172
    Cranberry, Orange and Port Glaze, for ham, 241
    Cranberry, Pear and Apple Relish, 159
    Cranberry, Rum and Raisin Conserve, 84
    Cranberry and Apple Jelly, 45
    Cranberry Christmas Vinegar, 206
    Cranberry Ketchup, 189
    Jumbleberry Jam, 24
    Quick Cranberry Butter, 113
    Zesty Cranberry Relish, 159
Cream Cheese Icing, 251
Creamy Herb and Garlic Dip or Salad Dressing, 218
cucumbers
    about cucumbers, 121, 123
    Authentic Bread and Butter Pickles, 126
    Carrot and Cucumber Relish, 145
    Cucumber and Dill Pickle Dip, 220
    Simply Good Dill Pickles, 125
Cumberland Sauce, 227
cumin, about, 173

currants
    Cumberland Sauce, 227
    Red Currant Jelly, 55
Curried Apple Chutney, 178
Curried Chutney Dip, 219
Curried Corn Relish, 151

D

Dark Seville Marmalade, 65
dips and spreads
    Creamy Herb and Garlic Dip or Salad Dressing, 218
    Cucumber and Dill Pickle Dip, 220
    Curried Chutney Dip, 219
    fruit butters, 105–16
    fruit "butters," 64
    Gingered Orange Spread, 224
    Quick dip using relish, 144
    Tartar Sauce, 226
Duck Breasts with Blackberry Cassis Sauce, 237

E

enzymes, 3–4, 122

F

Feisty Red Pepper Ketchup, 191
figs
    Fig and Lemon Chutney, 171
    Plum Orange Conserve with Figs, 82
Five-Fruit Ketchup, 188
French Tarragon Vinegar, 204
Fresh Fruit Salsa, 221
frozen fruit, making jam or jelly from, 19
fruit
    freezing, 19
    pectin, 18
    in pickling, 121
    pits and kernels, 28
    vinegars, 199
fruit butters
    Apple Butter, 110
    cooking in oven, 108
    honey in, 113
    Peach, Mango, Nectarine or Papaya Butter, 116
    Pear Orange Butter, 112
    Plum Butter, 114
    Quick Cranberry Butter, 113

fruit butters *(cont'd)*
    Wild Blackberry Butter, 111
fruit "butters," 64
fruit sauces
    Blackberry Orange Sauce with Port, 104
    Honeyed Applesauce, 98
    Honeyed Peach and Blueberry Compote, 101
    Pineapple, Strawberry and Rhubarb Dessert Sauce, 100
    Spiced Pear Sauce, 102
    Spirited Cherry and Raspberry Compote, 103
    Spirited Peach and Blueberry Compote, 101

G

garlic
    changing color in pickles, 123
    in infused vinegars, 199
    Pickled Garlic, 127
gel testing, 42
gifts from the pantry, 267
ginger
    about ginger, 177
    Chunky Apple Marmalade with Ginger, 71
    flavoring vinegar with, 203
    Gingerbread with Spiced Pear Sauce, 253
    Gingered Apple Preserves, 93
    Gingered Orange Spread, 224
    Gingered Pear Jam, 31
    Rhubarb and Ginger Chutney, 180
    Rhubarb Ginger Chutney and Walnut Loaf, 249
gooseberrries
    Summer Berry Jelly, 51
grapes
    Grape Jelly, 54
    Grape Pecan Conserve, 80
    Pickled Grapes with Tarragon, 139
    Wonton Crisps with Gorgonzola and Grape Salsa, 231
Green Beans Mexicana, 245
Green Tomato and Apple Chutney, 174
Guacamole, 222
    Chunky Salsa Guacamole, 148

H

hard water, treating, 121
head space, 9
herbs
    adding fresh herbs to jellies, 57
    in infused vinegars, 197

honey
    about honey, 101
    Honeyed Applesauce, 98
    Honeyed Peach and Blueberry Compote, 101
    Honey Lemon Jelly, 50
    Pickled Pears with Honey and Red Wine, 140
Hot Chili Pepper Vinegar, 209
hot peppers. *See* peppers

I

India Relish, 155
infused vinegars
    basic fruit vinegar, 199
    basic herb vinegar, 197
    blending flavors, 196
    Cranberry Christmas Vinegar, 206
    flavoring with ginger, 203
    French Tarragon Vinegar, 204
    Hot Chili Pepper Vinegar, 209
    Lovely Lavender Vinegar, 201
    Opal Basil Vinegar, 202
    in pickling, 203
    Raspberry Vinegar, 208
    Scarborough Fair Vinegar, 203
    Spiced Plum Vinegar, 210
    suggested flavorings, 198–99
    suggested uses, 197, 200

J

Jalapeño Pepper Jelly, 60
Jam-Filled Buttery Layer Cake, 260
jams
    Apricot Jam, 28
    Black and Blue Jam, 26
    Blackberry Jam, 22
    Butterscotch Peach Jam, 29
    from frozen fruit, 19
    Gingered Pear Jam, 31
    Jumbleberry Jam, 24
    Kiwi Lime Jam, 34
    Peach Melba Jam, 30
    Plum Apple Jam, 36
    Plum Jam, 36
    Rhubarb and Carrot Jam, 32
    Ruby Red Raspberry Jam, 22
    Soft Strawberry Jam, 21

Spiced Blackberry and Apple Jam, 25
Strawberry Lime Jam, 21
Strawberry Mint Jam, 21
Strawberry Orange Jam, 21
Strawberry Rhubarb Jam, 33
True Blueberry Jam, 26
jar lifter, 6, 12
jars, 6–8
jellies
    adding chopped herbs to, 57
    Apple Basil Jelly, 47
    Apple Lemon Balm Jelly, 47
    Apple Mint Jelly, 46
    Apple Rose Geranium Jelly, 47
    Basic Apple Jelly, 44
    Blackberry Jelly, 53
    Cranberry and Apple Jelly, 45
    easy steps, 40–42
    failure to set, 43
    gel tests, 42
    glaze for a fresh fruit tart, 53
    glaze for ham, 43, 240
    Grape Jelly, 54
    Honey Lemon Jelly, 50
    Jalapeño Pepper Jelly, 60
    jelly bag, 41
    Quince Jelly Scented with Vanilla, 48
    Red Currant Jelly, 55
    Red Pepper and Orange Jelly, 59
    Rosemary and Orange Jelly, 57
    Rosemary and Red Wine Jelly with Garlic, 57
    Rosemary and Red Wine Jelly with Orange, 56
    Spiced Apple Jelly, 44
    Summer Berry Jelly, 51
    troubleshooting, 43
Jim Jams, 255

k

ketchups
    Country Style Chili Sauce, 186
    Cranberry Ketchup, 189
    Feisty Red Pepper Ketchup, 191
    Five-Fruit Ketchup, 188
    Old-Fashioned Tomato Ketchup, 185
Kiwi Lime Jam, 34

l

Lamb Chops with Mint Vinaigrette, 244
Lemon Cheesecake, 258
lemons
    about lemons, 69
    Fig and Lemon Chutney, 171
    Honey Lemon Jelly, 50
    Lemon Cheesecake, 258
    Lemon-Lime Marmalade, 68
lids, 6, 9
limes
    Kiwi Lime Jam, 34
    Lemon-Lime Marmalade, 68
Little Crab Cakes with Fresh Fruit Salsa, 232
Lovely Lavender Vinegar, 201

m

mangoes
    Banango Chutney, 165
    Mango Chutney, 165
    Peach, Mango, Nectarine or Papaya Butter, 116
marmalades
    Amber Marmalade, 70
    Carrot Marmalade, 73
    Chunky Apple Marmalade with Ginger, 71
    Dark Seville Marmalade, 65
    Lemon-Lime Marmalade, 68
    marmalade glaze for ham, 240
    Marmalade Oatmeal Muffins, 252
    Orange Marmalade, 66
    Peach Orange Marmalade, 72
    Pumpkin Marmalade, 74
    Spirited Seville Marmalade, 65
    Traditional English Marmalade, 65
    Winter Marmalade, 76
    Zany Zucchini Marmalade, 75
Marvelous Meat Loaf with Chili Sauce, 242
Mason jars, 6–8
Mayonnaise Flavored with Fruit Vinegar, 217
Mexican Chicken Lasagne, 238
Michael's Pickled Onions, 134
microorganisms, 3–4, 10, 196
microwave, preserving with a, 13
mold, 4, 9, 10, 18, 43, 121

n

nectarines
Nectarine and Pepper Relish, 160
Papaya Nectarine Conserve, 83
Peach, Mango, Nectarine or Papaya Butter, 116
nuts, toasting, 83

o

Old-Fashioned Glazed Baked Ham, 240
Old-Fashioned Tomato Ketchup, 185
Old-Time Corn Relish, 150
onions
how to peel, 135
Michael's Pickled Onions, 134
oranges
Baked Banana Squash with Orange Marmalade, 246
Blackberry Orange Spread with Port, 104
Dark Seville Marmalade, 65
Gingered Orange Spread, 224
Orange Marmalade, 66
Peach Orange Marmalade, 72
Pear Orange Butter, 112
Plum Orange Conserve with Figs, 82
Plum Preserves with Orange Zest, 92
Red Pepper and Orange Jelly, 59
Rosemary and Orange Jelly, 57
Rosemary and Red Wine Jelly with Orange, 56
Spirited Seville Marmalade, 65
Traditional English Marmalade, 65

p

papaya
Papaya Nectarine Conserve, 83
Peach, Mango, Nectarine or Papaya Butter, 116
Pineapple and Papaya Chutney, 168
paraffin
about paraffin, 18
sealing bottles with, 196
peaches
Brandied Peach Preserves, 94
Butterscotch Peach Jam, 29
Peach, Mango, Nectarine or Papaya Butter, 116
Peach Melba Jam, 30
Peach Orange Marmalade, 72
Spiced Pear, Peach and Citrus Conserve, 81

pears
Cranberry, Pear and Apple Relish, 159
Gingerbread with Spiced Pear Sauce, 253
Gingered Pear Jam, 31
Pear Chutney, 166
Pear Orange Butter, 112
Pickled Pears with Honey and Red Wine, 140
Spiced Pear, Peach and Citrus Conserve, 81
Spiced Pear Sauce, 102
pectin
about pectin, 18
commercial, 18, 39–40
in jam, 18
in jelly, 39–40
peppers
Feisty Red Pepper Ketchup, 191
handling, 60
Hot Chili Pepper Vinegar, 209
Jalapeño Pepper Jelly, 60
Nectarine and Pepper Relish, 160
Pepper Relish, 158
Striped Pickled Peppers, 128
Sweet Potato Fries with Feisty Red Pepper Ketchup, 233
pickles
about cucumbers, 121
Antipasto Pickles, 136
Authentic Bread and Butter Pickles, 126
Michael's Pickled Onions, 134
Pickled Asparabits, 131
Pickled Asparagus, 130
Pickled Cherries with Tarragon, 139
Pickled Garlic, 127
Pickled Grapes with Tarragon, 139
Pickled Pears with Honey and Red Wine, 140
Pickled Rosemary Carrots, 129
pickling pointers, 123
pickling problems, 122
Simply Good Dill Pickles, 125
Spicy Pickled Green Beans, 132
Striped Pickled Peppers, 128
Sweet Spiced Pickled Beets, 138
pickling salt, 122
pickling spice, about, 125
pineapple
Amber Marmalade, 70
Pineapple, Strawberry and Rhubarb Dessert Sauce, 100
Pineapple and Papaya Chutney, 168

Pork Satay with Pineapple, 234
Winter Marmalade, 76
plums
    Plum Apple Jam, 36
    Plum Butter, 114
    Plum Chutney with Cinnamon and Coriander, 169
    Plum Jam, 36
    Plum Orange Conserve with Figs, 82
    Plum Preserves with Orange Zest, 92
    Sesame Plum Sauce, 225
    Spiced Plum Vinegar, 210
Pork Satay with Pineapple, 234
preserves
    Brandied Peach Preserves, 94
    Classic Strawberry Preserves, 89
    Gingered Apple Preserves, 93
    Plum Preserves with Orange Zest, 92
    Sweet Cherry Preserves in Almond Syrup, 91
preserving
    equipment, 5–8
    gel testing, 42
    high-acid foods, 4, 19
    at higher altitudes, 11
    low-acid foods, 4
    microwave, 13
    pectin, 18, 39–40
    pressure canning, 4
    processing, 10
    sealing, 12
    spoilage, 3–4, 13–14, 122
    sterilization, 8–9
    storage, 13–14
    techniques, 5–14
pressure canning, 4
processing, 10
Prosciutto Asparagus Roll-ups, 230
Pumpkin Marmalade, 74

q

Quick Cranberry Butter, 113
Quince Jelly Scented with Vanilla, 48

R

raspberries
    Peach Melba Jam, 30
    Raspberry Vinegar, 208
    Raspberry Vinegar Sorbet, 266

Ruby Red Raspberry Jam, 22
Spirited Cherry and Raspberry Compote, 103
Summer Berry Jelly, 51
red currants
    Cumberland Sauce, 227
    Red Currant Jelly, 55
Red Pepper and Orange Jelly, 59
red peppers. *See* peppers
relishes
    Beet and Red Cabbage Relish, 147
    Carrot and Cucumber Relish, 145
    Chow Chow, 146
    Chunky Salsa Guacamole, 148
    Cranberry, Pear and Apple Relish, 159
    India Relish, 155
    Nectarine and Pepper Relish, 160
    Old-Time Corn Relish, 150
    Pepper Relish, 158
    Ripe Tomato Relish, 157
    Salsa Fiesta!, 148
    Spicy Ripe Tomato Relish, 157
    Tartar Sauce, 226
    Zesty Cranberry Relish, 159
    Zesty Zucchini Relish, 152
rhubarb
    Rhubarb and Carrot Jam, 32
    Rhubarb and Ginger Chutney, 180
    Rhubarb Ginger Chutney and Walnut Loaf, 249
    Strawberry Rhubarb Jam, 33
Ripe Tomato Chutney, 173
Ripe Tomato Relish, 157
rosemary
    Blackberry, Rosemary and Red Wine Marinade, 223
    Pickled Rosemary Carrots, 129
    Rosemary and Orange Jelly, 57
    Rosemary and Red Wine Jelly with Garlic, 57
    Rosemary and Red Wine Jelly with Orange, 56

S

Salmon Fillets with Citrus Beurre Blanc, 243
salsa
    Chunky Salsa Guacamole, 148
    Fresh Fruit Salsa, 221
    Green Beans Mexicana, 245
    Guacamole, 222
    Little Crab Cakes with Fresh Fruit Salsa, 232
    Mexican Chicken Lasagne, 238

index |

salsa *(cont'd)*
    Salsa Fiesta!, 148
    Wonton Crisps with Gorgonzola and Grape Salsa, 231
salt, in pickling, 122
Scarborough Fair Vinegar, 203
sealing jars, 12
seasonings, in pickling
Sesame Plum Sauce, 225
Simply Good Dill Pickles, 125
Soft Strawberry Jam, 21
spice bag, 31
Spiced Blackberry and Apple Jam, 25
Spiced Pear, Peach and Citrus Conserve, 81
Spiced Pear Sauce, 102
Spiced Plum Vinegar, 210
Spicy Pickled Green Beans, 132
Spicy Ripe Tomato Relish, 157
Spirited Cherry and Raspberry Compote, 103
Spirited Peach and Blueberry Compote, 101
Spirited Seville Marmalade, 65
spoilage
    avoiding, 13–14
    causes of, 3–4
    in pickles, 122
sterilization of jars, 8
storage, 13–14
strawberries
    Classic Strawberry Preserves, 89
    Soft Strawberry Jam, 21
    Strawberry Lime Jam, 21
    Strawberry Mint Jam, 21
    Strawberry Orange Jam, 21
    Strawberry Rhubarb Jam, 33
Striped Pickled Peppers, 128
sugar
    berry sugar, about, 261
    in jam, 18
    in pickling, 121
Summer Berry Jelly, 51
Sweet and Sour Red Cabbage, 248
Sweet Cherry Preserves in Almond Syrup, 91
Sweet Potato Fries with Feisty Red Pepper Ketchup, 233
Sweet Spiced Pickled Beets, 138

T

tarragon
    French Tarragon Vinegar, 204

Pickled Cherries with Tarragon, 139
Pickled Grapes with Tarragon, 139
tomatoes
    Country Style Chili Sauce, 186
    Five-Fruit Ketchup, 188
    Green Tomato and Apple Chutney, 174
    Old-Fashioned Tomato Ketchup, 185
    peeling and seeding, 186
    Ripe Tomato Chutney, 173
    Ripe Tomato Relish, 157
    Salsa Fiesta!, 148
    Spicy Ripe Tomato Relish, 157
Traditional English Marmalade, 65
Triple Apple Galette, 256

V

vanilla
    about vanilla, 49
    Quince Jelly Scented with Vanilla, 48
vinaigrettes
    about vinaigrettes, 216
    Basic Fruit Vinaigrette, 216
vegetables, in pickling, 121
vinegar, in pickling, 121
vinegars. *See* infused vinegars

W

water
    in pickling, 121
    treating hard water, 121
Winter Marmalade, 76
Wonton Crisps with Gorgonzola and Grape Salsa, 231

Y

yeast, 4

Z

Zany Zucchini Marmalade, 75
Zesty Cranberry Relish, 159
Zesty Zucchini Relish, 152
zucchini
    Zany Zucchini Marmalade, 75
    Zesty Zucchini Relish, 152